Playing
Cleopatra

Playing Cleopatra

INVENTING THE FEMALE CELEBRITY IN THIRD REPUBLIC FRANCE

Holly Grout

LOUISIANA STATE UNIVERSITY PRESS

BATON ROUGE

Published by Louisiana State University Press
lsupress.org

DESIGNER: Michelle A. Neustrom
TYPEFACE: Calluna

COVER ILLUSTRATION: *Costume of Cleopatra for Ida Rubinstein,* by Léon Bakst, 1909.
Lobanov-Rostovsky Collection, Pushkin State Museum of Fine Arts.

LIBRARY OF CONGRESS CATALOGING-IN-PUBLICATION DATA

Names: Grout, Holly, 1976– author.
Title: Playing Cleopatra : inventing the female celebrity in Third Republic France /
  Holly Grout.
Description: Baton Rouge : Louisiana State University Press, 2024. | Includes
  bibliographical references and index.
Identifiers: LCCN 2023035415 (print) | LCCN 2023035416 (ebook) | ISBN 978-0-8071-
  8178-2 (cloth) | ISBN 978-0-8071-8186-7 (pdf) | ISBN 978-0-8071-8185-0 (epub)
Subjects: LCSH: Women in the theater—France—History. | Women—France—Social
  conditions—20th century. | Women—France—Social conditions—19th century. |
  Actresses—France—Paris. | France—History—Third Republic, 1870–1940.
Classification: LCC PN2622.W65 G76 2024 (print) | LCC PN2622.W65 (ebook)
LC record available at https://lccn.loc.gov/2023035415
LC ebook record available at https://lccn.loc.gov/2023035416

Contents

Illustrations

Acknowledgments

This project has benefited from the institutional support of The University of Alabama, the assistance of librarians in Paris, and the editorial board at the Louisiana State University Press. In addition to providing sabbatical leave for conducting the research necessary to produce this book, The University of Alabama also provided indispensable funding in the form of an ORED small grant and two Capstone International Travel Grants, while the History Department provided post-tenure research leave and funds for images. In Paris, the staffs at the Bibliothèque Nationale de France (especially the Arts and Spectacle salle at the Richelieu site), the Bibliothèque Arsenal, the Bibliothèque Marguerite Durand, and the Bibliothèque Opéra facilitated my work in the archives. This book would not have come to fruition without the investment of the Louisiana State University Press. I am sincerely grateful for my editor, Alisa Plant, who, from the beginning, enthusiastically supported this project. The anonymous reader's critical engagement with the manuscript tremendously improved the overall quality of the finished product. The brilliant LSU Press staff made the production process painless, and their talent and skill made this book even better than I imagined.

This project was also enhanced by the colleague feedback that I received at the Western Society for French History (WSFH) annual meeting in 2015, the Politics of Beauty Summer School and Conference held in Cambridge, England, in 2016, the IHTP/CNRS Seminar of Dress History at which I was invited to speak in 2017, and the Society for French Historical Studies/Georges Rudé Conference held virtually in 2020. I am especially grateful to Diane Negre for her incisive comments on the first version of what would become the Josephine Baker chapter as well as to the participants in the summer school group, from whom I learned a great deal. The Bernhardt chapter benefited from discussions held with fellow WSFH panelists Sara Kimble and Joelle Neulander, while my thinking on celebrity more broadly was enhanced by conversation with Society for French Historical Studies (SFHS) copanelists Dantzel Cenatiempo and Carol Harrison in 2020.

In addition to presenting parts of the material collected in this book at conferences, earlier versions of some of its content have been published previously. The discussion of celebrity memoir as source and genre appeared in "Authorizing Fictions: Narrating a Self in Mistinguett's Celebrity Memoir," *French Historical Studies* 42.2 (April 2019): 295–322. Selections regarding scholarship devoted to celebrity appeared in "European Celebrity in Historical Perspective," *Making Modern Social Science: The Global Imagination in East Central and Southeastern Europe after Versailles,* spec. issue of *Journal of Contemporary European History* 28.2 (May 2019): 273–82. Finally, a similar discussion of the etymology of "fame" and "celebrity" appeared in "Celebrity Matters," *Aeon* 16 (July 2019). My appreciation to the anonymous reviewers and editors of these journals whose feedback shaped my thinking on these issues.

So many generous colleagues and amazing friends made this book possible. Although long since relieved of her advising duties, Mary Louise Roberts continues to comment on my work and to offer sage career advice. I appreciate Lou's invaluable feedback on the first iteration of the introduction of this book. More than that, however, I am grateful for the many kindnesses she has shown me over the years, and I look forward to many more rendezvous in Paris, Madison, or wherever life takes us! Jenny Shaw, Jolene Hubbs, and Andrew Huebner have also graciously provided feedback on several drafts-in-progress. Jenny not only read every chapter of the manuscript, but she also encouraged me through my doubts, listened patiently to my musings, and put up with my ill-temper on bad writing days. Little did I know when I joined the faculty at UA in 2009, that the person in the office next to me would become my most supportive colleague and one of my dearest friends. I am a better scholar, teacher, and friend for knowing her. Jolene's many insightful suggestions tremendously improved my work, but it is her acerbic wit and compassionate friendship that daily enhances my life. Andrew's reasoned comments added clarity to my prose and, like his own work, reminded me to always look for the humanity in the history.

I have benefited significantly from the constant support of my department colleagues, especially Margaret Abruzzo, John Beeler, Heather Kopelson, Jimmy Mixson, and Dan Riches. The "UA Goddesses" cocktail club has provided hours of commiseration and much-needed conviviality. I cannot express how thankful I am for Sarah Moody, Dan Sweaney, and Matt Orndorff. They have brought joy and laughter into my life, and their constant support is one of the greatest gifts in my life. One of the silver linings of the global pandemic was getting to know wonderful people close to home. I am thankful for both the Reston Place neighborhood crew and the "Precious Few," who have reminded me that home and family are where you make them. I have been fortunate to maintain strong ties to Madison and to the incredible people there. Kathy and Sarabeth Colwell, Katherine Eade, Craig Katz and Kafryn Lieder, Bonnie Svarstad, Jeffrey Van Fleet, and Janice and Ron Volden filled my summer holidays with joy and lively conversation. I owe a special debt to the "little friends" (two- and four-legged, furry and feathered) who bring unconditional love and happiness into my life. That Jenni Cain, Cristy Gosney, Jean Johnson, Crystal Lykins, and Nicki Schuller continue to share their lives with me is a blessing beyond measure. How fortunate that our paths crossed so early in life and that our bonds remain so strong today. As always, I offer a very special and heartfelt thanks to the many students who continue to teach, to challenge and to inspire me.

I am forever indebted to my greatest cheerleader, Fred Grout. From an early age, Fred taught me to believe in myself, to value the art of learning, and to chase my dreams. He continues to be my biggest fan, and for that I am eternally grateful. Jeanine Mount inspires me as much today as she did when, as a little girl, I wanted to go to college, like she did. I wanted to become a professor, like she did. I wanted to create a life worth living, like she did. I'm still working on that third one, but I'm getting closer every day. My siblings Jamie and Stacey, my nephew Colt, and my mother, Ninette, have shown me more love and patience than I deserve. They remind me who I am, they accept my shortcomings, they celebrate my achievements, and they challenge me to become better. Finally, I am humbled by the legions of exceptional women who have enhanced my life. I hope that they find their echoes not only in this book but also in the woman who wrote it.

Playing
Cleopatra

Introduction

This is not a book about *being*. It is not about who Cleopatra, Sarah Bernhardt, Colette, and Josephine Baker *were*. It is not a collection of biographies, though the narrative that follows offers biographical information about each person. It is not a history of women in the theater, though theatrics and theatrical productions figure prominently in the text. It is not a book in search of universal truths, nor is it a work of fiction, for facts and falsehoods relentlessly intermingle in the lives, stories, and mythologies of these four women. It is not written in the declarative but in the interrogative, though sometimes statements may seem more transparent and questions more elusive than intended. No, this is not a book about *being*. This is, rather, a book about *becoming*. It is a book about *playing*, about *acting*, about *performing*, about *imagining*. The verbs inflecting the narrative are intentionally transitive. Collectively, they mark the processes through which Cleopatra, Sarah Bernhardt, Sidonie-Gabrielle Colette, and Josephine Baker enacted fantasies of exceptional womanhood to invent their celebrity and to claim their place in history.

On the surface it would appear that very little should unite the Cleopatra of ancient Egypt with the Bernhardt, Colette, and Baker of Third Republic France. And yet, upon closer inspection, these women shared much in common. Most notably, all of them achieved legendary cultural status, becoming celebrities in their own time and remaining recognizable in ours. Throughout their lives, they irreverently blurred distinctions between the person and the persona, they aroused curiosity, and they incited intrigue. They provocatively performed multiple versions of womanhood (sometimes simultaneously) that paradoxically reinforced and challenged extant gender norms. And they so

1

effortlessly resisted classification that their personalities often eclipsed their personal accomplishments. Cleopatra, the capable political leader, remains to this day overshadowed by her image as Marc Antony's femme fatale paramour. Bernhardt's notorious love affairs and eccentric lifestyle loom over her career as a formidable thespian. Although eventually welcomed into the French literary canon, Colette could never fully escape her bohemian days and pantomime routines from the café concert. Baker, despite her notoriety as an acclaimed entertainer and her reputation as an international humanitarian, remained for many a rubber banana skirt caricature. Precisely because these women refused to fit, to simply replicate the status quo, they both confounded and enchanted their contemporaries. It is for this reason as well that they continue to beguile us today.

These women, of course, were not the only ones to defy convention during their lifetimes, nor were they the only exceptional women to achieve celebrity status. So, why focus only on them? Why not include the equally remarkable Catherine de Medici, Elizabeth I, Georges Sand, Marie Antoinette, or Catherine the Great, for example? Why connect these women to one another, and why make them the subject of historical inquiry? In one sense, we should link them to one another because they were, in fact, connected on the Paris stage. Bernhardt, Colette, and Baker became associated, to different degrees and in a variety of ways, with the mythology and iconography of the Egyptian queen. Bernhardt literally played Cleopatra, starring in both Shakespeare's and Victorien Sardou's productions devoted to her. Colette evoked her in one of her more noteworthy stage performances, *Rêve d'Égypte*. Meanwhile, Baker so mesmerized audiences with her frenetic dance numbers, many of them staged in contrived colonial settings, that biographers bequeathed to her the title of "Jazz Cleopatra." They should also be linked, however, and perhaps more importantly, because they each held up a mirror to a powerful republic (Rome for Cleopatra, France for Bernhardt, Colette, and Baker), demanding that the polity and the men who claimed to represent it see itself through their racially ambiguous female eyes.

Through their various iterations of Cleopatra and their evocations of the iconographies associated with her, this book explores the ways in which Bernhardt, Colette, and Baker produced their celebrity by enacting a transhistorical fantasy of exceptional womanhood. This fantasy, anchored in the cultural illegibility of racially ambiguous female bodies, unsettled an already unstable category "woman"; it called into question the exclusionary politics of republican universalism; and it even challenged the logic of sequential time. International celebrities whose subversive acts rattled the status quo to such a degree as to have a lasting impact, these women, as we will see, were uniquely poised to carry out the disruptive work of mythmaking and of myth breaking. Unapologetically preoccupied with authoring their own life stories, pursuing their own desires, and fabricating their own public image, Bernhardt, Colette, and Baker enacted fantasies that became central to their own mythologies. At the same time as they engaged in these acts of self-production, however, they also drew upon Cleopatra's legacy to co-opt and coauthor narratives of womanhood that countered republican mythologies of race, gender, and national belonging.

An enduring symbol of ancient civilization and one of the world's oldest celebrities, Cleopatra offers a useful point of origin for considering the fantasy of exceptional womanhood. As her story was told and retold in the millennia after her death, her image was repeatedly recontextualized, modernized, sexualized, and racialized to such an extent that it has become impossible to distinguish the historical figure from her mythologized persona. Through these posthumous renderings, Cleopatra became a temporally and spatially unmoored figure. She was a story as much as a person, an idea imbued with tremendous cultural power. She also became a celebrity who generated fantasies of exceptional womanhood that others would adopt. This is not to suggest that Bernhardt, Colette, and Baker merely replicated fantasies produced by the Egyptian queen. Nor is it to claim that Cleopatra herself ever imagined or made the possibility of these future female celebrities inevitable. Rather, it is to propose that the fantasies of exceptional womanhood she produced endured to be rearticulated by these women in Third Republic France.

As *Playing Cleopatra* will demonstrate, Cleopatra's imagery as well as her privileged position in the collective imaginary provided a critical framework through which the French (and Westerners broadly) understood the powerful, racially unfixed woman. The queen's mythology was so salient and so accessible by the late nineteenth century (reproduced in the novels, plays, artwork, and commercial media of the age) that her name and her image became a shorthand for the racially indistinct, sexually provocative, politically influential woman. Through their engagement with her story and iconography, Bernhardt, Colette, and Baker harnessed Cleopatra's cultural potency, and, by "playing Cleopatra," they revealed the myriad ways that identity is (re)produced in the stories that individuals, collectivities, and even nation-states tell to, for, and about themselves. Through their self-generated fantasies of exceptional womanhood, moreover, these performers inadvertently produced new narratives of national belonging that exposed as contrived any definition of Frenchness that excluded women, nonwhite racial groups, or sexually fluid individuals. In short, they proposed a more inclusive vision of French identity, one that challenged the abstract individual central to the republic's own mythology.[1]

THE FANTASY OF EXCEPTIONAL WOMANHOOD

Despite scholars' efforts to add nuance to accounts of women's lives, the historical record continues to reify woman as a biological, sociological, psychic, and even imaginary category. Whether under the governance of patriarchy, under the purview of domesticity, or circumscribed by the gender politics of liberal democratic regimes (as in the case of Third Republic France), Western women have too often been defined through confining ideologies of sex difference. The prevalence of such ideologies means that women who reject the subordinate roles allocated them have been marginalized, regarded as troublesome, unruly, or, more generously, as "exceptional." An established trope of women's history and gender studies, the exceptional woman resides on the historical periphery, acting sometimes as a necessary social corrective, at others as an alarming cautionary tale. She undermines the regulatory norms of gender by divulging the arbitrary boundaries of sex difference, and she exposes tensions between the contingent production of womanhood and the persistent ideology of the eternal feminine.

Nevertheless, as a structuring narrative of subversive womanhood, the fantasy of exceptionalism has provided nonconforming women a place in history. It has done so by marking these women as "Other" in their own time but also by connecting them to one another, anachronistically, through a common fund of essentialized gender characteristics. In this capacity, the fantasy of exceptional womanhood offers a productive platform for considering linkages between the historical and the mythical. It likewise illuminates how women can be represented as both *of their time* and *timeless.* And it opens up a new conceptual space through which we might examine historical phenomena that, while connected to political, economic, and social structures, and reproduced in rational discourses and measurable markers of change over time, are ultimately rooted in the psychic, in the imagined, in that which can be recognized but not necessarily fully grasped.[2]

To access and assess that which might be only partially ascertained, this book examines how the fantasy of exceptional womanhood intersected with competing fantasies, particularly those related to the eternal feminine, to the eroticized, racialized Other, and to the abstract individual at the center of republican Frenchness. When the revolutionaries of 1789 congregated to build a republic strong enough to dismantle an absolutist monarchy, they envisioned a new relationship between the individual and the state. Based on a social contract, rather than rooted in divine right and heredity, this new government promised to promote human rights and to empower the common person. Despite its universalist claims, however, the republic's founding document, the Declaration of the Rights of Man and Citizen, extended political participation only to men. From its inception and across the various republics established thereafter, the disconnect between the rhetoric of 1789 and its practices became a source of consternation, especially for those groups (women, people of color, colonials) denied the full rights of citizenship.

In the conservative Third Republic, the desire to maintain republican institutions so as to hold antirepublican adversaries at bay superseded any appeal to shake up the status quo. Determined for the republic to succeed, after a tumultuous nineteenth century that witnessed the rise and fall of a second republic, two monarchies, a consulate, and two empires, republican men seemingly connected the government's fragility with their own. In the face of constant challenges from those who would see the republic fail as well as from those determined to expand representation within it, statesmen endeavored to subdue women by glorifying them as dutiful wives, republican mothers, moral arbiters, and, most importantly, as *passive* citizens. Of course, not all women were content with maintaining this ascribed status. By the late nineteenth century, New Women, suffragettes, and feminists advocated for new roles for women, demanding that they, too, enjoy the opportunities of public life and that they take on active roles in the polity. Although relatively few in number, these women caused enough commotion to make many men, across the political spectrum, uncomfortable.

Troubled by this onslaught of vocal, visible women, male novelists, artists, playwrights, caricaturists, and poets authored new fantasies of womanhood that enabled them to articulate their own political, cultural, and social anxieties.[3] From the mid-nineteenth century forward, the femme fatale, the *belle juive,* the *amazone,* the *filles d'Eve,* and the Venus Noire, hypersexualized, exoticized women who were sometimes violent, always sexually potent, and often racially Other, posed a phantasmagoric counter to the ideal republican woman.[4] Like their New Woman counterparts, these "bad girls" infiltrated French society through cultural media and were more alive in the imagination than in reality. Nevertheless, they provided a compelling symbolic language for articulating masculine fears of emasculation and political impotence.

It was within this context that the exceptional women in this book emerged. Although none of them identified as feminists, New Women, or even as women who desired the vote (Colette in particular thought women unsuitable for the franchise), critics catalogued them all alongside the femme fatale. Despite their own efforts to portray themselves as the republican ideal, to their detractors Bernhardt the *belle juive,* Colette the *amazone,* and Baker the Venus Noire could never quite measure up. By reducing these women to the femme fatale stereotype, critics attempted to neutralize their cultural influence and to write them off as unnatural perversions of womanhood. As we will see, however, Bernhardt, Colette, and Baker may have exhibited qualities and behaviors associated with the femme fatale, but they also rejected that label. At every turn, they proclaimed their fidelity to the republican ideal, and they acted in ways commensurate with status quo.

Bernhardt, Colette, and Baker did much more than simply reinforce or challenge the pervasive male-authored scripts that prescribed social roles within the republic; they also crafted new ones rooted in their own fantasies of exceptional womanhood. These new narratives troubled seemingly immutable identity categories and contested the linear notions of time that made such social categories appear fixed and indisputable. As unorthodox interlocutors who marched to the beat of their own drummer, these women interrupted time's forward march. For them, like Clio, the Greek muse of history, time was not only sequential (masculine) but also fluid and synchronous (feminine).[5] Whereas sequential time proposes a rational narrative of continuities and disruptions, synchronous time introduces contradictions, necessarily jumbles cause and effect, and exposes the fictions that construct reality.[6] It was through continuity, as well as through contradiction—specifically in the myriad ways that Bernhardt, Colette, and Baker insisted on their unique particularity even as they attempted to portray themselves as *just like* other women—that these women performed their most significant historical work. By enacting fantasies of exceptional womanhood that were both timely and timeless, they destabilized the categories of race, gender, sexuality, and national belonging at the core of French identity.[7]

To be sure, these women did not produce such commanding fantasies of exceptional womanhood because they were simply *not like* other women. Indeed, these four women confronted the same social, political, and economic obstacles designed to curtail the agency of all women. In Hellenic Egypt, Cleopatra deftly negotiated the contradictory expectations placed upon her as both a woman and a sovereign. Recognized as full citizens, Egyptian women worked outside the home, freely entered into contracts, petitioned the government, inherited and bequeathed property, and even served as heads of household. Roman women, by contrast, did not enjoy the benefits of full citizenship.[8] Elite women could conduct some of their own financial affairs, divorce their husbands, and achieve social power by acting as patrons; however, they could only indirectly influence affairs of state.[9] Importantly, Roman emperors brought their gender politics with them into the Fertile Crescent. It would be against their norms and through their telling of her story that Cleopatra entered into history.

In Third Republic France, Bernhardt, Colette, and Baker, too, navigated a complicated gender politics. Premised on a binary classification of sexual difference, the nineteenth-century liberal ideology of gender ubiquitous in western Europe, evoked biology to promote complementary roles for women and men. In republican France, a country that envisioned active citizenship explicitly as male and implicitly as white, the ideal woman's social role was primarily domestic and decorative. As men's subordinate helpmates, the standard-bearers of familial respectability, and the symbol of virtue for whom republican men sacrificed, women were summarily excluded from politics and discouraged from entering public life. The "true" woman stayed at home, devoted herself entirely to her family, and tolerated sex as an unpleasant procreative duty.[10]

Despite the restrictions placed on them, French women did gain some important legal advances between 1870 and 1939. The number of women in the workforce increased to about 50 percent; they were authorized to establish and maintain personal savings accounts; and they could eventually use the wages they earned without consulting their husbands. Women, including two of the three featured in this book, also participated in the various military conflicts that erupted on French soil, nursing the injured during the Franco-Prussian War, mounting the barricades during the Commune, and driving ambulances, acting as messengers, and taking over men's jobs in almost all sectors of the economy during the Great War. Though applauded for their wartime efforts, after each crisis passed, women were again relegated to the margins and denied the rights of citizenship, rights guaranteed to men simply by virtue of their sex.[11]

Some women refused, however, to remain on the sidelines. As feminists advocated for women's increased participation in politics and New Women demanded to live life on their own terms, Bernhardt, Colette, and Baker used the Paris stage to animate their fantasies of exceptional womanhood.[12] It was on the theatrical stage, in the media, and on the boulevards of the capital city, moreover, that these women became public women and women in public.[13] Here they became targets of ridicule and recipients of adoration, they invited scandal, they reveled in controversy, and they scrambled distinctions between public and private, real and fictive, personal and professional. Here these savvy self-promoters added their voices to the growing cacophony of those demanding change within the republic. And it was here that they contributed their own stories to an ever-expanding collective fantasy of exceptional womanhood whose reverberations would be echoed frequently in the twentieth-century female celebrity.

ECHOES AND ESSENCES

If the fantasy of exceptional womanhood metaphorically connects Cleopatra with Bernhardt, Colette, and Baker, then Joan Scott's notion of the "fantasy echo" suggests how they mobilized that fantasy to upset conventional narratives. Scott proposes that fantasy echoes insinuate a "commonality among women . . . that enable[s] them to transcend history and difference." As "incomplete reproductions," echoes, she continues, "only return fragments" that create "new gaps of meaning and intelligibility" so that each "echo undermines the notion of enduring sameness that often attaches to identity."[14] By playing Cleopatra, Bernhardt, Colette, and Baker tapped into the subversive behaviors and discourses generated by exceptional women across time, most notably those engendered by Cleopatra. Yet, as we will see, their fantasies, which provided powerful counternarratives to the republic's male-authored exclusionary scripts, *resembled* rather than *replicated* the original. Bernhardt, Colette, and Baker did not simply copy Cleopatra's fantasy of exceptional womanhood; they echoed it.

The women discussed in this book shared some important similarities that, taken together, made them exceptional: they were racially ambiguous, they were sexually fluid, they challenged accepted gender roles, and they were celebrities. Although one attribute at times overshadowed others, it was not a single characteristic but the interplay of all four collectively that underwrote their fantasies of exceptional womanhood. Just as we cannot understand the work of exceptional womanhood without recognizing the racial composition of the women deemed exceptional or by ignoring the racial attitudes of their audiences, neither can we appreciate the ways in which fantasy operated without examining how one's sexuality, gender, and celebrity status or the audience's sexism, homophobia, or fandom also contributed to its work. Given the attention paid to race, gender, sexuality, and celebrity at the time, Third Republic France offers an especially productive avenue for exploring how fantasies of exceptional womanhood initiated a reassessment of republican values. Not only does it offer up three powerful examples of this fantasy, but it also provides a context for understanding the contested identity politics of a young republic attempting to secure its own place in history. The republic came to understand itself through the articulated values of 1789, through the legal apparatus of the Napoleonic Civil Code (1804), and through its social customs, its culture, and its history. But it also came to know itself by what it was *not*. To this end, it constructed Others, like the exceptional women in this book, within and outside the Hexagon to measure itself against.[15]

At the same time, however, republicans came to appreciate, in perhaps unanticipated ways, the richness of certain "Other" civilizations. Indeed, in this moment many western Europeans possessed a seemingly unquenchable thirst for all things Egyptian. In their zeal, they Orientalized the Egyptian Other, and they reimagined its most commanding symbol, Cleopatra. Several nineteenth- and early twentieth-century events, including Napoleon's campaign into the region (1798–1801), the deciphering of hieroglyphs after studying the Rosetta Stone (1822), the raising of obelisks, the opening of the Suez Canal (1869), and the discovery of King Tutankhamun's tomb (1922), not only sparked interest in travel to Egypt and in the collection of its artifacts but also inspired a new style that evoked Egyptian themes, materials, and scenes in art, fashion, and theater.[16] As ancient originals were copied or adapted, travel narratives and explorers' sketches published, and the research of archaeologists and Egyptologists popularized, Cleopatra emerged as the "spectral legacy of Egypt" within the Western cultural imaginary.[17] Cultural producers commodified Cleopatra's image and fetishized her foreign female body. Furthermore, like the explorers, scientists, and statesmen of their time, they mixed Romantic sentiment with imperial ambition.[18] In this regard, Cleopatra symbolized the transcontinental country of her origin as well as the pleasures and promises of the exotic Other. Through her iconography, Westerners manufactured fantasies of the East that enabled them to legitimize their grandiose political aspirations, to shore up their exclusionary definition of national identity, and to reassert their perceived cultural superiority.[19]

The imperial mission was especially important to the French, who had recently suffered defeat at the hands of the newly unified Germany and whose lust for "the Orient" was in part guided by its desire to remain relevant in international affairs. In the 1870s and 1880s, this proved an especially complicated task for a nation rebuilding itself after the collapse of its own domestic empire and struggling to reconcile imperial domination with a republican ideology premised on universal liberty.[20] In addition to these considerations, the Third Republic was internally plagued by bitter political rivalries, preoccupied with demographic decline, and unsettled by fears of moral contamination and social degeneracy. As the twentieth century took shape, the beleaguered republic suffered through a catastrophic world war and was forced to recuperate through an influenza epidemic, the rise of extremist political regimes across the continent, and a global economic downturn that crippled the national economy.

Amid such turmoil, French men and women sought refuge in the theaters, dance halls, and cafés of Paris. As both objects and purveyors of fantasy and as reincarnations of a fictionalized Oriental past, Bernhardt, Colette, and Baker offered overwrought audiences a much-needed reprieve from the trials of modern life. By temporarily transporting viewers beyond place and time, they offered a means for imaginatively escaping the present, and they fostered a shared identity among audience members, who recognized themselves as *not like* the women onstage. Although spectators came from all over the world and represented a variety of classes, racial groups, and sexual preferences, Parisian crowds were overwhelming heteronormative, middle class, and white. By spectacularizing the racially and sexually ambiguous working female body, by making the Other an object of display, these entertainments reinforced differences between viewers and viewed. Through the Orientalized stage performances of women who were not quite French, not quite white, not quite heterosexual, not quite man's submissive companion, and not quite the foreign characters they portrayed, Bernhardt, Colette, and Baker ultimately presented audiences with a nebulous Other against which to define themselves.[21]

At the same time, these performances also enflamed popular debates, reflected contemporary anxieties, and projected new fantasies of womanhood and Frenchness. Under the Third Republic, champions of the white, heterosexual, bourgeois status quo maintained that woman possessed certain qualities, bestowed by nature, that she could not transcend. From Aristotle's locating womanhood in a precariously "wandering womb" to Rousseau's assertion that, because of her reproductive capacity, "a woman is a woman all of the time," philosophers had qualified woman's subordination and explained her perceived intellectual inferiority as simple facts of nature. During the eighteenth and nineteenth centuries, physiologists, physicians, and other men of science preoccupied with explaining anatomical sex difference extended these arguments by inextricably linking woman's sex to her individual character and social function. These men used the fact of the female body to lend credence to the idea that a "feminine essence"—a repository of natural, embodied characteristics—indicated woman's absolute otherness from man.

As purveyors of fantasy, Bernhardt, Colette, and Baker paradoxically upheld and undermined the prevailing assumptions regulating sex difference. On the one hand, admirers reduced them, in some ways through their connections to Cleopatra, to their timeless feminine essence. As eroticized sexual playthings, they were physically attractive objects of masculine pleasure (made for man's delight, in Rousseau's parlance). As spectacles of male ocular enjoyment, they were pleasing. And, as emotive, emotional, even histrionic creatures, their sense was often overshadowed by their sensibility. On the other hand, critics portrayed them as perversions of "true womanhood." They may have submitted to male pleasure, but they were not passionless housewives. They played at purity, piety, and virtue onstage, but they did not necessarily adhere to these prescriptions in real life. And, perhaps most dangerously, they challenged the biological fact of the racially fixed female body. Cloaked in the costumes of the Other, appearing in drag, and themselves racially indeterminate figures, they exposed the illusion behind the most fundamental tenet of anatomical difference. Through this last act, they threatened to loosen womanhood from its corporeal trappings and to reveal dislocations between the sexed body and gender identity, as well as between the raced body and Frenchness. If the biological fact of the body no longer existed, then, as Scott maintains, there could be "no essence of womanhood . . . only successive iterations of a word that doesn't have a fixed referent and so doesn't always mean the same thing."[22] As *Playing Cleopatra* will show, through public performance, literally by spectacularizing the racially and sexually ambiguous female body, Bernhardt, Colette, and Baker defied the fixity of that body and suggested that if there was no essence of womanhood, there was also, perhaps, no embodied essence of Frenchness.[23]

FAMOUS FIGURES

It was not merely as women, but as famous figures, that Cleopatra, Bernhardt, Colette, and Baker entered into the collective imagination. It is precisely because they were celebrated objects of public attention, deemed worthy of media coverage and documented in text and on film, that they have provided scholars with the archival material necessary for investigating exceptional womanhood's assorted genealogy. At the same time that their exceptionalism enabled them to illuminate the often-hidden dynamics of power through which women have challenged the status quo, it also provided a lens for examining the myriad ways that celebrity itself has been gendered.[24]

To unravel the tangled relationship between womanhood and celebrity, we must understand the latter's etymology.[25] Since its inception, celebrity has been linked to visibility, reputation, and fame. Derived from the Latin *fama*, fame was first connected, through Virgil's epic poem the *Aeneid*, to Roma, the goddess of rumor and spreader of news who used "her wings and her multiple mouths to tell all."[26] Fame passed through Old French and Middle English to connote, by the thirteenth century, an individual's public estimation and, by the fourteenth century, one's popular acclaim. From the outset, fame was almost exclusively associated with the masculine—the emperor, the hero, the great man of letters, or the adventurer. Fame was bestowed upon an individ-

ual because of his good deeds but could also recognize his elevated hereditary position: the king was famous simply because he was king.[27] By the eighteenth century, to be famous was not simply to be known but to be revered,
respected, or admired—perhaps even feared. In this way, fame conferred cultural capital onto its recipients.

More imprecise than fame, celebrity, from the Latin *celebrem,* implied
both the celebration of an individual and a reciprocity between the esteemed
and the public. Because it could not be achieved without an audience, celebrity was *collectively* constituted. It was regarded as transitory, opaque, and,
increasingly, as feminine. And, unlike fame, it struggled against critiques of
excess and superficiality.[28] It was also a product of considerable transformations in the public sphere, chief among them the development of a new con-
cept of the self, the rise of publicity, and the commercialization of leisure.[29]
Elevating individuals to the public stage, celebrity bestowed new forms of
capital—commercial, cultural, social, discursive, even political. As persuasive
cultural brokers, celebrities like Bernhardt, Colette, and Baker embodied and
contested the values, interests, and assumptions of the dominant culture. But
always reliant on public opinion for their status, they had also always to play
to audiences. To achieve and to retain their notoriety, they coauthored and
co-opted collective fantasies, and they awakened, encouraged, enticed, and
frustrated personal desires.[30]

In the nineteenth century, celebrated individuals became "known" through
the intertwined mechanisms of the mass media and the mass market. Indeed,
widespread industrialization, unprecedented urbanization, technological in-
novation (especially in print production and photography), and the advent
of rapid forms of communication transmitted information faster and farther
than ever before. These developments, alongside the expansion of discretionary spending, the growth of literacy, especially after passage of the Ferry Laws
(1881 and 1882 that made free, secular education compulsory for both sexes),
and the demand for leisure among the middle and then the working classes,
coalesced to create the conditions necessary for the emergence of a commer-
cialized celebrity culture.[31] As men and women were drawn to urban centers
for work in industry, individuals came into close, regular contact with one another as never before. Proximity and anonymity, moreover, placed more em-
phasis on the visual. *Seeing* and *being seen* became ways for strangers to identify and to distinguish themselves as well as ways to create community.[32] What

was happening on city streets was mirrored in the thriving mass press. Growing in volume and diversifying in scope, local, regional, and national newspapers increasingly added *fait divers* (human interest stories), *roman-feuilleton* (serialized fictional stories), advertisements, theater reviews, and photographs of prominent individuals and noteworthy events to their reportage.[33] In this way, the press both reflected and shaped public interest, and it became an indispensable vehicle for the creation and dissemination of celebrity.[34]

It was through the media—the press, the lifestyle magazine, the *cartes de visite,* the poster, the trading card, and even the postcard—that celebrity became a "powerful social force."[35] The press, moreover, proved a great democratizer, bringing stories and images of not only the wealthy and influential but also of the exceptional and the entertaining into the private household. By replacing the unique with the ubiquitous, moreover, the media deprived the esteemed of cultural permanence by shining a light on ambitious attention seekers.[36] In this way, the media created and catered to a new specular economy that made fame accessible to ordinary people both through the spotlight and through consuming information about those who desired it.[37]

The media and the market provided the institutional frameworks and technological apparatuses necessary for the development of celebrity culture, and they also provided a platform for the celebrity to foster personal connections with her audience.[38] Throughout their careers Bernhardt, Baker, and Colette were photographed "at home," interviewed about their personal preferences, and were subjects of gossip whose "dirty laundry" was routinely aired for public consumption. The media simultaneously humanized and lionized these women, portraying them as mischief makers, talented entertainers, and aspirational models of female achievement. In its reportage, the media demonstrated the ways that these women challenged the limits of social probity, even as they embodied the values of the dominant culture.[39] It presented Bernhardt, Colette, and Baker as unparalleled cultural phenomena who were also fallible human beings, ordinary women who looked and acted *just like* everyone else.[40]

In Third Republic France, Bernhardt, Colette, and Baker were more than mere celebrities, however; they were superstars.[41] These especially talented female stage performers rose to the highest echelon of stardom because they were culturally illegible forces of nature with tremendous crossover appeal. They resonated with diverse audiences because of their uncanny ability to cross genre and media (appearing in film, theatrical productions, text, art, and commercial advertisements) and because of their chameleon-like ability to seem both exotically Other and quintessentially *just like us.* They attracted public attention because they crossed boundaries of sexual propriety, racial difference, gender norms, and class affiliation. In their work as in their lives, inseparable entities themselves, they crossed the line between fact and fiction, public and private. On the surface, because they authored memoirs, gave interviews, and offered opinions on everything from music to cooking, they presented themselves as open books, completely accessible and knowable to the public they charmed. However, their memoirs were written in the service of their celebrity, their interviews were often contrived, and their opinions changed by the hour. These women were enigmas, crafty storytellers who spellbound audiences by stoking their desires, by playing in and on their own fantasies. Despite the many ways that they were otherwise marginalized in a republic that regarded women and people of color as second-class citizens, these women took center stage in the collective imagination. In the process, they wove themselves into the fabric of French republicanism, becoming, like Cleopatra, an emblem of the very age they both defined and defied.[42]

UNRELIABLE NARRATORS

To explore how celebrity articulates the fantasy of exceptional womanhood and vice versa, this book examines how both were produced in the media, in the marketplace, and in the imagination. To this end, I read autobiographies, biographies, hagiographies, theater bills, novels, plays, and press reportage alongside posters, advertisements, paintings, film, and caricatures devoted to Cleopatra, Bernhardt, Colette, and Baker to recover the manifold ways that celebrity and womanhood made one another. Each of these women has garnered tremendous scholarly attention. The goal is thus not to provide an exhaustive engagement with this scholarship or to offer new interpretations of each woman's own works. Rather, the aim is to show how, by reading their performances alongside one another, through the various media that helped produce them, and under the rubric of the fantasy of exceptional womanhood, we might better understand how they used their celebrity to effect political and cultural change.

At the same time that these women engaged in this work, they also established a promotional template that future female celebrities would follow. Beyond a doubt, Bernhardt, Colette, and Baker were talented performers and multifaceted human beings who lived complicated lives. But they were also expert saleswomen who understood the commercial value of a well-crafted persona. They were shrewd self-promoters who harnessed new technologies—the mass press, the cinema, radio—to keep themselves in the public eye, and they were gifted storytellers whose fascinating personalities sustained the public's fickle attention. By courting intrigue and packaging scandal as newsworthy tidbits ripe for public consumption, they distinguished themselves from their contemporaries and established a formula for attracting media attention that future celebrities would emulate.

Given their dedication to creating a public persona, getting at these women's stories is a tricky endeavor. Although abundant and accessible, none of the sources examined in this book are value-neutral. All of them, whether newspaper reviews or fine art portraits, were created with a purpose: to sell or to promote; to elicit an emotional, moral, or intellectual response; to persuade; to confound; to deceive; to incite fantasy. Precisely because they tell no truths, even when they explicitly profess to do so, these sources tease us now as much as they taunted contemporaries when they first appeared. Given their multifarious functions as well as their proclivity to conceal as much as they reveal, we must approach these sources cautiously, recognizing their explanatory limitations even as we mine them for historical meaning. Our inability to take them at face value, however, does not negate their worth or foreclose opportunities for analysis. As we will see, these sources reveal competing discourses around celebrity and womanhood that enable us to uncover the narrative structures through which the fantasy of exceptional womanhood found expression.

Cleopatra produced no surviving autobiography, but Bernhardt, Colette, and Baker all engaged in storytelling the self. Bernhardt's *Ma double vie* (1907) and *The Art of the Theater* (1924); Colette's autobiographical fiction *La Maison de Claudine* (1922), *Sido* (1929), and *La Naissance du jour* (1928); and Baker's coauthored autobiographies including *Les Mémoires de Joséphine Baker* (1949) with Marcel Sauvage and *Josephine* (1976) with Jo Bouillon exemplify the ways in which these women narrated their celebrity.[43] Historians, literary critics, and, most recently, scholars working in media and celebrity studies have recognized autobiography and memoir as valuable sources.[44] Nevertheless debates continue to arise regarding how exactly they should be interpreted. Critics of the genre distrust autobiography's inherent subjectivity and its reliance on individual rather than collective measures of time. They also maintain that memoirs are riddled with personal fictions, fabricated stories that obscure the reality of historical situations. Focused on an individual, memoir necessarily and artificially privileges a subjectively centered self. Yet because it is a form of storytelling, it also threatens to transform the author's self into fiction.[45]

Unraveling an autobiography's dubious truth claims is even more challenging, of course, when that autobiography was penned by (or in the name of) a celebrity. Intended for the public, celebrity memoirs are especially problematic because they anticipate external scrutiny at the same time that they propose to reveal the hidden work involved in creating the celebrated self.[46] Mediating between the persona and the product, the celebrity autobiographer not only narrates a life lived but also animates, and packages for mass consumption, a life imagined.[47] Whether we engage memoir as a "self-sufficient text," or try to bring it into "intertextual relationship with other evidence," or even read it as nothing more than a necessarily "fictive structure," we must understand it above all as a performance.[48] For Bernhardt, Colette, and Baker, writing the self was part of the act; it was the place where fact and fiction intermingled; and it was a primary vehicle for disseminating their own fantasies of exceptional womanhood.

So, how do we make sense of the stories told by our admittedly unreliable narrators? I propose that we acknowledge their roles as storytellers and consider the ways in which they engage the dominant narratives of their time. Each woman in this book has been the subject of numerous biographies, academic and popular works of nonfiction, and fictional renderings. Each has told stories, and stories have been told about her. However, no one has yet brought these stories together, no one has identified the common threads of exceptionalism running through them, and no one has analyzed these women's personal exploits as constituting acts through which constructions of womanhood might be better apprehended. By reading intertextually (across contemporary sources produced by and about these women) and intercontextually (examining sources produced about these women across time), *Playing Cleopatra* explores the multifarious contradictions within the fantasy of exceptional womanhood. It does so not to suggest that there is something essential and natural about womanhood itself, but to divulge womanhood, celebrity, and identity as fantastic fabrications.[49]

If, as Léopold Lacour predicted, "Cleopatra is ceaselessly reborn, the eternal symbol of man's vulnerability to the power of woman," then in the performances of Bernhardt, Colette, and Baker we witness that rebirth and we anticipate the reverberations, the echoes, destined to follow.[50] Cleopatra's image saturated the cultural media of nineteenth-century France, and yet Lacour's declaration in the October 21, 1890, issue of *Le Figaro* seemed especially prescient. Understood in the context of growing feminist agitation (the first international congress for women's rights convened in Paris in 1878) as well as in the ascent of the New Woman, and an unhealthy fixation on demographic decline and moral degeneracy, the politically powerful Cleopatra vividly symbolized man's vulnerability as well as woman's empowerment. At stake in the Third Republic iterations of her was not only man's relationship to woman but also the individual's relationship to the state, as masculine fragility could easily be read as republican weakness.

On the heels of the Boulanger debacle, which threatened to overthrow the republic in 1889, the nation hosted an extraordinary universal exposition that attempted to signify the republic's enduring strength. Celebrating the past by commemorating the one-hundredth anniversary of the storming of the Bastille, the exposition also looked to France's future, envisioning itself, in the image of the Eiffel Tower, as a modern nation. Ten years later, however, it would not be the iron tower but the colossal (twenty-one-foot!) statue *La Parisienne* that welcomed visitors to the exposition. Positioned atop the Porte Monumentale, the brightly adorned ceramic icon graced the fair's eastern entrance located at the Place de la Concorde. The site of many guillotine executions (including that of the king and his family) during the Revolution, in the 1830s the square was fitted with a three-thousand-year-old Egyptian obelisk anchored by two Roman-inspired water features. Metaphorically situated at the intersection of Paris, Egypt, and Rome, *La Parisienne*'s ambiguous, hybrid figure made her a complicated allegory of the nation. Decorated in Byzantine motifs, she was adorned in the latest fashions. She symbolized the republic, but she wore a crown. She introduced the world to the latest technological gadgets and industrial advancements, but she was depicted in promotional material surrounded by the flora and fauna of the natural world. She embodied Paris for the provinces and France for the rest of the world. At the same time that she did all of this, she also referenced current debates about woman's place in the republic. Should *La Parisienne* be read as the ideal republican woman or, in her very public display and imposing figure, did she reference the dangerous femme fatale? Positioned at a geographical and metaphorical crossroads, was she a gracious hostess who welcomed the world into the heart of France or was she a tenacious gatekeeper tasked with keeping them out? Lurking behind *La Parisienne*'s image, as made clear by her residence at the Place de la Concorde, was the spectre of Cleopatra. Whether in her own image or echoed in that of *La Parisienne,* the racially unfixed, sexually promiscuous, powerful female allegory continued to signify man's vulnerability to woman. Situated at the entry of the world's fair and recast beneath the imperial gaze of a nascent republic eager to establish its political legitimacy, her elusive femininity, open as it was to multiple interpretations, signaled the republic's fortitude as well as its fragility.

Like *La Parisienne,* Bernhardt, Colette, and Baker tapped into pervasive cultural discourses of female empowerment, echoing Cleopatra to fashion their own fantasies of exceptional womanhood. Cleopatra's iconography and mythology permeated the Third Republic; that it was appropriated by the female performers at the center of this book, then, is not altogether surprising. What is compelling, however, is the extent to which these frameworks, and the fantasy of exceptional womanhood that underwrote them, influenced how the young, vulnerable republic saw women, saw race, and even saw itself. In this period, national insecurities expressed themselves through debates about gender roles, sexuality, race, and the meaning of Frenchness. The Cleopatra myth provided French audiences a shared language and safe point of reference for framing these debates. Moreover, the echoes of it found in the self-fashioning and playacting of Bernhardt, Colette, and Baker comprised a vibrant cultural space for working through anxieties around the perceived emasculation of men, the growing influence of women in public, and the demand for political participation among those excluded from power. Through these women, Cleopatra was not literally reborn, of course, but the fantasy of exceptional womanhood rooted in cultural illegibility that she originated was reinvigorated. As Cleopatra's echoes, Bernhardt, Colette, and Baker mobilized fantasy as an ideological weapon, and they used it as a strategy for challenging the exclusionary politics of republican France.

Acknowledging that echoes distort over time, the chapters that follow explore how these fantasies of exceptional womanhood resonated in new ways with a French public engaged in reassessing feminine sexuality, racialized beauty, and national identity. As what Michel de Certeau identifies as "ever-unfinished *acts* of elucidation," Baker's echo of Cleopatra's fantasy of exceptional womanhood is more distorted than Colette's, whose is more distorted than Bernhardt's.[51] Through these imperfect reverberations, we witness the fantasy transform and we see the ways in which female performances function as acts of articulation as well as articulating acts that bring myth into language. Read within a broader cultural context that evoked Cleopatra's mythology as a referent for a feminized, racialized Other, Bernhardt, Colette, and Baker's subversive acts engaged broader debates regarding the meaning of womanhood, celebrity, and Frenchness.

To illustrate how these debates transpired, the following chapters examine the ways through which these women fashioned celebrity. The intent is not to arbitrarily collapse temporalities, to posit a one-to-one correlation between one historical moment or figure and another, but rather to explore how the fantasy of exceptional womanhood expresses itself across time, and to think critically about how knowledge is produced and disseminated through celebrated figures. Chapter 1 establishes what we think we know about Cleopatra before tracing the myriad ways that Westerners have interpreted her since her death. The remaining "echo" chapters, 2, 3, and 4, devoted to Bernhardt, Colette, and Baker, respectively, are catalogued chronologically and formatted identically. The first part of each chapter examines how these unreliable narrators engaged in multivocal storytellings of the self. These sections illuminate how each woman narrated her own fantasy of exceptional womanhood and demonstrate how they situated themselves in and beyond time. The second section of each chapter builds upon these stories as context for analyzing how each performer echoed Cleopatra onstage. For example, Bernhardt literally *played* Cleopatra, Colette *played at* her, and Baker more subtly *played with* her. The third section of each chapter further explores the fantasy as it reverberates through the cultural illegibility of the performers under consideration. By examining how each woman's racial, sexual, and gender ambiguity shaped their celebrity as well as their reception, these segments examine the cultural and political work of fantasy in constructing identity. Together these chapters demonstrate how, as Cleopatra's echoes, Bernhardt, Colette, and Baker produced fantasies of exceptional womanhood that enabled them to circumvent the republic's exclusionary politics at the same time as they laid the groundwork of modern celebrity. They also suggest that Hollywood did not create the modern celebrity as we know her; Third Republic France did.

1

Cleopatra

A "MOST WOMANLY WOMAN"

> [Cleopatra] . . . the most complete woman ever to have existed,
> the most womanly woman and the most queenly queen, a person to
> be wondered at, to whom the poets have been able to add nothing,
> and whom dreamers find always at the end of their dreams.
>
> —THÉOPHILE GAUTIER, *Une nuit de Cléopâtre,* 1838

Théophile Gautier's adulatory exaltation of Cleopatra as the "most womanly woman," the most "queenly queen," and the most "complete woman ever to have existed" is noteworthy not only for its hyperbolic prose but also because the esteemed writer praised a person whom he had never met, who lived and died centuries before his own lifetime, and who governed a foreign land that he had visited but that he never called home. Gautier's tribute is even more remarkable when we consider how little is known generally about either Cleopatra the queen or Cleopatra the woman. The historical record offers only glimpses into particular episodes of her reign, and it frequently filters pivotal events through the lens of her political adversaries in Rome. Thus, although the name Cleopatra has transcended centuries, the woman and queen who bore that name remains elusive, hidden, and, in many regards, completely unknowable. In light of these facts, how could Gautier so confidently venerate the Egyptian empress? How could he so effortlessly disentangle her from those "other poets" who added nothing to her allure? Did he, could he, like so many before and after him, find her only at the "end of [his] dreams"?

Gautier's fascination with Cleopatra is not altogether surprising when understood within the context of the widespread enthusiasm for all things

Egyptian that pervaded nineteenth-century French culture. Napoleon's much-celebrated military campaign into Egypt in 1798 and the numerous publications that it inspired reawakened French interest in the region and reignited colonial fantasies of the exotic, which were dormant but rarely extinguished in the Western imaginary.[1] That Cleopatra would feature prominently in these (predominantly) white male fantasies of the East is also not unexpected given her complicated relationship to political authority and to sexual agency. Indeed, for many nineteenth-century novelists, artists, playwrights, and poets, Cleopatra epitomized the promises, the perils, and the promiscuity of both the Orient and the Other.[2] Viewed through the twin prisms of Romantic sensibility and imperial ambition, Cleopatra, for nineteenth-century Europeans, seamlessly united discourses of desire and empire.

In many ways Gautier's fantasy of Cleopatra exemplifies Edward Said's classic definition of Orientalism. According to Said, Orientalism signifies a discursive construction of difference, "a style of thought based upon an ontological and epistemological distinction made between 'the Orient' and (most of the time) 'the Occident.'"[3] From the eighteenth century forward, and particularly in the interactions between France, Great Britain, and the East, Orientalism provided a conceptual panacea for understanding, even legitimizing, Western dominance in parts of the non-Occidental world.[4] As Said explains, Orientalism functions primarily through the constant construction and shoring up of seemingly arbitrary binaries: a rational, familiar, moral, and Christian West contrasts with an illogical, foreign, erotic, and heathen, East.[5] A variable yet somewhat comprehensive discourse, Orientalism, for Said, exploits racial, ethnic, and national differences through which Westerners came to demarcate and ultimately to claim authority over the Other. In short, it provided a fantasy of the Other through which the West came to see and know itself.

Yet, the stereotypes underwriting Orientalism are problematic, not least because they presume the superiority of European cultures, thereby misrepresenting both East and West to one another and to themselves. They potentially obscure commonalities between the two, moreover, by artificially privileging race over other perceived markers of difference. Arguing that colonial discourses are sustained by ideologies of gender as well as those of race, Reina Lewis considers Orientalism a fluid, dynamic, and permeable lexicon riddled with "enunciative positionalities" that "reveal some of the fictions of discourse and of imperial power."[6] Whereas Said's notion of Orientalism posits a fixed register of colonial dominance and limits the ideological work made possible by Cleopatra's fantasy of exceptional womanhood, Lewis's more robust definition multiplies its discursive possibilities. Modern Europeans understood Cleopatra as both an "Oriental" and as a woman. It was through the categories of race *and* gender, then, that her fantasy of exceptional womanhood permeated the Anglo-European imagination. Under the aegis of Orientalism, Cleopatra functioned as a historically situated Eastern kaleidoscope through which the West defined itself and envisioned the Other. As a fantasy of exceptional womanhood that both reinforced and challenged this ideology, she unmasked Orientalism's inherent contradictions and exposed the arbitrary differences separating East and West.

To demonstrate how Cleopatra's fantasy of exceptional womanhood found expression across time, this chapter explores the myriad ways that she has been identified, imagined, and invented since her birth in 69 BCE. The subject of more than two hundred plays and novels, forty-five operas, five ballets, forty-three films, and no fewer than 230 works of art produced in the seventeenth and eighteenth centuries alone, Cleopatra has become a mainstay of the Western imaginary. The chapter begins by piecing together what we think we know about Cleopatra as derived from available artifacts and through the (admittedly prejudicial) ancient accounts of her life and reign. Next, I trace Cleopatra's legacy through the early modern period, examining how depictions of her onstage and in print, most notably in Shakespeare's play *Antony and Cleopatra,* shaped her modern hagiography. From here, the chapter moves to France, assessing how nineteenth-century French cultural elites reframed her within a masculine, Orientalist gaze. Highlighting how twentieth-century stage and screen productions transformed her into an international icon, the penultimate section of the chapter explores how she embodied feminine beauty and sexuality in an international mass market. The final section circles back to the Third Republic. It previews the chapters that follow, setting the stage for Bernhardt, Colette, and Baker by enumerating the primary ways that Cleopatra's brand of exceptional womanhood appealed to French audiences. Ultimately, it was as a culturally illegible woman that Cleopatra has provided a shorthand for debating issues of race, sex, and state power. Through the iconography of a "most womanly woman," and the fantasy of exceptional womanhood she signified, Cleopatra offered Westerners, the French chief among them, an enchanting Other against which to measure and to multiply the possibilities of the self.

Born around 69 BCE, Cleopatra VII would reign as Egypt's last Ptolemaic monarch from 51 BCE until her death twenty-one years later at age thirty-nine. Few contemporary sources documenting Cleopatra's life and career have survived, yet there are some facts on which scholars agree. She ascended her deceased father's throne at the age of eighteen and initially ruled in uneasy concert with her ten-year-old brother. The family bloodline was three-quarters Macedonian and one-quarter Egyptian. Although no portraits remain of her, two-dimensional coinage produced during her reign depicted Cleopatra with a pronounced nose and chin and a penetrating gaze.[7] The degree to which she embodied the beauty standards of her age remains a source of controversy—some contemporaries attest to her physical attractiveness while others detract from it, with one source describing her as short, another as masculine in comportment if not in appearance.[8] No such disagreement exists, however, concerning the queen's mental acuity. Educated in her father's court by the tutor Philostratos, Cleopatra became fluent in nine languages (including Egyptian, Greek, and various regional dialects). She was a skilled orator and an avid reader. In her lifetime, she was regarded as an accomplished equestrian and hunter, a savvy diplomat and capable administrator, a shrewd naval commander, an amateur pharmacologist, a talented linguist, and an erudite author.[9]

Cleopatra descended from a long line of powerful female rulers, and she resided in an Egypt renowned for the extensive political, legal, and economic rights afforded to women. Unlike their Roman counterparts, Egyptian women were not second-class citizens but autonomous individuals capable of entering into contracts, initiating lawsuits, and operating businesses without male supervision. They inherited equally, served as priests and moneylenders, and owned land, livestock, homes, and slaves. Egyptian women tended to marry later than their neighbors, but they exercised greater rights within marriage. If unsatisfied with a partner, they could demand a divorce. Upon dissolution of the union, they could expect to retain the marital dowry, maintain the familial residence, and secure custody of the children. These liberties confounded foreigners, especially Romans, who, although they granted women citizenship, made that status conditional on male guardianship.[10]

The empire that Cleopatra inherited from her father was allegedly fraught with financial difficulty, and it was undeniably less geographically expansive than it had been in the third and second centuries BCE. Once on the throne, however, Cleopatra mobilized Egypt's vast natural resources, strengthened connections among the people under her domain, and entered into political alliances that enabled territorial expansion. To revive the economy, she capitalized on traditional sources of revenue—commodities such as grain, vegetable oil, papyrus, textiles, and aromatics and land that could be cultivated or leased—and expanded Egyptian coinage. She also initiated several important building projects. She repaired the main gymnasium, the library, and the Lighthouse of Pharos and constructed an entire precinct within the city of Alexandria dedicated to Julius Caesar. This last project not only commemorated her amorous liaison with the influential statesman but also visibly positioned her kingdom within the sprawling Roman world. Allying herself first with Caesar and then with Marc Antony, Cleopatra curried favor with Rome but also enlarged her dominion, subdued rival monarchs, and established herself as the strongest ruler in the eastern Mediterranean by 37 BCE.[11]

Although posthumously venerated and disparaged for her rumored sexual prowess, Cleopatra engaged in only two certifiable sexual liaisons during her reign. That each of these relationships produced children (potential dynastic heirs) and involved two of the most powerful Romans of the age, attests less to the queen's lusty carnal appetites than to her willingness to align sex with statecraft to ensure her political survival. Cleopatra birthed four children, one to Caesar (named Caesarian/Ptolemy XV) in 47 BCE and three to Antony (twins Alexander Helios and Cleopatra Selene, born 40 BCE, and a son Ptolemy Philadelphus, born 36 BCE), whom the couple formally recognized and bequeathed regional leaderships to in 34 BCE.[12] Although Caesarian's parentage was somewhat disputed, especially among her political adversaries, it was well-documented in official records.[13] Cleopatra's insistence on the paternity of her child as well as her clever naming of him, moreover, asserted her offspring's legitimacy as heir to both the kingdom of Egypt and to the republic of Rome.

Cleopatra's connections to Julius Caesar and Marc Antony, particularly her status as mother to their children, complicated rather than clarified her relationship to Rome. On the one hand, by producing Roman heirs, she ensured her own authority over the eastern Mediterranean, effectively overshadowing many of her political rivals in that region. On the other hand, her children's legitimacy threatened the ambitious Octavian, with whom Marc Antony shared power upon Caesar's death. In addition to these maneuverings, Cleopatra's affair with Antony instigated the crumbling of the Second Triumvir (comprised of Antony, Octavian, and Lepidus), an alliance previously secured through Antony's marriage to Octavian's sister Octavia. In response to this betrayal, Octavian would aggravate popular uncertainty regarding Caesarian's paternity and mobilize Cleopatra's extramarital entanglement with Antony to launch a vicious propaganda war. In image and in verse, Octavian and his allies discredited and emasculated Antony, depicting him as Cleopatra's weak-kneed, love-obsessed plaything. At the same time, they openly challenged Caesarian's claim as heir and increasingly portrayed Cleopatra as both a cunning seductress and a barbaric foreigner. Eventually this war of words escalated into the bitter military conflict at Actium. The ferocious battle that ensued there would culminate in Octavian's triumph, lead to the deaths of Antony and Cleopatra, and, ultimately, facilitate the creation of the Roman Empire.[14]

Despite being a clever self-promoter (aligning herself with great men as well as with the goddess Isis) and a masterful impresario of political theater (choreographing lavish spectacles and seducing foreign emissaries with endless banquets and opulent processions), Cleopatra could manage but never completely control her public image. Not that she did not try. Cleopatra understood the optics of power and the importance of public visibility.[15] For example, she used the occasion of Caesarian's birth to connect herself not only to Rome but also to Isis. The goddess of agriculture and harvests as well as of marriage and maternity, Isis was, like the queen, also a single mother. From as early as 47 BCE, Cleopatra explicitly linked the popular cult of Isis to legitimate Egyptian state power. She did so by appearing at official functions dressed in the divinity's image, by petitioning Caesar to construct a Temple of Isis in Rome (although Romans had long been ambivalent about the cult), and, if the rumors were true, by using an asp in her suicide, which recalled the goddess's cobra-encircled crown.[16] Portraying herself as an ephemeral mother-goddess, as both of this earth and beyond it, she conjured an almost supernatural fantasy of exceptional womanhood. More than a mere mortal, more than even a powerful queen, she aligned herself with the gods. Through the cult of Isis, and specifically through her theatrical terrestrial embodiments of her,

Cleopatra vividly wove together Egypt and Rome, past and future, mortal and divine in the fabric of her own person.

She supplemented such extravagant displays with ceremonies portraying herself as the great liberator of Asia as well as with equally grand gestures that linked her to Rome.[17] At the Donations of Alexandria in which she eagerly played the wife to Antony, she won his allegiance at the same time that she claimed for herself the title Philopatris (She who loves her country). Through this single act she cemented her relationship to Roman power. She also publicly acknowledged her Hellenic ancestry while celebrating her Egyptian identity. Even in defeat, Cleopatra relied on spectacular gestures to advance her political agenda. Hoping to distance herself from the disempowered Antony in the aftermath of Actium and eager to secure Caesarion's rise to power, she entered into secret negotiations with her enemy Octavian. She declared her fealty to the new leader not through a simple letter of obedience, which would have been customary at the time, but through an extravagant set of gifts: a gold crown, a jewel-encrusted scepter, and a life-size throne. Once Octavian refused to recognize Caesarion, however, Cleopatra abandoned her efforts and reneged on her promise. Rather than face humiliation as part of Octavian's own triumph spectacle, the dispossessed queen attempted first to starve herself and eventually succeeded (most likely with poison rather than by asp) in taking her own life. Through this final dramatic action, Cleopatra ostensibly brought the Ptolemy dynasty to an end. Octavian married off her only surviving child, Cleopatra Selene, to Juba II. He sent the couple away to rule Mauretania, a part of northwest Africa roughly spanning modern-day Algeria and Morocco, territories that would fall under French dominion by the nineteenth century.[18]

From this moment forward, Cleopatra's story would be told primarily by men, some who knew her, many who did not, all who interpreted her life in light of their own agendas (political, literary, or artistic) and in accordance with the customs of their own time. The earliest of these biographers and the originator of the first Cleopatra myth was her archenemy Gaius Octavius, Octavian himself.[19] Determined to undermine Antony and to discredit Cleopatra, Octavian's account embellished their characters and purposefully misrepresented actual events. It was under his pen that Cleopatra became the beautiful temptress, the toxic foreign seductress who threatened to destroy Rome. It was also through his storytelling that the acclaimed warrior Antony was reduced to a lovesick fool, defeated not by a former ally and fellow Roman but by his own carnal feebleness. By depicting Cleopatra and Antony in these roles, Octavian aligned foreignness with femininity to villainize his enemies. As Cleopatra's cuckold, Antony was doubly disempowered. His inability to resist the African temptress who figuratively, if not literally, poisoned him with her sex, rendered him metaphorically weak (feminine) and foreign (Other) himself. An external threat who used her feminine powers to insinuate herself into the heart of Rome (and Romans), Cleopatra represented, for Octavian, the dangers Westerners faced when mixing with the "Oriental Other."[20]

Following Octavian's lead, ancient recitations of the Cleopatra and Antony story explored themes of hypersexual femininity and impotent masculinity. Drawing on contemporary records and eyewitness testimony, Plutarch's *Life of Antonius* (110–15 CE) attributed Antony's downfall entirely to his romance with Cleopatra. Evoking common Roman prejudices about the queen, Plutarch fashioned Cleopatra as an enchanting vixen who used both her physical beauty and her keen wit to seduce the impressionable Roman. Although her beauty "was not, in and of itself, completely incomparable, nor was it the sort that would astound those who saw her," Plutarch explained, "interaction with her was always captivating, and her appearance, along with her persuasiveness of discussion and her character that accompanied every interchange, was stimulating."[21] In Plutarch's account, Cleopatra seduced not merely with her woman's body but with the tone of her voice, the flattery of her tongue, and her penchant for amusements, playing dice, hunting, and drinking, activities coded as masculine.[22]

Despite Plutarch's somewhat begrudging acknowledgment of Cleopatra's agreeable attributes, the queen was seldom portrayed positively in ancient narratives.[23] As Christiane Ziegler points out, Lucan, Josephus, Cicero, Virgil, Horace, Propertius, and Ovid would all condemn her as "an enemy of Rome, a dissolute foreigner, the ruler of an Oriental empire, and—greatest anomaly of all in a society that scorned the female sex—a woman wielding absolute power."[24] Indeed, shortly after her death, Horace designated Cleopatra the "fatale monstrum," and it is from his *Satires* that the fable regarding the queen's supernatural ability to dissolve pearls in vinegar originated.[25] Perhaps even more damning, however, was the polemicist Flavius Josephus's demonic portrayal of her in *Against Apion*.[26] Although primarily concerned with the plight of Jews in Judea, Josephus relied upon accounts from Herod and Nikolaos of

Damascus (two of Cleopatra's competitors) to accuse the queen of a variety of horrific crimes including fratricide and sororicide, plundering tombs, betraying Antony and, most damning for Josephus, refusing famine relief to Jews.[27] Filtered through the Roman lens, Cleopatra would be cast as Medea, Helen of Troy, even the Furies themselves, who represented the ultimate feminine challenge to (male) Western civilization. Thus, by the time that Cassius Dio wrote *Roman History* in the third century CE, providing the only continuous, if flawed, account of the last Ptolemaic era, the die had been cast. Fact and fiction, real and surreal, good and evil, had already inextricably intertwined to establish a fantasy of exceptional womanhood in which the racially ambiguous, sexually provocative, politically threatening Cleopatra would enter into history as well as into myth.

SHAKESPEARE'S CLEOPATRA

Through the late Middle Ages, male authors and artists routinely repackaged Augustan stereotypes of the Egyptian monarch. Like their ancient predecessors, they, too, evaluated Cleopatra's merits through contemporary lenses. To her most brutal critics, like Boccaccio in his fourteenth-century work *De Claris mulieribus/On Famous Women,* Cleopatra remained the merciless ruler, the lusty harlot, and the "whore of Oriental kings," responsible for the downfall of good men and, by association, of Western civilization.[28] More sympathetic Renaissance painters, however, emphasized the sovereign's physical beauty over her political prowess—even if they did so by styling her incorrectly as a plump blonde (the beauty standard upheld in their own age).[29] Perhaps the most compassionate rendering of Cleopatra came from Chaucer, who catalogued her affair with Antony as a matter of courtly love and portrayed the queen not as a vicious vixen but as a sentimental paramour.[30]

By the seventeenth century, Europeans, especially those in the Anglophone world, would come to know Cleopatra not only through these older works but also, and sometimes exclusively, through Shakespeare's play *Antony and Cleopatra.* Written sometime between 1603 and 1607 and staged first at the Globe Theater London in 1608, Shakespeare's work drew heavily upon Thomas North's 1579 translation of Plutarch's *Life of Mark Antony.*[31] Despite the critical acclaim and popularity of his work in England, Shakespeare did not arrive in France until Voltaire translated and adapted *Julius Caesar* in 1731.

Voltaire's adaptation was followed by Pierre-Antoine de la Place's ten-volume collection devoted to the English theater (1746–49), which featured several of Shakespeare's works, including a modified translation of *Antony and Cleopatra*. From the 1770s onward, translations of Shakespeare's works proliferated across France. De la Place's work was followed by Pierre Le Tourneur's 1776 collection and by Jean-François Ducis's sanitized stage productions of *Hamlet*, *Macbeth*, and *Romeo and Juliet*. It would not be until François-Victor Hugo's meticulous fifteen-volume translation of Shakespeare's original work (published between 1859 and 1866) that French audiences encountered an unmodified version of Shakespeare's plays. Given the extent to which *Antony and Cleopatra* would influence modern perceptions of the queen, as well as the degree to which future artists and authors would rely upon it as a source for their own depictions of Cleopatra and Antony, it is worth briefly recounting the plot of Shakespeare's tragedy.[32]

The play opens in Cleopatra's palace as a smitten Antony is recalled to Rome. Cleopatra encourages his return, regarding it as an opportunity to reassert his authority. She cannot anticipate, however, that Antony will enter into a pact with Octavian by marrying his sister. Jealous of her new rival, Cleopatra savagely interrogates the messenger charged with relaying news of the union. Meanwhile, Antony and the other triumvirs celebrate their alliance with Sextus Pompey before Antony departs for Athens. Behind Antony's back, Octavian and Lepidus declare war on Pompey, which divides the triumvir. When Antony returns to Alexandria, he and Cleopatra officiate the Donations ceremony, crowning themselves sovereigns of Egypt and rulers of the eastern third of the Roman Republic. The triumph offers only a momentary distraction, however, as Antony prepares for war against Octavian. At Cleopatra's insistence, and ignoring the counsel of his commanders, he challenges Octavian by sea rather than on land. At the Battle of Actium, Cleopatra's fleet retreats unexpectedly, and, outflanked by the enemy, Antony's convoy is forced to follow. When Antony's army is defeated in the desert, he resolves to kill the deceptive Cleopatra. Learning this news, Cleopatra attempts to outmaneuver him by faking her own death. Her plan works too well, however, and when Antony discovers that she is dead, he fatally stabs himself. Unwilling to surrender to Octavian or to live without Antony, in the final scene Cleopatra dramatically commits suicide by asp.

Describing the story of Cleopatra and Antony as a romance, a tale of passion and desire, Shakespeare fashioned Cleopatra as a capricious coquette, an embattled lover, and a spirited femme fatale.[33] But he also portrayed her as a formidable African queen whose power arose not only from her sexuality or her political ambition but also from her racial and cultural ambiguity. In the opening lines of the play, the Roman centurion Philo bemoans how Antony's

> goodly eyes,
> That o'er the files and musters of the war
> Have glowed like plated Mars, now bend, now turn
> . . . .
> Upon a tawny front.

Philo's discomfort with Cleopatra's "tawny front" suggests that it is her dark skin as much as her feminine sexuality that threatens Rome. Shakespeare doubles down on this threat, having Cleopatra herself erase any doubt regarding her racial origins. While pining away for Antony in scene 5 of the same act, she hopes that her lover will

> Think on me
> That am with Phoebus' amorous pinches black,
> And wrinkled deep in time?[34]

Cleopatra's hybrid ancestry long perplexed (and continues to confound) those who told her story.[35] Was she Hellenic? Macedonian? African? Rather than insist upon her whiteness, as others had done almost as a default, Shakespeare twice, through "a tawny front" and "amorous pinches of black" affirmed her blackness. He may have chosen to do so because his contemporaries evoked Black racial identity as a shorthand for those of African descent. Or perhaps he realized that her sexual allure resided to no small degree in her racial otherness. Regardless of what guided his decision, the effect was the same: for Shakespeare, Cleopatra's race, like her sexuality, was central to her political challenge to Rome.[36]

Shakespeare further underscores the importance of Cleopatra's racial identity by having her rewrite the myth of its origins. Greek storytellers attributed dark skin to a cosmic misfortune, blaming its creation on Apollo's half-mortal son Phaeton, who, in his impetuous zeal to prove his power, drove his chariot too close to the sun. Rather than accept the negative connotations that accompanied this version of the story (that is, blackness was both a celestial mistake and a warning against efforts to prematurely usurp power), Shakespeare's Cleopatra declares that the skin color of her people derived from her coupling with the Sun god himself. By making this claim, Cleopatra erases the notion that blackness was an unfortunate accident, and she aligns herself once again with the gods. Produced through consensual intercourse between herself and a deity, blackness, in Cleopatra's creation myth, was a blessing not a curse. Through Cleopatra's version of her racial origin story, Shakespeare rehabilitates blackness. He roots it in masculine sexual desire (Apollo's lust for the mortal queen) and in the *intentional* (not accidental and therefore inferior) mingling of a god with a mortal. In so doing, however, he also participates in the sexualization of the dark-skinned Other and somewhat restores an otherwise emasculated Antony. For, if the Sun god himself could not resist Cleopatra's sexual charms, how could Roman mortals be expected to do so?[37]

Shakespeare further complicates Cleopatra's relationship with Antony by exploring the former's gender fluidity. In the second act of the play, Cleopatra and Antony engage in a drunken game of dress-up. Cleopatra recalls this lighthearted game to her confidante Charmian:

> That time?—O, times!—
> I laughed him out of patience; and that night
> I laughed him into patience; and next morn,
> Ere the ninth hour, I drunk him to his bed,
> Then put my tires and mantles on him, whilst
> I wore his sword Philippian.[38]

In this episode, cross-dressing connotes an inversion of gender roles with political implications. In the guise of both sexual foreplay in which Cleopatra seizes Antony's sword, and as an allusion to the myth of Mars and Venus, wearing the clothes of the opposite sex symbolically empowers the Egyptian monarch by feminizing the Roman warrior. Although the scene is recounted rather than performed for the viewer, it operated as more than just juicy gossip that added intrigue and possibly comic relief to the tragic plot. Through this story, Shakespeare highlights how Cleopatra's shape-shifting enabled her to overpower men. It was through seduction, drunken pleasure and not battlefield combat that she subdued Antony; thus, it was not only her naval fleet but also her feminine wiles that Romans need fear.[39] Pleasure and peril were, it seems, two sides of the same coin where Cleopatra was involved.

Frequently performed onstage and reissued in print, adaptations of *Antony and Cleopatra,* like those resurrected from the Augustan authors, often reflected contemporary concerns. Through each reinvention Cleopatra provided both a blank canvas for imagining the exotic East and a metaphor for female power.[40] Although they rarely strayed too far from Shakespeare's narrative outline, eighteenth-century interpreters characterized the play as a political parable, whereas nineteenth-century Romantics focused on its themes of sexual violence. Perhaps not surprisingly, Victorian editions centered issues of marriage and (in)fidelity. In these interpretations, Cleopatra evoked either a disempowered model of womanhood (the docile, and ultimately failed, wife) or a too-powerful (the threatening vixen) version of it.[41] Sometimes portrayed in both roles simultaneously, Cleopatra came to embody the conundrum of Victorian womanhood: she paradoxically reinforced and challenged the tropes of domesticity, and she blurred the housewife/harlot dichotomy central to the period's prescribed gender order.[42]

In the centuries following the play's debut, its staging as well as its intended meanings underwent constant reappraisal. Following the first major revival by David Garrick at Drury Lane in 1759, *Antony and Cleopatra* became a formidable theatrical spectacle. Nineteenth-century productions featured extravagant scenery, lush gardens, and sumptuous costumes that both encapsulated and rivaled the opulence of the ancient queen's own court. John Philip Kemble's 1813 Covent Garden performance included a breathtaking funeral procession (involving forty-five actors) that culminated in an oration over the lovers' tombs. William Charles Macready's Drury Lane 1833 rendition showcased the Battle of Actium with intricately detailed replicas of the queen's fleet. Samuel Phelps's 1849 staging at Sadler's Wells inserted an Egyptian and an Amazonian guard into Cleopatra's entourage. And, although he cut the play down to twelve scenes, Chesterton added to his 1873 Drury Lane production a ballet, thirty choirboys, an Amazonian procession, and an elongated recreation of Antony and Cleopatra's first meeting on the queen's lavish barge. Showcasing England's most notable actresses—Isabel Glyn, Cora Brown Potter, and Lillie Langtry—in the starring role, these elaborate stage productions represented Cleopatra as an overindulgent, lascivious foreign queen, an exotic (although pale-skinned) Eastern Other who could add fuel to British imperial fantasies in a modern age of empire.[43]

To varying degrees, twentieth- and twenty-first-century reenactments continued to play on each of these tropes. Like their predecessors, they staged *Antony and Cleopatra* as a romance, a political scandal, and as a warning against mingling sex with state power. For their part, modern Shakespearian scholars have examined the play for what it suggests about how the intertwined politics of race and gender have informed (and continue to shape) cultural struggles between East and West. As noted earlier, whereas Cleopatra was often personified by white actresses, Shakespeare, unique for his time, envisioned his Macedonian queen as "black."[44] Moreover, because Cleopatra, as she had been portrayed from the Augustan period forward, shared, according to Arthur Little, "a race with *black* men and a gender with white *women*," scholars contend that her political power resides primarily in her hybrid body.[45] Cleopatra's sexual power, and by extension her political threat to the Roman, Western world, derives from the potent mix of racial ambiguity and gender fluidity that renders her culturally illegible.

Although most productions from the seventeenth through the twenty-first centuries featured a white actress as Cleopatra, the costumes and jewelry these actresses wore connoted her racial difference. Gauze, silks, gold or silver breastplates, elaborate metallic headpieces, arm bracelets, and other costuming signified Cleopatra's geographic origins and represented her racial otherness to European audiences. Through acts of cultural appropriation steeped in stereotypes—these were after all European perceptions of how an Egyptian/African queen would appear—Cleopatra became a doubly hybrid figure, mingling Eastern materials with the Western imagination. Embodied by white actresses who were simply fashioned as racial Others, stage Cleopatras continued to evoke the queen's ambiguous identity—neither black nor white, neither Eastern nor Western, and neither entirely female nor male.[46] The fusion of Eastern materials with Western stereotypes further confuses the identity categories of race and gender, adding to Cleopatra's mythology by amplifying rather than resolving her cultural hybridity.

Recognizing the disruptive potential of Cleopatra's mixed identity, Shakespeare used the queen's story to align England with Rome. His play insinuated a contest between a civilizing, white masculinity (Caesar and, to a lesser extent, Antony, whose own status changes over the course of the production) and an archaic, nonwhite femininity (Cleopatra).[47] The bastion of order and efficiency and the bureaucratic hub of imperial authority, Rome, like the London of Shakespeare's day with its female queen and imperial ambitions, contrasts with the seemingly listless, sensual, even hedonistic Alexandria.[48] Not surprisingly, it is in Alexandria that Cleopatra disarms Rome's most virile leader, transforming him into an enfeebled, if not entirely emasculated, disciple. In an important twist, Shakespeare troubles a facile East/West divide by depicting Egypt not only as a source of blackness/otherness but also as a place for England's own racial origins.[49] Egypt would become part of the Roman Empire, and Rome was the birthplace of Western civilization. As a descendent of this civilization, England was linked both to Rome and to Egypt, whose bloodlines it incestuously intermingled.

CLEOPATRA IN NINETEENTH-CENTURY FRANCE

The British were not alone in their fascination with Cleopatra, their curiosity about ancient Egypt, or their desire to demystify and ultimately to possess the East.[50] In the nineteenth century, the foreign queen and her verdant homeland animated the imaginations of French statesmen, artists, authors, and, to some extent, the general population. In 1798 the then military general Napoleon Bonaparte led a massive campaign against British forces in Egypt.[51] Determined to obstruct Britain's access to India and to establish colonial holdings of its own, Napoleon's expeditionary force also included an entourage of 167 engineers, humanists, mathematicians, surveyors, and draftsmen eager to study the country's topography, to document its monuments, and to explore its great pyramids. These efforts coalesced in the twenty-one-volume *Description de l'Egypte* published between 1809 and 1829. The collection featured visual depictions of historical sites and contemporary landscapes alongside entries from a variety of noteworthy European authors. The materials contained in the compilation opened Egypt up to further foreign research, laying the groundwork for modern Egyptology, and it inspired numerous novels, plays, and works of art.[52] As specialists confidently catalogued their findings, they used their technical dominance over Egypt to assert their cultural superiority. Whether they regarded the North African territory as a potential colony, like the Old Regime's lost holdings in the Americas, or as a possible satellite republic, like those continental areas annexed by Napoleon's armies, the French overwhelmingly supported the Egyptian campaign. They increasingly considered it their duty, moreover, to restore that country's lost glory by infusing it with French civilization.[53]

During the industrial age, travel to Egypt became easier while the desire to go there became more widespread. Middle-class (and eventually working-class) tour groups went sightseeing to ancient settlements, visited biblical ruins, and collected all sorts of souvenirs, from pottery to jewelry, antiques to tchotchkes.[54] Egyptologists, archaeologists, and other adventurers excavated hidden cities and forgotten tombs, while authors and artists composed travel narratives, copied or adapted ancient texts, and sketched the local scenery. These endeavors collectively stimulated demand for foreign commodities back home. Egyptian artifacts and wares soon filled museum expositions and world's fairs. They were also often featured in magic lantern shows, panoramas, dioramas, photographs, and documentaries. Before long, Europeans were ensconced in the passionate throes of a full-blown "Egyptomania."[55]

Relishing the lurid delights of his 1840s tour, the then relatively unknown Gustave Flaubert confided in his diary, "first night on the Nile . . . cannot bring myself to go to bed; I think of Cleopatra."[56] Of course Flaubert, whose own sensual experiences in Egypt would shape the fantasies of the notorious Emma Bovary in his best-selling novel *Madame Bovary* (1856), was but one of many nineteenth-century French authors enchanted by the wonders of the Fertile Crescent and its affiliated populations. Decades before Flaubert's voyage, Victor Hugo romanticized the eastern Mediterranean in a volume of poetry entitled *Les Orientales* (1829), and Honoré de Balzac explored Orientalized Jewish beauty through the prostitute Esther in his 1838 novel *Splendeurs et misères des courtisanes.* By the time that Flaubert embarked upon his journey, moreover, his travel companion, Maxime Du Camp, had already published his own travelogue, *Souvenirs et paysages d'Orient,* in 1848. Cleopatra herself featured a bit more prominently in Rachilde's (pen name for Marguerite Vallette-Eymery) scandalous novel *L'Heure sexuelle* (1898). An example of Decadent fiction, Rachilde's racy *L'Heure sexuelle* portrayed Cleopatra as a Parisian prostitute and as the male protagonist's erotic fixation.[57] Although not always as explicitly focused on Cleopatra as Rachilde's work, all of these texts, which fetishized the erotic, feminine Other, helped set the stage for her cultural revival in France.

Featured in the paintings of Jean-Léon Gérôme, Jean-Auguste-Dominique

Ingres, Alexandre Cabanel, and Gustave Moreau, among others, Cleopatra embodied for many nineteenth-century French visual artists the mysterious East.[58] In their depictions, painters signaled Cleopatra's foreignness by surrounding her with Eastern commodities and artifacts, and they often positioned her alongside Black servants.[59] Like many of those before them, they also envisioned her as a hybrid figure. However, for many of these artists, what interested them most about Cleopatra was her ability to transcend time. For them, Cleopatra represented both Pharaonic Egypt, which was old and enigmatic as well as the contemporary Orient, which was new, vibrant, and sensuous.[60] On the artist's canvas, Cleopatra was not merely an ancient historical actor but also a phantasmagoric mirage, a disembodied apparition, as much alive in the present as she was in the past.

Nineteenth-century visual artists regularly set their work in pre-Christian Greece or Rome, or they took as their subject the harems and slave markets of the Islamic Middle East, in order to paint the nude female subject without offending the presumably prudish sensibilities of bourgeois viewers.[61] Not surprisingly, Cleopatra featured prominently in several of these works. Gérôme's *Cleopatra and Caesar* (1866; also known as *Cleopatra before Caesar*), for example, captures the pair's first meeting. In the painting, a cunning Cleopatra infiltrates Caesar's private quarters by stowing herself away in a rolled-up carpet (figure 1). Yet her political calculation—her success at achieving a private audience with the most powerful leader in the Mediterranean—is absent in Gérôme's rendering of the conference. Indeed, by portraying the very setting of Cleopatra's debut as a dark, sultry palace boudoir, reminiscent of contemporary brothels, Gérôme insinuates a subtext of exotic conquest that accompanies this particular form of political intrigue.[62] This point is reinforced by the fact that Cleopatra emerges, alongside a presumably enslaved, brown-skinned male, before an audience of voyeuristic Roman men. Their collective gaze penetrates the diaphanous costume barely covering her nude body, whose whiteness is accentuated by the lighting of the room as well as by the juxtaposition of the dark-skinned servant at her feet. Her head is slightly tilted, her eyes cast downward, her breasts bared. Her pose is both open and submissive, as if she is offering herself up for the onlooker's pleasure. Suggestively compared to both the prostitute and the harem girl, in this painting Cleopatra becomes an object of male pleasure, a sexual fantasy rather than a leader of state.

FIG. I. *Cleopatra and Caesar* (also known as *Cleopatra before Caesar*), Jean-Léon Gérôme, 1866.

What is even more striking than the overt sexualization of Cleopatra in this scenario is that the episode itself probably never happened. In fact, the entire idea of the carpet performance originated in a mistranslation of Plutarch's *The Parallel Lives* series undertaken by John and William Langhorne in 1770. In this "scholarly" edition of the text, revered at the time as a more historically precise, if less engaging, account than North's sixteenth-century version, the translators detailed an episode in which Cleopatra encounters Caesar wrapped in bed sheets, not carpets. We also know that Cleopatra and Caesar's initial rendezvous occurred not in Rome but in Alexandria. It transpired not in the context of a torrid affair in which smitten lovers listlessly wallowed in

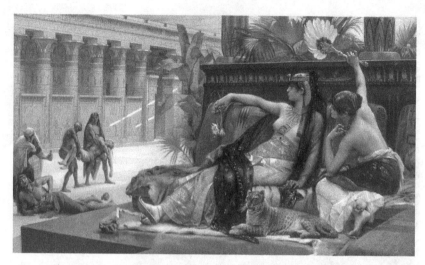

FIG. 2. *Cleopatra Testing Poisons on Condemned Prisoners,* Alexandre Cabanel, 1887.

domestic tranquility but amid intense military and political maneuverings. At the moment of their meeting, Caesar's forces were engaged in Pompey, and Cleopatra herself was embroiled in a bitter contest of wills with her brother Ptolemy XIII. Given the precarious circumstances under which the pair's clandestine meeting unfolded; it is likely that Cleopatra sought to win Caesar's favor. However, she probably did so to secure him as a political ally, not to pursue him as a sexual conquest.

Whereas Gérôme's work abstracted Cleopatra's relationship to political authority, Alexandre Cabanel's *Cleopatra Testing Poisons on Condemned Prisoners* (1887) explicitly connected sex to power by representing the queen as the ultimate femme fatale (figure 2). In yet another harem-like setting, a bare-breasted Cleopatra tended by her half-nude female servant (herself light-skinned but somewhat racially indeterminate) and accompanied by a tame leopard rather than a domesticated house cat arbitrarily dispenses justice within her kingdom. As in Gérôme's work, in Cabanel's Cleopatra is once again bare-breasted, and her white skin, where it is exposed (breasts, arms, face, and feet), is illuminated. Yet whereas Gérôme's Cleopatra was the object of the male gaze, Cabanel's gazes at the men around her. Cabanel does not deny Cleopatra's authority here; it is she, after all, who has poisoned the prostrate men now languishing in her palace, and it is she who owns the power of the gaze. However, in the manner in which he constructs his scene, he does somewhat undermine it. Rather than occupy a conventional seat of power—a throne, a dais, even an elevated judiciary bench—Cabanel's Cleopatra is languorously sprawled across what looks like a large bed. She may own the gaze; however, it is diverted sideways, toward the scene of punishment rather than cast forward and toward the viewer. She is posed, like so many courtesans of the age, as a reclining odalisque. Despite the authority she exercises in the scene itself, Cabanel's Cleopatra remains the eroticized Oriental woman. She is made legible to contemporary audiences not only as a figure of authority but also as an object on display.[63]

Although Gérôme's painting debuted in the waning days of the Second Empire, whereas Cabanel's was displayed during the heady early days of Third Republic, both highlight how masculine fantasies of the femme Orientale could simultaneously convey and conceal the numerous political concerns and cultural anxieties plaguing nineteenth-century France. In an era mired in political revolution and social unrest, Orientalist depictions of Cleopatra constructed an erstwhile but not forgotten foreign Other against which the enduring power of France might be measured. After the upheavals of 1848, defeat in the Franco-Prussian War, and the bloodbath of the Commune, the French sought symbols of reconciliation around which to unify the nation.[64] Cleopatra emerged as one of those symbols. Furthermore, amid changing definitions of gender, family, and race that accompanied an age of vast industrialization, rapid urbanization, and wide-scale emigration, the hypersexualized, acquiescent, and available femme Orientale reassured male viewers of their prowess, offered them escape from the trials of daily life, and fueled their imperial desires. Indeed, these paintings, especially in their depictions of blended nonwhite bodies, revealed how imperial ambitions and aspirations to maintain French power could be pursued not only through the acquisition of foreign lands but also through the sexual subjugation of foreign female bodies.[65]

By the late nineteenth century, the connection between imperial domination and sexual conquest was well-established in the European mind. What is less obvious is why Cleopatra, a racially ambiguous, politically powerful, independent woman, should become a chosen vehicle for carrying out such important ideological work. Neither Black nor white, neither doting housewife nor promiscuous harlot, Cleopatra disrupted as many conventional narratives of race, class, and gender as she reinforced. If the erosion of these norms preoccupied the French status quo, as we know it did throughout the century, why express national anxieties through a figure whose cultural identity was so fluid and whose historical reputation so fraught? Perhaps the answer lies in the question: precisely because Cleopatra could be read in so many ways, she appealed to everyone.

As European powers, especially France and England, jockeyed for international influence and endeavored to assert their political and economic authority across the globe, fascination with Cleopatra only intensified. Periodically emerging in works of art and literature, the queen came to life more fully by century's end and entered public consciousness more consistently through her portrayal on stage and screen. A staple of the theater, Shakespeare's *Antony and Cleopatra* continued to attract audiences, especially when the lead was played by Europe's most revered actresses: Isabella Glyn, Lillie Langtry, and Sarah Bernhardt. But Cleopatra was also somewhat divested of her Shakespearian trappings. In the last decades of the century her story was reimagined by George Bernhard Shaw in *Caesar and Cleopatra* (1899) and by Victorien Sardou in *Cléopâtre* (1890). In 1899, French director Georges Méliès first captured Cleopatra on film in a four-minute horror short entitled *Cleopatra's Tomb*. It would be through a variety of cultural reproductions like these that Cleopatra, the woman and the myth, would enter into a new century.

CREATING THE "CLEOPATRA LOOK"

Although she might have been long forgotten, cast away alongside other fading artifacts of a lost world, Cleopatra the woman, the queen, and the myth materialized in a range of twentieth-century cultural productions. Early in the century, she could be found onstage in the highbrow performances of the Ballets Russes one night and featured in the skits of tawdry British burlesque shows and bawdy French *quartier* cabarets the next.[66] Jumping enthusiastically onto the Egyptomania bandwagon, costumed merrymakers and irreverent student organizers of the avant-garde Bal des Arts made Cleopatra the subject of several naughty tableaux vivants. Meanwhile, fashion houses manufactured ornate textiles and artisans crafted jewel-encrusted accessories designed to invoke the Orient, while commercial cosmetic companies mass-produced Cleopatra's image to peddle beauty products across the globe.[67] None of these efforts, however, resurrected Cleopatra in the modern mind as persuasively as the new medium of cinema. The canvas, the stage, and the text kept

Cleopatra alive in the popular imagination; the cinema made her a modern celebrity.

Russian choreographer Michel Fokine's one-act ballet *Cléopâtre* opened at the Théâtre du Châtelet on June 2, 1909. Based on his *Une Nuit d'Égypte*, which débuted a year earlier in St. Petersburg, Fokine's *Cléopâtre*, starring the breathtaking Anna Pavlova in the role of Ta-hor and the as yet unknown but soon to be formidable Ida Rubinstein as Cleopatra, captivated Parisian audiences. Theatergoers were impressed by the ballet's exquisite choreography, but they were also mesmerized by its sumptuous costuming. Designed by Léon Bakst, Rubinstein's "glittering metal bustier and girdle," reminiscent of Maud Allan's *Salomé* wardrobe, outshone the production's desert scenery, its enormous pharaoh statues, and its faux Egyptian architecture.[68] Alongside a bevy of scantily clad dancers whose jewel-covered "fleshings," a combination of skin-toned silk or jersey inserts, and body makeup, Rubinstein's Cleopatra, like so many stage Salomés before her, performed the erotic dance of the veils. Although anachronistic and ahistorical, Cleopatra's dance perpetuated a narrative of hyperfeminine sexuality that Westerners had attributed to the East, through the figure of the femme Orientale, for hundreds of years.[69] In conjunction with Nikolai Rimsky-Korsakov's popular *One Thousand and One Nights* symphonic suite (1888), moreover, the ballet stimulated French demand for "the exotic" in fashion, in the decorative arts, and in interior design.

Following the success of *Cléopâtre*, in 1910 the Ballet Russes performed *Schéhérazade*, an updated version of *One Thousand and One Nights*. Enthralled by these productions, Parisian fashion designer Paul Poiret introduced hobble skirts and hosted his own extravagant dress party, which he called "The Thousand and Second Night."[70] Shortly thereafter he launched his "harem" pantaloons in 1911 and his "lampshade" tunics of 1913—two wildly popular confections that not only encouraged a proliferation of Orientalist motifs, colors, and embellishments in high fashion but also cemented Poiret's status as Europe's premiere couturier.[71] In the early decades of the twentieth century, Poiret created numerous costumes for the stage, and, with his distaste for the corset and insistence on flattening the female form through straight lines and abstracted silhouettes, he upended Western fashion, creating streamlined, Eastern-inspired styles that would become the trademark of the postwar modern woman.

Revived by Sergei Diaghilev in 1918, *Cléopâtre* the ballet once again caused a stir because of its costuming. Designed this time by Sonia Delaunay, the new costumes constrained Cleopatra in a tight-fitting sheath dress constructed of muslin-lined silk taffeta, a dramatic departure from Bakst's fluid fleshings. Although Delaunay's design included the beading, gems, and stones regularly associated with Eastern outfitting, its tapered hobble skirt, straight waist, and high bodice resembled contemporary Parisian couture, especially that manufactured by the House of Poiret. By conflating these fashions, Juliet Bellow argues, Delaunay shifted the audience's attention "away from the fictionalized, otherworldly setting of the ballet to the contemporary context of the Champs-Élysées and to the social anxieties that site conjured." By connecting the ancient queen to the newly emancipated, highly visible postwar Parisienne, Delaunay's Cleopatra confused time and place and sent contradictory messages about woman's position in both. Indeed, the stunning fashions of the Ballets Russes so captivated female audiences that they sparked demand for similar styles in women's clothing. Once adorned in these hybrid creations, French women articulated their modernity by literally cloaking their bodies in styles of the past. In this way, Cleopatra, in Bellow's words, "occupied an important position in the cultural imaginary of the early twentieth century, incarnating fears and fantasies, aspirations and expectations about modern women."[72]

In the same way that Poiret's and Delaunay's costumes blended the modern and the ancient, art nouveau jewelry transformed contemporary European stage actresses into historical female figures—most notably, Theodora, Salomé, and Cleopatra. Designers René Lalique and Alphonse Mucha, who would consequently style Sarah Bernhardt for her role as the queen, both created such ornamentation for the stage and carried the motifs over into their broader collections.[73] Combining sinewy lines and disjointed female forms with bright, expensive stones, animal hybrids, and vibrant colors, art nouveau jewelry articulated Western male (after all, the craftsmen were men) fantasies of the sexually potent femme Orientale. Even more fascinating is that French women celebrated this new style of ornamentation, contributing to the broader rage for all things foreign. By incorporating art nouveau jewelry into their daily wardrobes, French women appropriated Eastern culture and womanhood, replicating and subverting the same cultural and racial stereotypes that underwrote French men's sexual fantasies of the racial Other.

As culture producers inundated the entertainment world and the fashion market with Eastern motifs and styles, German archaeologist Ludwig

Borchardt's 1912 recovery of Nefertiti's bust and English Egyptologist Howard Carter's unearthing of King Tutankhamun's tomb in November 1922 kindled demand for all things specifically Egyptian.[74] Covered widely in the international media, these expeditions, along with the rediscovery of the ruins of Nefertiti's city, El-Amarna, contributed to a resurgence of Egyptian themes in the fine and decorative arts. They also made Egyptian-inspired jewelry, accessories, collectibles, costumes, and fashions more popular than ever. In December 1919, the women's periodical *Femina* included two advertisements showcasing Cleopatra's image, one for "Ramses River Powder" and the other for "Sphinx's Secret." Four years later, the April 15, 1923, issue of French *Vogue* featured a line of Egypt-inspired dresses under the title "Paris Reads the Riddle of the Egyptian Sphinx," while a new line of "Luxora" garments were marketed as both Egyptian and Parisian—or, as both past and future oriented.[75] Made of precious stones, Cartier's 1925 Egyptian sarcophagus vanity case enabled a woman's public toilette; this compact cosmetic casket empowered the fashionable Parisienne to flaunt her sexuality and her modernity once again by evoking the past. Additionally, the fashion house Callot Soeurs developed a two-toned green silk gown whose extensive beading and tunic style further popularized Egyptian motifs in European fashion.[76]

Twentieth-century films devoted to Cleopatra not only reinforced connections between Eastern female sexuality and Western modernity but further globalized her image by connecting her to the Hollywood star system. Released in France, Denmark, Finland, and the United States in 1910 and featuring Madeleine Roch in the title role, the French silent *Cléopâtre,* based on Sardou's play, premiered two years after an American version of Shakespeare's *Antony and Cleopatra,* in which the Canadian actress Florence Lawrence played the lead. From this point forward, most of the Cleopatras who appeared on film were produced in America. To some extent, this shift was part of broader developments within the film industry itself. Before 1914, France (and Italy) led the industry, managing worldwide distribution networks and boasting production companies that adapted the newest techniques to create the highest-quality products. However, the Great War curtailed the growth of the French film industry. The war damaged or completely destroyed some industrial complexes, and these would have to be rebuilt after 1918 if prewar firms were to recover. Rebuilding would be difficult because corporations, including the two industry powerhouses Gaumont and Pathé, lost substantial capital during the war and were subject to government regulation in ways that American companies, which would dominate the postwar market, were not. Predictably, the French film industry never quite recovered from these catastrophic developments. Following the war, it became dependent on exports, especially those from America that boasted not only the latest technologies but that also catered to the tastes of increasingly younger, working-class, and female theatergoers.[77]

It would also be America that would manufacture the most popular cinematic Cleopatras of the twentieth century. Embodied by some of Hollywood's most fashionable actresses—Theda Bara, Claudette Colbert, Elizabeth Taylor—the highly stylized Cleopatra that emerged in the postwar era came to be identified by her jet-black bobbed hair, her heavily kohl-rimmed eyes, her flowing "harem-girl" robes, her revealing bodice, and her ostentatious jewelry. In film, fashion, and theater, this contrived Cleopatra "look" drew on stylized, eroticized Western stereotypes of the femme Orientale and packaged these images for international mass consumption.[78] Curated in Hollywood's standardized visual lexicon, this commercial Cleopatra added to a well-established, collective mythology that was itself primarily a contrivance of the Western imagination.

The biggest box office attraction of 1917, Theda Bara's *Cleopatra* was the most advertised and talked-about film of that year. Drawing on nineteenth-century Orientalist tropes for her personal styling as well as for the film's set, Fox Studio portrayed the queen, and the actress who enlivened her, as the ultimate femme fatale. The first Hollywood star to have her image manufactured by a studio press, Bara's publicity materials depicted a vaporous vixen clutching an asp to her chest, a sinewy siren lounging beneath a shadowy sphinx, or a boudoir enchantress, horizontal and draped in little more than bed sheets. Featured alone, publicity stills captured Cleopatra's exotic otherness not by surrounding her with racially ambiguous servants or in contradistinction to her Roman male adversaries but through props—bedding, costumes, jewelry, snakes. By centering the actress in this way, studios emphasized Cleopatra's singularity and connected her image explicitly to the modern female star. For her part, Bara promoted her vicarious identification with the ancient queen. "I know that I am a reincarnation of Cleopatra," she claimed. "It is not a mere theory in my mind. I have positive knowledge that such is the case. I live Cleopatra, I *am* Cleopatra."[79]

FIG. 3. *Cleopatra* starring Claudette Colbert, 1934.

Despite her bravado, Bara's Cleopatra would be eclipsed by two new Cleo-patras, each played by future Academy Award winners: Claudette Colbert and Elizabeth Taylor.[80] Acclaimed filmmaker Cecil B. DeMille cast Paramount ac-tress Claudette Colbert, who had played a convincing seductress in his *The Sign of the Cross* two years earlier, for his epic 1934 production. Adorned in a jet-black wig, bejeweled, heavily made up, and scantily clad, Colbert brought the same vamp persona to Cleopatra, and through her performance, she ce-mented the queen's reputation as history's ultimate femme fatale (figure 3). The film was an instant success, earning a standing ovation on opening night, acquiring five Academy Award nominations (including Best Picture), and gar-nering critical acclaim for both the cast and the director.

Capitalizing on its success, the studio financed extensive publicity cam-paigns for both the film and its star. In so doing, it inadvertently launched a

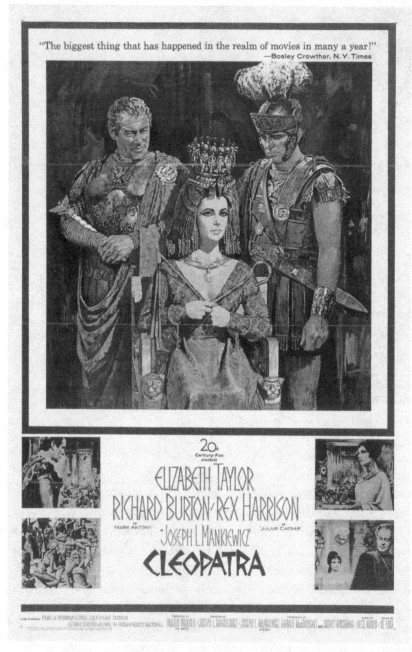

FIG. 4. *Cleopatra* starring Elizabeth Taylor, 1963.

variety of commercial endeavors: in London, Selfridge's department store introduced a "Cleopatra" hat, and Dolci's shoe store created a Cleopatra sandal. In the States, Macy's developed an entire clothing line inspired by the fashions worn in the film, and both Lux soap and Marcovitch Egyptian cigarettes used stills of Colbert in their respective product advertisements.[81] Through her latest avatar, Colbert, Cleopatra monopolized the modern marketplace. And, although encountering economically embattled audiences, spectators enmeshed in the throes of global financial hardship, Cleopatra continued to offer ordinary people opulence, extravagance, and glamour. Once again, she met dreamers at the end of their dreams.

These dreams, however, were heavily prescribed by the context in which they transpired. Hollywood's Cleopatra, as embodied in the figures of Bara and Colbert, was racially coded as white. Renowned onstage and off for their stunning appearance and sensual sexuality, these actresses projected a standard of female beauty that, despite Cleopatra's racial hybridity, excluded nonwhite others. The Orientalist frame through which studios packaged these Cleopatras—styling, set, tie-in products—could not erase the fact of the actress's white body, only mask it. Rather than celebrating the queen's racial origins, Hollywood's Cleopatras hid them behind white faces. For the rest of the century, onstage and onscreen, America's Cleopatras, all played by white actresses, would reinforce the message that Western beauty required the erasure of blackness.[82]

Even as the civil rights movement gained momentum and chants of "Black is beautiful" echoed on American streets, Joseph L. Mankiewicz's blockbuster, which would make Elizabeth Taylor the most recognizable cinematic Cleopatra of the twentieth century, only strengthened the perception that beauty, even exotic beauty, equated to whiteness (figure 4). Plagued by production issues, scandalized by an off-camera affair between Taylor and her leading man, Richard Burton, and single-handedly responsible for almost bankrupting the Twentieth Century Fox Film Corporation, costing the studio $31 million, Cleopatra would become the most talked-about film of 1963.[83] Indeed, the 248-minute period piece generated almost as much attention for what was going on around it as it did for the quality of the production itself. Although it would receive nine Academy Award nominations, winning four including Best Picture, and earn an astronomical $57.7 million at the box office in the United States and Canada (and selling an estimated 5.4 million tickets in France and

Germany), the film elicited mixed reviews, including one from Taylor herself, who claimed that it "lacked reality and passion."[84]

Repackaged once again, this time in the guise of a Hollywood starlet notorious for her power over men both onscreen and off, Cleopatra retained her femme fatale status in the collective imaginary. In both adopting and perpetuating the "Cleopatra look," Taylor, like those actresses before her, not only played a role but also revealed how masquerade might be deployed as a powerful feminine weapon.[85] That the modern actress need not physically resemble the Hellenistic queen but rather evoke her in a look, take on her (perceived) affect, comport herself in ways contrived by current audiences rather than in ways transcribed in the historical record suggests that neither womanhood nor race was fixed in time or in the body. Rather, they were both constructs, appropriations of the Other made in the name of the self.[86] As far as Hollywood was concerned, Bara, Colbert, and Taylor need not be Egyptian to play Cleopatra, they needed to know only how to play at her in ways that contemporary audiences would understand.[87] Thus it was through a fantasy of exceptional womanhood derived from cultural illegibility and fashioned through public opinion, that both actress and queen found celebrity.

Into the twenty-first century, Cleopatra continued to embody the ultimate fantasy of Eastern otherness, of exotic femininity, of uninhibited sexuality, and even of empowered womanhood. As early modern England, nineteenth-century France, and the twentieth-century United States reinvented Cleopatra, each made her a value-laden metaphor, "a conveyor of meaning," who spoke as much about the present as she did about the past.[88] Although no archival materials written in her hand remain, the desire to know and to tell her story persists. Through the cultural products of other storytellers, she has emerged a hybrid figure—a combination of facts and fictions, a racially indeterminate subject, a culturally illegible icon—who is not easily defined. Her mythology has also been interpreted to suit the needs of the time in which it was reproduced: Elizabethans made her tale one of passion and fidelity; Romantics one of sexual violence; Hollywood one of glamour, danger, lust.[89] In these ways, Cleopatra has entered into history through the fantasies of others, and through them she has also been transformed time and time again into a fantasy of the Other.

As a Euro-American cultural production of the femme Orientale, moreover, Cleopatra has shared a lineage with Salomé, Judith, and Delilah from the Old Testament as well as with Circe and Medea from ancient mythology. An Eastern figuration of the femme fatale, these femmes Orientales threatened Western patriarchal structures and signified the dangers of autonomous femininity. Portrayed as sinister villains, violent usurpers of male authority, and seductive temptresses, these women have occupied a privileged symbolic position in the Western imagination. That their images proliferated at critical historical moments, like during the Third Republic, when real women vocally and publicly demanded greater access to education, employment, and enfranchisement, is not at all surprising. As Lacour so astutely observed in 1890, Cleopatra emerged precisely at those moments of masculine vulnerability when women, it seemed, might actually upset the tenuous balance of power upon which male authority rested.

Yet to reduce Cleopatra to a fantasy of the Other, to see her only as the West's exoticized femme Orientale, would deny the important cultural work that her mythology, image, and iconography has performed for more than a millennium. Cleopatra's influence over the Western imaginary has derived as much, if not more so, from the fantasy of exceptional womanhood she evokes. She is exceptional because she was an enigmatic queen. Both Mediterranean and African, a mortal who thought she was divine, and a woman who earned her place in a world of powerful men, Cleopatra challenged fixed identity categories. In the myriad fantasies generated about her, she belongs to no one and to everyone. She is of her time; she is timeless. In her we see others; in her we see ourselves. Like the modern celebrities who would enliven her onstage and onscreen, Cleopatra, as we know her, is almost entirely a product of the various publics who have (re)created her. We know her only as a reproduction, a facsimile, a sign whose referents multiply indefinitely.

It was through these multiplications that Cleopatra's fantasy of exceptional womanhood resonated in new and important ways in Third Republic France. As the young republic recovered from a century of military, political, economic, and social upheavals, as it continued to contend with challenges to its authority from both the Left and the Right, and as it endeavored to claim its place on an international stage in the age of empire, republicans promoted historical figures that could unite the nation. Despite the fact that she was not French and although she was a racially ambiguous foreign monarch whose downfall preceded the transformation of the Roman republic into an empire, the French found in Cleopatra's fantasy of exceptional womanhood useful narratives for constructing their own identity. On the one hand, they revered her as an emblem of the same Western civilization from which France itself emerged. In this way, republicans connected their own civilization with the ancient world, perpetuating the myth of an eternal France. On the other hand, by cataloguing her alongside her African counterparts, subjecting her to the colonial gaze, and enabling them to assert their cultural superiority, she helped legitimize their desire to create a Greater France. Monarchists liked that she was a queen; Bonapartists that she maintained an empire. Men found her exotic sexuality titillating while women could imagine through her new models of womanhood. Cleopatra played to all of these fantasies. Importantly, the fantasy of exceptional womanhood she signified would be itself played out by three of the republic's most popular celebrities: Sarah Bernhardt, Colette, and Josephine Baker.

2

Sarah Bernhardt

"INCREDIBLE MIRAGE!"

The Queen of Egypt has armed herself for seduction: clothed in the richest tunic; long hair cascading like a golden helmet over her shoulders; scepter in hand, she sits, resplendent with beauty and sparkling jewels.

—*Le Figaro,* October 24, 1890

Although familiar to them all, the Cleopatra described here belonged to neither Plutarch nor Octavius, to neither Shakespeare nor Shaw. This Cleopatra, recounted by a *Figaro* theater critic shortly after the opening performance of Victorien Sardou's five-act play by the same name, belonged entirely to the woman who played her—the sensational Sarah Bernhardt. In 1890 a number of Cleopatras took center stage: Lillie Langtry performed Shakespeare's adaptation at the Royal Princess Theater in London, while Fanny Davenport headlined Sardou's version in New York City; both followed Cora Potter's popular Shakespearian rendition from the year before. Despite the notoriety that each of these actresses brought to the role, it would be Bernhardt's Cleopatra against which all others would be measured.[1]

What was it about Bernhardt that made her Cleopatra so mesmerizing, so memorable? She might have played the role so convincingly simply because she shared with her character so many striking similarities. Both women's biographies were invented and contested. Both women were simultaneously adored and reviled. Both manipulated pageantry and spectacle to produce larger-than-life public personas. In complex and incongruous ways, both women have been upheld as models of "true womanhood," and they have been cast as saboteurs of that model. Both have embodied idealized notions of feminine beauty, and both have epitomized dangerous perversions of it. Both have played the game of sexual politics, and both have reimagined the politics of sex. Both experienced racial prejudice, and both used that bias to invent the self on her own terms.[2]

As this chapter will demonstrate, these competing attributes not only link Bernhardt and Cleopatra through a transhistorical fantasy of exceptional womanhood; they also illuminate how such women signified collective cultural values and became vehicles for expressing social anxieties. Bernhardt's Cleopatra resonated with audiences because it tapped into broader fantasies and fears regarding the hypersexualized female Other. Anchored in each woman's cultural illegibility and articulated through the contradictions above, Bernhardt's Cleopatra made visible and visceral anxieties about sex, race, class, gender, and Frenchness current in the Third Republic. Drawing on the Orientalist tropes available to her, Bernhardt resurrected a familiar Cleopatra. However, by conflating the queen's racial ambiguity with her own and by amalgamating liberated sexuality with state power, star power, and female empowerment broadly, she complicated the category of otherness against which French republicans defined themselves.

By the time she played Cleopatra in 1890, Bernhardt was an experienced thespian whose talent, professional skill, and notorious offstage persona had garnered international recognition. A veritable golden age for both the theater and the press, the fin de siècle offered entertainers like her unprecedented opportunities for attracting public attention. Between 1884 and 1914, no fewer than forty-five theaters operated in Paris, and in 1888, it was estimated that more than a million Parisians frequented the theater at least once a month, while half that number attended weekly. Although theater revenues fluctuated across the period, they more than doubled from thirty-two to sixty-eight million francs. At the same time that the conventional theater flourished, a variety of working-class amusements emerged. Boulevard theaters, café-concerts, panoramas, and music halls offered alternative forms of entertainment.[3]

Despite the proliferation of these new venues, it was in the hallowed theaters of Paris that Bernhardt first came to public attention. A mesmerizing world of unfettered artifice, the theater, with its sumptuous sets and contrived props, its engrossing musical scores, and its arresting performers, along with its penchant for mimicry, parody, and satire (all genres that challenged social convention), created fantasy worlds through which actresses like Bernhardt could craft public personas that seamlessly blended fact with fiction. Enacting a seemingly endless variety of characters, Bernhardt could appear domestic and domesticated, frivolous and ornamental, pleasing and passive one moment, wanton and wild, shrewd and cunning, headstrong and hypersexual the next. Indeed, through the characters she personified on stage, Bernhardt disseminated alternate realities wherein the norms of gender, race, and class could be easily traversed.[4]

Performers like Bernhardt not only gained notoriety on the stage, but they also garnered attention in the press. At the same time that the theater reached its apex of popularity, the press—a beneficiary of technological developments in print and image making as well as of the lifting of censorship laws and a soaring literacy rate due in large part to compulsory schooling under the new republic—practically tripled its circulation between 1880 and 1914. Whereas subscription-based boulevard journals like *Le Figaro, Le Gaulois, Gil Blas, L'Éclair, Le Temps, L'Écho de Paris,* and illustrated weeklies like *L'Illustration* and *La Vie Parisienne* had covered the theater since the middle of the nineteenth century, new mass-produced dailies like *Le Petit Journal, Le Petit Parisian, Le Matin,* and *Le Journal* eventually included celebrity coverage as well.[5]

A shrewd self-promoter, Bernhardt recognized early on how to manipulate both the stage and the media. It was thus not only through her acting but also through her actions, publicizing her offstage antics, inviting the press into her (carefully choreographed) private life, and involving herself in the most important political issues of her day, that she manufactured her public image. In all of these endeavors, she curated her celebrity by making a spectacle of her indeterminate otherness. The public wanted to know: Was she Jewish? Catholic? French? Was she heterosexual? Homosexual? Was she female? Male?[6] By playing up those attributes that made her culturally inscrutable, the *"Fantastique,"* the *"Divine"* Bernhardt intentionally fused and confused the artificial identity registers that circumscribed Frenchness.

Between 1862 and 1923, the more than six decades that coincide with Bernhardt's illustrious acting career, few performers on the planet rivaled her in popularity or acclaim. Bernhardt played more than 125 different roles on stages across Europe and the Americas, she appeared in eleven films between 1900 and 1923, and she was an effective theater manager and a sensational publicist. Like the previous chapter, this one, too, begins by piecing together what we think we know about the woman at its center. Although Bernhardt actively crafted her life story, her biography is no less riddled with uncertainty. Reading Bernhardt's memoir alongside biographical texts written about her, media reviews, and press interviews, the first part of the chapter explores the invention of Sarah Bernhardt. The chapter then examines how, through her portrayal of Cleopatra, Bernhardt confounded ingrained, if arbitrary, distinctions between us and Other to upend contemporary notions of race and gender. The final section teases out the various cultural meanings inscribed in Bernhardt's performance, considering how the actress, as a fantasy echo for Cleopatra and as a culturally ambiguous woman in her own time, monopolized her illegibility to create her celebrity. By enacting a fantasy of exceptional womanhood rooted in racial ambiguity, Bernhardt engaged the identity politics of the Third Republic at the same time that she provided a model for modern female celebrity that others would emulate.

INVENTING SARAH BERNHARDT

Sarah Bernhardt came to public attention on the Parisian stage; however, it was also in the press and through memoir that she narrated the fantasy of exceptional womanhood central to her celebrity. Through these media she capitalized on her otherness, calling attention to her ethnic ambiguity, sexual fluidity, and gender nonconformity to distinguish herself from the status quo. Although fascinated by her eccentricities, the public embraced Bernhardt because in her they also saw themselves. Confiding that she fought an innate desire to please, evoking the merits of motherhood, and entering into an ill-fated marriage, Bernhardt adopted the trappings of domesticity. On the surface it would appear that she did these things to conform to the cult of true womanhood and to affirm her Frenchness. Yet given her penchant for performance and her keen insight into giving people what they wanted, it is equally likely that she manipulated these conventions to ensure her commercial success. Symbolizing the Other and recalling the self, she revealed difference itself as a fiction. In this way, she made indecipherability the hallmark of her celebrity.

Through the public stage of the media and memoir, moreover, Bernhardt brought the contradictions of her fantasy into the private lives of ordinary citizens. Whereas the stage provided at least the façade of separation between performers and spectators—the theater was a communal space entered into by the public—the media and memoir more easily traversed arbitrary divides between public and private. Whether sold by subscription or hawked daily on the streets of urban centers, periodicals circulated freely through the public sphere. They were not confined to one location or to one audience. Memoirs functioned much like periodicals in the ways in which they crossed boundaries between public and private to confer intimacy between reader and text. However, unlike periodicals that might be encountered by happenstance, memoirs were more often intentionally purchased or borrowed. Much lengthier and filled with information about only one person, memoirs also required a greater personal investment from readers. Bernhardt used both of these media to peddle a fantasy of exceptional womanhood that intentionally blurred person with persona. She did so, as we will see, to create a life story as fantastic as the performer who lived it.

If reconstructing Cleopatra's biography is tricky due to the paucity of surviving sources documenting her life, then recounting Sarah Bernhardt's life story is challenging precisely because so much has been written about her. Contemporaries filled newspapers, magazines, diaries, and journals with lively tales of her professional ventures and juicy recitations of her personal escapades. Bernhardt herself supplemented these voluminous records, sometimes augmenting, at other times undermining, them with her own vividly woven fabrications. What we are left with is not a single, comprehensive if contradictory life narrative but rather countless versions of the Bernhardt story: those spun by Bernhardt herself; those imparted by her critics and her supporters; those chronicled by the media (past and present); and those culled by biographers, scholars, and fans searching for snippets of truth amid uncertainty. In many ways, the only Sarah Bernhardt we can claim to *know* is the "Sarah Bernhardt" invented for popular consumption.

Despite a certain degree of ambiguity surrounding the exact place and date of her birth, most biographers agree that Bernhardt (née Sarah Marie Henriette-Rosine Bernard) was born in the Latin Quarter of Paris on either October 22 or 23, 1844.[7] She was the first of three illegitimate daughters born to Julie Bernard (aka Judith or Youle), a Dutch Jewish courtesan who, along with her sister Rosine (Sarah's namesake) entertained some of city's most notorious elites.[8] Julie gave birth to two more daughters, a perky blonde named Jeanne and an unruly imp named Régina, who devoted herself to her eldest sister. Bernhardt likely never knew her father, and although she would make dubious claims about him, his identity remains shrouded in mystery.

Notwithstanding the many glaring absences in her life narrative, however, we do know when some of the key events of Bernhardt's life transpired. She converted to Catholicism on May 21, 1856 (at age eleven). She was accepted into the acclaimed Conservatoire de Paris, the national school for theater, drama, dance, and music founded in 1795, and she became an official member of the esteemed Comédie Française in 1859 (at age fifteen). She gave birth to her only child, Maurice, on December 22, 1864 (at age twenty). Her breakthrough performance came in her *travesti* role as a young male minstrel in François Coppée's one-act play *La Passant* in 1869 (at age twenty-five). A self-proclaimed patriot, Bernhardt nursed wounded soldiers through the Siege of Paris in 1870. Ever the risk-taker, she traveled over Paris in a hot-air balloon during the 1878 International Exposition, and, at age sixty-eight, she unapologetically made her film début in *Queen Elizabeth* or *Elizabeth, Queen of England* in 1912. Acclaimed for her talent and venerated as a national treasure, the French government bequeathed upon her the prestigious Legion of Honor in 1914. Suffering from excruciating knee pain, she demanded a surgeon amputate her right leg in 1915. She died of uremia, a condition defined by diminished renal function and metabolic abnormality, on March 26, 1923 (at age seventy-eight). And, always the pioneer, she was the first woman ever to appear on a French postage stamp in 1945.[9]

Bernhardt was not only one of the Third Republic's most recognizable actresses, but she was also one of its most prolific businesswomen. She acquired and directed her own theater and theater company.[10] She negotiated her own contracts, toured Europe and the Americas numerous times, and she engaged in subsidiary careers as both a sculptor and author. Throughout most of her life, in addition to maintaining a studio and exhibiting work at the salon, she authored her memoirs, *My Double Life;* published an acting manual, *The Art of the Theater,* and a best-selling farcical tale, *In the Clouds: A Chair's Impressions, as Told to Sarah Bernhardt;* penned three plays; and produced a rudimentary novel, *The Idol of Paris.* Amid all of this, Bernhardt found time to entertain countless lovers (both male and female), to collect exotic animals, and even to acquire one disastrously ill-suited husband, an errant Greek aristocrat and temperamental stage actor named Aristides Damala.[11]

Despite her impressive forays into the male-dominated worlds of art and theater, however, Bernhardt was not entirely immune from the gender politics of the age. Like her middle-class contemporaries, she considered women natural dissemblers, fickle decorative objects who sought above all to please. Like them, too, she achieved the highest social status awarded to women by becoming a wife and a mother. Even when acting out in ways decidedly *not* like the conventional women of her time, moreover, she chose to play classic characters (like Cleopatra) rather than take on more controversial New Woman roles.[12]

Yet even as Bernhardt's behaviors made her appear *just like* her bourgeois audiences, they also revealed the ways in which she was nothing like them. Although she adored her illegitimate love child, her marriage to the wayward Greek was in many ways a sham that undermined rather than exalted the virtues of marital domesticity.[13] While some considered Bernhardt's lithe figure and auburn locks assets that made her physically attractive, others considered her slight body too thin, her curly hair too unruly, and her sinewy form and expressive features too dark, too Semitic. When left to her own devices, she turned what contemporaries might consider typical feminine frivolity into unabashed, excessive eccentricity. She did not merely indulge in luxurious bed linens or collect the occasional domesticated house pet; rather, she had herself photographed sleeping in a coffin and converted her entire residence into a zoo for exotic wildlife. And, although she portrayed conventional characters onstage, they were often, like her, powerful, seductive, flirtatious, and assertive. Added to these subversions was her flagrant appropriation of the masculine. She appeared onstage not only as Théodora, Phèdre, or Lady Macbeth but also as Jeanne d'Arc, Prince Charming, and Hamlet. Behind the scenes, she conducted her own financial affairs and directed her own career. If all of this was not enough to challenge woman's secondary status and to disqualify arguments regarding the necessity of her passive citizenship, Bernhardt exercised political agency by publicly supporting Alfred Dreyfus through one of the most contentious episodes in modern French history.

Given Bernhardt's colorful experiences, it would seem that the actress would have no need to embellish her personal life story. Yet she would do so at every turn—in the press, in her memoir, and in the stories that she told about herself to any audience who would listen. Onstage she played a wide range of characters, but in the media, Sarah Bernhardt always played Sarah Bernhardt. This playacting is nowhere more evident than in her memoir, *My Double Life* (1907). Throughout the engrossing text, she portrays herself as strong-willed, stubborn, selfish, impetuous, candid, and histrionic. She freely acknowledges her desire to occupy the center of attention and admits that her penchant to please sometimes tempered her headstrong willfulness. Rather than explain away these contradictory personality traits as commonplace feminine defects, however, she insists on the ways in which they prepared her for her profession. Indeed, in her version of her story, every single life event, no matter how minor it may have appeared at the time, prepared her to become Sarah Bernhardt.

Allegedly chronicling her first thirty-five years, *My Double Life* presents Bernhardt as nothing less than an enfant terrible. Bernhardt's childhood was seemingly filled with danger: as a toddler, she fell into a fire while under her nurse's care in Quimperlé. She broke multiple bones chasing down her Aunt Rosine's carriage in a fit of hysterics. Throughout her youth she engaged in daredevil activities, even taking a fall that left her bedridden for several weeks. She attended boarding school and then convent school until age fourteen. On the rare occasions in which she returned to her mother's house, she recalled being entertained by various "godfathers" and "uncles." These figures passed in and out of her young life, and they, along with other family friends, would pressure her at age fifteen to choose her life's path: the marriage bed or the theatrical stage.[14]

Uninterested in the suitors brought before her, Bernhardt entered the Conservatoire. Upon her arrival, she confessed that she "began to feel the need to create a personality for myself. It was the first awakening of my will. I wanted to be someone." "On September 1, 1862, the day of my début," she writes of her first appearance at the Théâtre-Française, "I found myself planted in front of the theater posters . . . on the corner of rue Duphot and the rue Saint-Honoré. It said on the poster for the Comédie: 'The début of Mademoiselle Sarah Bernhardt.' I don't know how long I stayed there drawn by the letters of my name, but I remember that each person who stopped seemed to look at me after reading the notice."[15] That the young actress should include a scene of herself lingering over the illuminated letters of her name is not surprising given her stated preoccupation with becoming somebody. That she should recount the first time that she encountered "Sarah Bernhardt," as the public would grow to know her, suggests that the somebody to whom she aspired was already aligning with the somebody else she was becoming.

In her memoir, Bernhardt portrayed herself by turns as a dutiful daughter and sister; a staunch patriot and devout Catholic; and as a sickly though passionate workhorse bent on her own fulfillment. Bernhardt went out of her way to enact the role of the obedient daughter and loyal sister, accounting for a distracted stage performance by explaining concern over her ailing mother's health. During her scene, Bernhardt noticed that her mother looked "deathly pale" and was taken away from the theater. In an attempt to recover herself, Bernhardt confided that she "put a little more powder on, but the public, not knowing what was taking place, were annoyed with me, thinking I was guilty of some fresh caprice, and received me still more coldly than before. It was all the same to me, as I was thinking of something else."[16] It was not a lack of concentration or stage fright that disrupted her performance but genuine concern over her mother's welfare that distracted her.

In a similar vein, she also cast herself in the role of devoted sibling. Despite having suffered a recent house fire, Bernhardt opened her home to her infirm sister Régina and presided over her deathbed. After Régina died, Bernhardt attempted to capture her sister's spirit in sculpture: "Then I undertook the bust of my young sister Régina . . . a more perfect face was never made by the hand of God! Two leonine eyes shaded by long, long brown lashes, a slender nose with delicate nostrils, a tiny mouth, a willful chin, and a pearly skin crowned by meshes of sunrays, for I have never seen hair so blonde and so pale, so bright and so silky." Aware that critics and fans alike would read her memoir, Bernhardt's aim in telling this story was as likely intended to draw attention to her work as an artist and to her suffering as a bereft sibling, as it was meant to extol her deceased sister. "But this admirable face was without charm; the expression was hard and the mouth without a smile," she continued. "I tried my best to reproduce this beautiful face in marble, but it needed a great artist, and I was only a humble amateur."[17]

Bernhardt's skill as a sculptress may have had its limits, but her fervent love of country seemingly knew no bounds. In addition to repeatedly declaring her affection for Napoleon, Bernhardt, in her telling of it, single-handedly saved Paris during the Prussian siege. Collecting overcoats, negotiating with the prefect of Paris for provisions for her makeshift hospital at the Odéon, staffing and running said establishment, and often feeding and tending to patients herself, Bernhardt emerges in her memoir as a one-woman Red Cross. As conditions worsened during the siege, she burned the chairs and props of her beloved theater for warmth, called in favors and bargained with butchers to get meat for recovering patients, and neglected her personal needs to serve the cause. Given the extent of her involvement in provisioning Paris and witnessing the sacrifices of those around her, Bernhardt regarded the armistice as "a slap in the face to Parisians." She claimed that she had no choice but to abandon the city when the "wretched Commune" overturned law and order, bringing with it "a lot of blood! What a lot of ashes! What a lot of women mourning! A malaise infected the whole of France but especially Paris."[18]

Scholars and contemporaries alike have speculated that Bernhardt so vehemently vocalized her patriotism because, as the daughter of a Jew and a Catholic convert, her Frenchness could be (and was) called into question. Bernhardt acknowledged this interest in her religious identity when recounting an interview with "a female reporter in a tailor-made skirt, with her hair cut short," on her first American tour in 1880–81. In a "clear, sweet voice," the reporter asked Bernhardt whether she was "of the Jewish religion or whether you are a Catholic, a Protestant, a Mohammedan, a Buddhist, an Atheist a Zoroastrian, a Theist, or a Deist." Visibly irritated by the question, she curtly responded, "I am a Catholic, Mademoiselle." When the reporter pressed, Roman or Orthodox, Bernhardt jumped out of her seat, interrupting the work of the sketch artist charged with rendering her image for the accompanying story. "When he had finished I asked to see what he had done, and, perfectly unabashed, he handed me his horrible drawing of a skeleton with a curly wig," she inveighed. "I tore the sketch up and threw it at him, but the following day that horror appeared in the papers, with a disagreeable inscription beneath it."[19] Read alongside the artist's rendering of Bernhardt as excessively slender with too curly hair, the American reporter's disingenuous query regarding "Roman or Orthodox," thinly disguised a far more pointed question: Was Sarah Bernhardt a Christian or a Jew? And, by extension, was she truly French?

Bernhardt's encounter with the American journalist would prove neither the first nor the last time that members of the press scrutinized her religious affiliation or racial origins. Nor would it be the last time that the actress so vocally expressed her irritation with people and situations beyond her control. Indeed, Bernhardt's response above was only one of many outbursts in a long line of tantrums thrown to express her displeasure: "Often, when I was a child, I wished to kill myself in order to vex others." She brought this sort of philosophy with her into the theater as well, railing against perceived injustices dealt her by employers and coworkers. After Comédie Française director Émile Perrin denied her a desired role, she felt that "same bitter and childish sentiment" bubbling up. Using her health as an excuse to get her way, she reflected, "I shall certainly fall senseless vomiting blood, and perhaps I shall die! And it will serve Perrin right.... Yes, that is what I thought. I am at times very foolish."[20]

Perhaps it was foolishness or merely a desire for attention that persuaded the actress to publicize several of her rather odd behaviors. She recounts a manicurist entering her rooms to do her nails who discovers in her napping in her coffin. "But seeing me in my coffin she rushed away shrieking wildly. From that moment, all Paris knew that I slept in my coffin, and gossip with its thistle-down wings took flight in all directions." In another episode, at the time of her sister's death, the undertakers called to collect her body "found themselves confronted with two coffins, and losing his wits, the master of ceremonies sent in haste for a second hearse." Bernhardt, who either woke up or decided that it was time to put an end to her charade, intervened only at the last minute and not soon enough to avoid "the papers" that "got hold of this incident. Of course, the "incident," as she was well aware, would make her the talk of the town.

Bernhardt characterized her coffin as little more than a piece of furniture, purchased in anticipation of her own untimely demise (she was convinced since childhood that her feeble, illness-prone body would renounce her at an early age). As such, it complemented the rest of her domestic décor, which reflected the "ornamental, exotica" of the high Victorian period. Her lavishly decorated homes overflowed with furniture, rugs, and works of art and were packed with "curiosities picked up on her travels."[21] To maintain her extravagant domicile, she employed scores of servants, maids, and secretaries, who were charged not only with looking after her homes but also with attending to her ever-increasing entourage of wildlife. While on tour in London, for example, she purchased a "cheetah in a cage, the dog-wolf in a leash . . . six little chameleons in a box, and Cross-ci Cross-ça on my shoulder, fastened to a gold chain we had bought at a jeweler's." These "new guests," as she called them, moved into her London home, joining the three dogs, a parrot, and a monkey named Darwin who were already in residence there.[22] Although delighted by her new acquisitions, Bernhardt conceded that the other members of her household, and many of her terrified visitors, were decidedly less enthusiastic about the new lodgers.

Bernhardt's professional life was as filled with drama as her personal life. Presenting herself as an artist dedicated to her craft on the one hand and as a business-minded professional capable of managing her own affairs on the other, she elicited the respect as well as the ire of many of her colleagues. Although she may have won friends at the Odéon, the theater she "most liked," where players "only thought about putting on plays" and rehearsed "in the morning, the afternoon, all the time," she openly disdained the "starchy, gossipy, jealous little group" with whom she worked at the Comédie Française. Reviling their frivolous discussions about "dresses and hats" and "a thousand things that had nothing to do with art," in her memoir, Bernhardt publicly undermined the esteemed theater's reputation and questioned the performers' talent, values, and commitment to work.[23]

Not only would Bernhardt openly disparage those in her trade whom she found lacking, she would even cast a critical eye upon those who helped make her. According to Bernhardt, relations with Perrin, which proved dicey at the best of times, deteriorated alongside her growing success. While the director was "pleased that I was successful, for the sake of the theatre; he was happy at the magnificent receipts of *Ruy Blas,*" Bernhardt contends, "he would have much preferred that it had been another than I who received all the applause. My independence, my horror of submission, even in appearance, annoyed him vastly."[24] It did not help matters between them that Bernhardt cleverly leveraged her success in Victor Hugo's play, which was roundly regarded as the playwright's triumphant return to the French stage, in future contract negotiations. When the Comédie Française was shuttered for repairs in June and July 1879, Perrin made plans to take the company to London for six weeks. Although he successfully scheduled enough actors to fill the roles, when told that Bernhardt would not accompany the troupe, managers at the Gaiety Theater balked, explaining that they had sold many tickets on the promise of her appearance. In an unenviable position, Perrin had to collaborate with Bernhardt to pull off his London venture. Aware of his predicament, Bernhardt refused to sign on to the scheme unless she was made a "*sociétaire* [the highest rank with the company] with one entire share in the profits." The Comédie committee initially refused her demand, but eventually members agreed to her terms and named her a *sociétaire* for life.[25]

Bernhardt's success in Hugo's *Ruy Blas* positioned her to make professional demands and marked a pivotal moment in the rise of her celebrity. "This 26 January," she wrote, "rent the veil which had, until then, obscured my future, and I realized that I was destined for celebrity. Until that night I had been the students' little fairy. But on that night I became the Chosen One. Breathless, dazed, delighted by my success." Characterizing her now dear friend and ardent admirer Victor Hugo as the "Messiah" and the "greatest poet of the last century," she credited him with placing "on my forehead the crown of crowns."[26] In a rare moment of humility, Bernhardt shared the spotlight with someone else. That she chose to do so with one of the most celebrated figures of the nineteenth century speaks perhaps to her cunning as well as to her prudence.

As Bernhardt's star continued to ascend, she openly acknowledged the ways in which her fame interfered with her personal and professional relationships. Whether she was genuinely concerned about the former's effect on the latter, however, is somewhat less clear. By the time of the Universal Exposition in 1878, she was aware of the strain her popularity caused: "My celebrity had become irritating for my enemies, and a little too resounding, I admit, for my friends." Nevertheless, she admitted that "at that time all the acclaim amused me tremendously."[27] In typical Bernhardt fashion, she insisted that she "did nothing to attract attention," arguing that she was merely "set apart" by "my rather strange tastes, my thinness, my pallor, my individualistic way of dressing, my disdain for fashion, and my couldn't-care-less attitude. I was not conscious of it." As if to drive home her point, she maintained that she "never" read newspapers and so remained blissfully unaware of what was said about her. By ignoring the press, both good and bad, and by surrounding herself "by a court of male and female worshippers," the anointed "Chosen One" professed to live in a "sunny dream."[28]

Despite her claims to the contrary, Bernhardt knew all too well that in the press she was very much talked about. Nevertheless, she vehemently denied enjoying the publicity that she so actively courted. "The public is very much mistaken in imagining that the agitation made about celebrated artistes is in reality instigated by the persons concerned," she explained. "Irritated at seeing the same name constantly appearing on every occasion," she continued, "the public declares that the artiste who is being either slandered or pampered is an ardent lover of publicity." Painting herself, and celebrities generally, as "victims of the said advertisement," she duplicitously disavowed her love of the spotlight and refused to take responsibility for the publicity generated about (and sometimes by) her.[29] This type of false modesty was not unique to Bernhardt but a hallmark of the double bind of female celebrity at the fin de siècle.[30] Whereas men could bask in the public recognition that they received, especially in regard to their artistic works, women were expected to downplay their achievements and to appear unconcerned with the public commentary they elicited. A woman's fame, moreover, was acceptable only to the extent that the public believed that she neither welcomed attention nor orchestrated it.[31] Undoubtedly aware of this conundrum, Bernhardt played a double game. By acknowledging how she was "supposed" to regard the press, she portrayed herself as its victim. But by manipulating that perception, she also transformed herself into a collaborator free to tell her own story.

The pronouncements that she "never" read stories written about her notwithstanding, Bernhardt nevertheless peppered her memoir with press excerpts.[32] One case in point is her reproduction of selections from the renowned theater critic Francisque Sarcey's appraisal of her opening-night performance in *Mademoiselle de Belle-Isle.* The review, which appeared five days after the play's premiere in the November 11, 1872, issue of *Le Temps*, was anything but favorable. Although not intimately acquainted with Sarcey, Bernhardt belied her professed disinterest in publicity by confessing that she knew he followed her "career with great interest." By reproducing only extracts from the review, moreover, she determined how she would be portrayed in her memoir, if not in the news item itself. The duplicated selection begins by acknowledging the public's "curiosity" about the "true or false stories" circulating around Bernhardt's private life before moving into a long description of her "disappointing" appearance. A costume that "exaggerated" her slenderness, powder that made her "terribly pale," eyes that "had lost their brilliancy," and finally a powerless voice incapable of "carrying away an audience" rendered her efforts in the first three acts little more than a "convulsive tremor."[33] Sarcey conceded that "roused by the coldness of the public," Bernhardt would recover for the fifth act, but by that time her performance's deficiencies had far outweighed its merits.

Given that she could select from thousands of news articles and reviews written about her, why would Bernhardt include what might be considered "bad press" in her memoir? On the one hand, incorporating negative appraisals of her performances enabled Bernhardt to appear humble. In this way, she portrayed herself as the struggling artist who, through pure grit and hard work, persevered. On the other hand, by excerpting the review in the way that she did, Bernhardt ostensibly rewrote it; she retold the story on her own terms. The night in question, after all, was the same one when Bernhardt was distracted by concerns for her ailing mother, performing on the back of another heated conflict with Perrin, and facing the potential of yet another failure at the Comédie Française. The odds against her, she valiantly recovered herself for the second performance. The insinuation here is that, had Sarcey attended subsequent renditions of the play, he would have been most impressed by her outstanding performance. In editorializing the review, Bernhardt intended to do more than simply redeem a lackluster showing. She also, as she had done with Hugo, associated herself with excellence in her field, the most revered theater critic of the moment, Francisque Sarcey. By cleverly reinterpreting Sarcey's review, then, Bernhardt shaped how she would be seen in posterity if not in the November 11 issue of *Le Temps.*

Perhaps it was important for Bernhardt to appropriate the words of others in her memoir because, despite her best efforts, she had relatively little control over what was published about her. Not only did she encounter critical reviews in the mainstream media, but she also had to contend with racist caricatures of herself. The press commented on Bernhardt's Jewish heritage throughout her career, but associations between the actress and her race were rendered more frequently and expressed more viciously after 1898, when she became a fervent Dreyfusard. As the nation bitterly divided over whether the Jewish artillery officer charged with treason had in fact colluded with the enemy by covertly passing intelligence to the German high command, Bernhardt passionately and publicly defended the officer's innocence. In so doing, she provoked the wrath of anti-Dreyfusards and anti-Semites who regarded Jews as threats not only to national security but also to Frenchness itself. Quick to demonize her and keen to blunt her cultural influence, the anti-Semitic press characterized Bernhardt as a neurotic, sickly, money-hungry megalomaniac, and it caricatured her image using racist stereotypes including a needle-thin physique, an exaggerated nose, a grayish, dirty complexion, dark, beady eyes, and a serpentine (spineless) frame. In short, it cast her as the latest version "la Juive errante," the pathological wandering Jew who belonged to no country and therefore could not be trusted to represent, to defend, or to preserve French values.[34]

Arguably the single most vitriolic text written about her came in the form of a counterfeit biography authored by Marie Colombier, her former colleague and travel companion. Published in January 1884, Colombier's scathing *The*

Memoirs of Sarah Barnum used Bernhardt's Jewish origins to attack her talent, her lifestyle, and her character. Rather than author a gossipy tell-all recounting her experiences with Bernhardt, Colombier penned a hyperbolic mockumentary thinly disguised as memoir. Indeed, by entitling her work *The Memoirs of Sarah Barnum,* she craftily revealed the pose of the text. Usually authored by the individual whom they depict and expected to reveal life experiences (even if those instances are evoked to cast the subject in a necessarily too rosy light), memoirs are typically not authored by a person's nemesis whose agenda it is to slander them. The impertinent Colombier conveyed her mission when she substituted Bernhardt's last name with "Barnum." A clear allusion to P. T. Barnum's traveling circus and freak show that deemed itself the "greatest show on earth," the use of "Barnum" as Sarah's surname was intended to malign the actress by aligning her with attention-seeking misfits and curious oddities who pandered to the easily amused. At the same time, the name provided Colombier with the pretext of plausible deniability: she could insist it was not *Sarah Bernhardt,* but *Sarah Barnum,* who was the subject of her book.[35]

Colombier's assault on the actress only began with the title of her work; she filled the more than 150 pages devoted to her rival with insults and innuendos that gave even Octavian a run for his money. Whether attacking her talent, her character, her appearance, or her morality, Colombier linked all of Bernhardt's deficits to her Jewish identity. A "real daughter of Israel," Colombier's Sarah was "coldly corrupt, vicious by habit, naughty by liking, eager for gain by instinct, sensational through idleness and a wish to throw dust in everyone's eyes, [and] envious by temperament." An "artificial woman" jealous of other females, vain though "her beauty had nothing attractive," the rootless troubadour was, in Colombier's accounting, "destined to remain an imperfect woman." Cruel to her siblings and vicious toward her colleagues, Barnum, who would have "buried all Israel to obtain" personal and professional advantage, could only mask "her violence, idiosyncrasies, her fantastic caprices, her cold wickedness" with a feigned charm calculated to conceal the "bad feminine feelings" that were "most deeply seated with her."[36]

If her personality won her no favors, her appearance proved even less impressive. Using every anti-Semitic and Orientalist trope available to her, Colombier criticized Barnum's extreme thinness as well as her "eccentric" toilette. She wondered at the public's fascination with the "exotic creature" who, rather than embodying the elegance of French civilization, pandered to the "Oriental tastes of the vulgar herd." She imagines Barnum "standing before a mirror," "her height seemingly increased by a wrap with an extravagant trail, her physiognomy made tragic by the powder on her cheeks, the strange scaffolding of her hair, and the infatuation of her pale face in the multiplied turns of her muslin cravat with its exaggerated bow; the serpentine and flowing lines of her body . . . took the fleeting indecision of spectral shadows."[37] Emphasizing Bernhardt's "pale face," a feature anti-Semites associated with disease and decay, Colombier portrayed Bernhardt as a hollow spectre, a soulless creature lurking in the "shadows." She doubled down on this insult by highlighting the "serpentine" and "flowing lines" of Bernhardt's body. The actress's signature sinewy "S" curve did not connote sensuous femininity for Colombier but unmasked a raw, racialized, and dangerous foreign sexuality.

These were not traits unique to Bernhardt, Colombier disingenuously conceded, but essential characteristics of her race that passed down across generations. Built "large and slender, slim to quite a ridiculous extent, the young female comedian had a strangely characteristic head. The traits were correct and pure, whose lines recalled to mind, but still softened and refined, the Jewish face of the mother." Indeed, Madame Barnum, although "elegant in carriage" and "shrouded in laces," could not mask her "Jewish look," and even a "clear complexion" could not compensate for "her Oriental eyes." The origin and marker of her Otherness, Bernhardt's body was not culturally illegible for Colombier; rather, it was a glaring neon sign that pointed indisputably to the Other. Driven by an equally inherited "love of money" and unable to escape her racial heritage, moreover, Barnum pursued publicity "to the point of mania." Desperate to be talked about, to be wealthy, and to be loved, Barnum gave herself to Paris as her mother had given herself to the paying customers who frequented her boudoir. Intoxicated by all the attention paid her, onstage and through her outlandish antics off of it, she willingly made herself the public's "thing, its doll," and "it amused itself with her."[38]

Colombier's anti-Semitic satire was but one in a chorus of racist attacks launched against Bernhardt. The nationalist right and the anti-Semitic press relentlessly evoked the ambiguity of her origins to question her nationality. Colombier and the brutish writers of Édouard Drumont's vitriolic paper *La Libre Parole* would not be the only or the last to assault Bernhardt in this way. In their rabidly anti-Semitic tract *Les Femmes d'Israel* (1898), Drumont's cronies Raphaël Viau and François Bournand denied the relevance of Bernhardt's conversion to Catholicism, arguing that "whether initiated into the worship of God by Gemara or by the catechism, Sarah Bernhardt is neither more nor less than a Jewess, and nothing but a Jewess."[39] By locking her into her Jewish identity, Viau and Bournand attempted to enclose her within a single, fixed category; they evoked the immutability of her Jewishness to mark her as untrustworthy, incapable of loyalty to the republic.[40] As "nothing but a Jewess," Bernhardt, they argued, could not transcend her race, and because of that, she would never be truly French.

One of the ways that Bernhardt countered these charges was to invite the media into her private life and by playing roles, like Jeanne d'Arc, that associated her with the glory of France. She reiterated her love of country by performing in two early twentieth-century films, *Sarah Bernhardt at Home* (1912) and *Mothers of France* (1916). *Sarah Bernhardt at Home* features the actress participating in local festivals, decorating her home, and pontificating on her craft while relaxing in Brittany. Shooting the film in the provinces, a common practice among journalists at the end of the nineteenth century who often interviewed actresses outside of their Parisian domiciles, Bernhardt asserted her Frenchness by demonstrating that she belonged as much in the countryside as to the cosmopolitan capital city. At home in the provinces, she metaphorically reclaimed France as *her* home. Although not focused on her real-life story, *Mothers of France,* shot during the Great War, upheld Bernhardt as a paragon of French womanhood. Backed by the French Ministry of War, the film, which featured Bernhardt as an army commander's wife, was designed to encourage Americans to join the war effort. Focused on Bernhardt's character, who has sacrificed both her husband and her son to the cause and nurses the wounded at the front, the film illustrates the collective hardship faced by the French people. A hero rather than a victim, Bernhardt symbolizes French strength and resilience. Nowhere in the film is Bernhardt's Frenchness or her womanliness disputed; in fact, by selecting her as its star, the ministry promoted her as a living symbol of French republican womanhood.[41]

Commodified plaything, errant daughter of Israel, shrewd publicist, unconventional libertine, devoted family member, fervent patriot, industrious artisan, and passionate artiste, Sarah Bernhardt seemed to reincarnate the mythical many-headed hydra.[42] Whether beloved as la Divine, la Fantastique, L'Incomparable, "the eighth wonder of the world," or bemoaned as la Juive errante, in Third Republic France, the chameleon-like Bernhardt colonized the collective imagination.[43] A gifted dissembler, Bernhardt relentlessly teased the public showing it by turns what it did and what it did not want to see. In so doing, however, she left herself open to interpretation and to appropriation. Importantly, admirers, feminists, and New Women countered the anti-Semite's dystopic fantasy of Bernhardt with a fantasy of their own. For many of her French fans, Bernhardt embodied elements of true womanhood: she was decorative, pleasing, sensual, a worthy spectacle, an alluring amusement, a "woman" above all else. To those less inclined to support this conventional model of womanhood, Bernhardt offered the possibility of perpetual reinvention.

In the midst of the Dreyfus Affair, Daniel Lesueur, a female reporter for the feminist daily *La Fronde,* portrayed Bernhardt as a fantastic spectre, an ephemeral sprite positioned outside of humanity. "In our somber era, our days of conflict and ugliness," Lesueur breathlessly maintained, "she arises, luminous, on the threshold of an invisible temple. . . . Does she not stand outside of any one race, any one time, any one civilization . . . ? The enigmatic smile of Cleopatra, of Theodora, of Joan of Arc has floated on her lips. One by one, their souls have animated her. Was she born in our century?"[44] For forward-thinking women like Lesueur, Bernhardt offered a model of womanhood circumscribed not by the myth of the eternal feminine but expressed through a fantasy of exceptionalism in which cultural illegibility provided a pathway to self-realization. In their celebration of her achievements as well as in their mimicking of her autonomous acts, New Women, like the *frondueses,* enacted alternate forms of womanhood and transformed Bernhardt's exceptionalism into their own fantasies.

PLAYING CLEOPATRA IN THIRD REPUBLIC FRANCE

In the autumn of 1890, Victorien Sardou's five-act play *Cléopâtre* premiered at the Théâtre de la Porte Saint-Martin. An established Parisian playwright—by this time the author was almost forty years into his creative career—Sardou penned the play explicitly for Bernhardt. Historically researched, well financed, and headlined by la Divine, the play promised to be yet another link in a long chain of Sardou's theatrical triumphs.[45] No expense was spared on the opulent set design or on the elaborate period costumes, which together

FIG. 5. Sarah Bernhardt in *Cléopâtre,* 1891.

created a stimulating visual smorgasbord of replicated artifacts and contrived Eastern panoramas. At the same time, however, the production's completely Euro-American cast and the characters' vernacular dialogue provided a modern, Western twist on the drama that the playwright hoped would resonate with contemporary audiences.

Drawing from the works of both Plutarch and Shakespeare, Sardou's Cleopatra blended East and West, past and present, masculine and feminine. She was also, as the interpretatively rich publicity materials for the production insinuated, a bundle of contradictions (figure 5). In this image, Bernhardt's set jaw, penetrating stare, and unyielding expression contrast notably with the fluid draping of her tunic and the soft textures of the damask blanket and pillows upon which she rests. Captured in a semi-reclining pose in which she props up her head with her bent right arm, Bernhardt's Cleopatra appears as though she has just awakened from a nap or as though she is watching some form of entertainment. The intimacy of the scene is belied only by the queen's barely visible crown, which is itself lost in the tussled curls of Bernhardt's hair. Although Bernhardt painted her body for the role, she is shown here without a trace of color on her white skin. Indeed, the lighting from the left side of the image highlights the alabaster whiteness of her cheek, her left arm, and even her bent elbow. Rather than obscure the player behind the character, images like this one emphasized the actress who enlivened her, inviting audiences to envision Cleopatra exclusively through the lens of Sarah Bernhardt. Although Bernhardt played Cleopatra on the stage, she continued, in materials promoting the production, to play Sarah Bernhardt.

Bernhardt frequently superimposed her own personality onto the character that she played. It was no great leap, of course for audiences to envision her Cleopatra as a hypersexualized figure whose carnal prowess rivaled her political proficiency. Like the racially ambiguous, sexually promiscuous woman who played her, Cleopatra was imagined by French audiences as an exotic and erotic femme Orientale, a formidable public woman governed by her passions. As the play opens, Dellius, a Roman legionnaire, notes that Cleopatra became the queen of Egypt not only through hereditary birthright and political acumen but also, and perhaps more artfully, through her sexual seduction of Caesar. "Today she is in the full flowering of her beauty," he explains. "And, moreover, this beauty, radiant and triumphant, is it not at the result of a strange charm which she releases and intoxicates us with? Is this an African philter, trickery or magic?" After characterizing the monarch's charm as some sort of "African" magic, he continues, "no one in vain receives the caress of her glow, the enchanting music of her voice, the voluptuous treachery of her beauty." Through Dellius's description, audiences first encounter Sardou's Cleopatra as an intoxicating though potentially dangerous figure. As Marc Antony enters into the discussion, the legionnaire connects these traits to her accomplishments as a musician, dancer, poet, and philosopher and links them with her uncanny ability to debate science with both the "gravity of a queen" and the "mad gaiety of a child." "All languages," he cautions, "are familiar to her and all are masks. Artificial and clever, she will charm you with her candor, or soften you with her tears . . . all these women are united in a single woman—all poisons concentrated in one. That's Cleopatra."[46]

At this moment, Bernhardt's Cleopatra takes center stage. Floating regally down the Cydnus River before her first audience with Antony, who is portrayed as "a man in the strength of his age," Bernhardt's Cleopatra emerges "dressed in a tunic of transparent linen," slightly hidden behind a "gold cassock" and veil, "bracelets" jingling "at her wrists . . . [r]ings sparkl[ing] on each of her fingers," holding "a scepter in the form of a cross." While Bernhardt is flanked by "two huge Nubian slaves" extending ostrich feathers behind her, the audience gains full view of the actress, whose "face and arms [were] stained brown."[47] The production's inclusion of "Nubian slaves," who were likely themselves white performers in body paint, to frame a "stained" Bernhardt is telling.[48] The juxtaposition reinforced a pervasive colorism in which the darker one's skin, the more s/he was considered Other—an assumption often upheld by Westerners to justify the domination and enslavement of the Other on racial grounds. As a signal of Cleopatra's racial ambiguity, Bernhardt's painted skin acknowledged such associations at the same time that it exposed, through racial parody, its limits. Bernhardt literally "stains" her skin, a word that recalls biblical origin stories of blackness. Yet by using stain to make her body appear "Black," Bernhardt denaturalized race, implying that, like the paint she used to create her character, it too was something that could be put on. Bernhardt's staining was more than an insensitive exercise in blackface, however; it was also a strategic move that enabled her to obscure her racial otherness as a Jewish woman while highlighting Cleopatra's identity as an African one. These racial displacements, somewhat ironically, reinforced Cleopatra's otherness while making Bernhardt appear to her French audience as more rather than less like us.[49] In other words, by staining her skin to portray a Black Cleopatra, Bernhardt emphasized her own whiteness, challenging those who would read her Jewishness as racial difference.

A similar sleight of hand reappears in the opulence of the spectacle, in Bernhardt's lavish wardrobe, and in her confusing choice of hair color. "Her head was covered—almost crushed—by an immense wig of auburn hair, falling in thick locks all over her shoulders. She wore one of those tunics . . . which seems to have been contrived only with a view of making her look as much as possible like a Tanagra statuette."[50] In Bernhardt's Cleopatra, stained skinned indicated the queen's African origins, while a "wig of auburn hair" that made her resemble "a Tanagra statuette," signaled her Hellenic roots. The wig competed with Bernhardt's stained skin, begging the questions: Was Cleopatra Black? Was she Mediterranean? Was she both? Neither? And what about Bernhardt herself? Where did she fall on the racial register?

Indeed, audiences, critics, and other actors were so perplexed by Bernhardt's portrayal of Cleopatra's racial ambiguity that they were uncertain as to how to read her dark skin and auburn hair. Before the play opened, a correspondent for the London evening paper the *St. James Gazette* attended a dress rehearsal in which s/he noted that the actress spent hours "trying on costumes and seeking among the headdresses that which appeared to her the most appropriate and the most consistent with historical truth." The observer then explained, "The Cleopatra who will appear on the 15th will have red hair and brown complexion. That these [traits] characterized Cleopatra seems" a conclusion drawn from "serious researches, made to reproduce as closely as possible the real appearance of that bold, attractive, powerful, and cunning woman."[51]

Unconcerned with the historical accuracy of Bernhardt's portrayal, Anglo-American actresses who had played Cleopatra questioned the red hair and brown skin on aesthetic grounds. American-born Russian actress and soprano Geneviève Ward conceded that "Madame Bernhardt is . . . quite right to represent Cleopatra as having a dark complexion." But, she questioned, would the skin tone "harmonize with red hair? Surely the colour is generally associated with a clear and vivid complexion. But then, again, it is a common practice among certain dark races to dye the hair of a warmer tinge." It is unclear whether the "dark races" to which Ward refers applied to Cleopatra or to Bernhardt herself; however, her comment reveals her sentiment that actresses should present themselves in the most flattering light regardless of the character they play. More sympathetic in her appraisal, the wildly popular English actress Ellen Terry suggested that if Bernhardt did wear red hair, "it's sure to be right. Everything Sarah does *must* be right."[52] Focused on the overall effect of the spectacle, Terry and Ward illustrated how commonplace dramatic (mis)appropriations of the racialized East had become by the end of the century. In their suggestion that Bernhardt's interpretation of Cleopatra "must be right," they deferred to her professional expertise, dismissing the pillaging of non-Western cultures and the racial play that accompanied it as a matter of theater.

Whether a matter of theater or a matter of history, Sardou's Cleopatra derived her power from her potent sexuality as well as from her racial hybridity. Sardou indicates Cleopatra's cultural illegibility early in the play when she announces to Antony that she is a "daughter of Egypt and Greece, I am of another race. The African sun, which has gilded my brow, has kindled flames in my breast."[53] It was thus as a "daughter of Greece" that Bernhardt's Cleopatra obtained her red hair and as a "daughter of Egypt" that she derived her brown skin. Articulated through these geographically specific racial markers, Cleopatra's sexual power appears to reside in a physical beauty developed explicitly from her hybridity. Antony is enchanted by her precisely because she is "of another race," somehow comfortably familiar and mysteriously Other.

The racial tension Antony identifies is exacerbated by his inability to determine what kind of woman Cleopatra is. Almost immediately after referring to her as a "woman, true woman," he calls her a "sorceress" who tempted Caesar with "the witchcraft" induced through her "lotus eyes."[54] In his eroticization of her illegible beauty, Sardou's Antony shared much in common with contemporary European theatergoers for whom the Orient represented a world of unfettered masculine desire. And, like his audience, Antony also found the uncontrolled female sexuality of the oversexed foreign woman unsettling. Antony certainly fetishized his love interest in terms that late nineteenth-century French audiences would understand. A "sorceress" made for man's delight as well as a "true woman" who provided a safe haven in a dangerous world, Bernhardt's Cleopatra embodied the two dominant female stereotypes of the time: harlot and housewife. At the same time, however, Antony detected "witchcraft" behind Cleopatra's "lotus eyes" and "caressing voice," suggesting that he also recognized in his paramour elements of the dangerous femme fatale. As played by Sarah Bernhardt, Sardou's Cleopatra was simultaneously a worthy partner and an untrustworthy vixen. She was *just like* many of the women in the audience and also nothing like them. She repelled and enticed her male audience, and in her potent figure, she vividly linked masculine desire with imperial aspiration. As the lusty harlot, Cleopatra represented the wild adventures promised by the imperial mission. As the domestic/domesticated woman she exemplified the rewards of colonial submission. In this way, Bernhardt's femme Orientale revealed the power of the Other not only to seduce and to tempt but also to rebuff, to resist, and, potentially, to surmount and to subdue.

As the voluptuously outfitted flotilla sweeps airily across the stage, Bernhardt's melodic voice enchants Antony, who appears "capable of the basest weakness under feminine influence, and yet a brave soldier ready to sacrifice his life for the discharge of his martial duties."[55] Mesmerized by her lyrical recitations, Antony quickly falls under the queen's spell. The hypermasculine warrior is so enraptured by Cleopatra that he abandons his diplomatic campaign and returns with her to Egypt by the end of the first act. Recalling the drama years later, critic Henry Bauer noted that the scene was "pretty, pleasing to the eye" but that it was "Bernhardt's grace" that conjured "the majesty . . . of that Cleopatra who seemed a radiant deity among men." Bernhardt's performance restored the "great seductress," who epitomized "the adorable magician proclaiming the triumph of woman, in turn seductive, flirtatious, terrible and moving." Ignoring all of the chat over her red hair and stained skin, Bauer addressed the accuracy of Bernhardt's portrayal as a matter of performative skill. "She composed the character as only a supremely intelligent artist, having seen and understood the antique," he extolled, "can create a figure."[56]

The second act finds "Antony, stretched on cushions of red hair, dressed in an Egyptian robe," reclining alongside Cleopatra as the pair partake in a grand banquet. Comprised almost entirely of a ballet performed by the queen's "Nubian dancers," the act uses the image of dancing Black bodies to metaphorically consummate the couple's love affair.[57] In the scene, as in the earlier one in which they appeared, it is the Nubians rather than Bernhardt who signify the exotic. Drawing attention away from the protagonists, who engage in very little dialogue in the scene, the ballet suggestively masks even as it explicitly evokes the transcultural sex act. Bernhardt's Cleopatra seduces Antony from behind the veil of Black performing bodies, and, in the process, she exposes her double otherness. Cleopatra shared a culture with the dancers around her, but she shared her body with the Roman who (through his communion with her) penetrated that culture. Emerging at the intersection of these two worlds, Bernhardt's Cleopatra appears to belong to both and to neither. Her power thus resides in her uncanny ability to fit into and to transcend both—in her complete cultural illegibility.

Like so many Western men, Antony is bewitched by the woman and the foreign land she represents. "Your beauty," he tells her, "seems more strange in the shade of these forests of granite or in the dazzling brilliance of burning horizons. . . . Your deep eyes, your enigmatic smile, your serpentine suppleness—you are truly Egyptian, Isis always veiled in the shadows, living enigma, the Sphinx." No longer only a "true woman," in Antony's eyes, Cleopatra is now also a true Egyptian. By linking her to Isis he merely envisions Cleopatra through one of the lenses through which she saw herself. However, by calling her a "Sphinx," a term that generically references the mythical creature with a woman's head, a lion's body, and a falcon's wings but that colloquially connotes an enigmatic person, he fixates on her otherness. In response to his musings, Cleopatra attempts to erase the mysterious differences between them by situating her otherness in her womanhood. She tells Antony that she loves him with "all my soul" and that she accepts him as "my master, my King."[58] Through these declarations, she reasserts the gender hierarchy familiar to nineteenth-century French audiences. Bernhardt's Cleopatra does not deny her amorous influence, but she insinuates that despite cultural and racial differences men and women can be sexually compatible, even, one might say, complementary. By restoring the gender balance, relationships of power that were temporarily disrupted, are harmoniously reinstated. In this instance, gender trumps race as the stabilizing force, it tames the femme Orientale, and evokes the triumph of Western civilization over the Eastern Other.

By act 3, Bernhardt's Cleopatra settles into a domestic relationship with Antony, and she asks him directly if he is "happy" with the "home" that she has made for him. A seemingly innocent question, this inquiry invoked two of the central inversions occurring throughout the play. First, because the question is posed in Cleopatra's domicile in Alexandria, it centers the East, identifying Egypt as "home." In this scenario, the West becomes peripheral; it is the implied Other. It was the seductive Eastern woman who transitioned from mistress/femme fatale into dutiful domestic partner, while the prudent Western male abandoned all reason and possessed the Other only through his own submission to it. Although Cleopatra is not lawfully married to Antony, the couple nevertheless creates a de facto domestic household in the East. In so doing, they rendered the foreign and exotic, native and familiar. A woman and a man could, ostensibly, play house anywhere. At the same time that they collapsed distinctions between the Western "us" and the Eastern "them," they also muddled European conceptions of womanhood by illustrating how the non-Western woman could enact bourgeois domesticity—how she could convincingly play wife and servant to Antony's master and king. A gifted shapeshifter, Bernhardt's Cleopatra portrayed the uneasy and potentially troubling elision between virtuous Western matron and depraved Eastern ingenue—an obfuscation that simultaneously tantalized and traumatized fin-de-siècle audiences.

In ways reminiscent of France's own nineteenth-century social contract, the sexual contract between Cleopatra and Marc Antony cements the couple's romantic union as it also provides the cornerstone of their political alliance. Domestic harmony is disrupted, however, when Cleopatra sends Antony back into battle to secure her own political aims. The third act opens with a love-lorn Cleopatra pining away for her absent warrior and desperate for news regarding his campaign abroad. In a moment of self-doubt that allies her with the passive housewife, Cleopatra chastises herself for sending him away. "He would still be here!" she laments. "Me at his feet . . . when I would wake so I could see him in his turn and his sword at his side when he called me his Serpent of the Nile." When a messenger finally brings news of her lover's adventures, she learns, to her horror, that while in Rome, Antony has subdued Octavian by marrying his sister. Through this union, Antony removes any pretense that Cleopatra might be anything more than a mistress or an expedient political ally. Cleopatra reacts to this news by lashing out in a white-hot rage. "Putting her foot on the shoulder of the crouching Messenger," she threatens to have the unfortunate envoy beaten and tortured. "Whip him with rods of iron. Then, throw him in a pit of serpents," she orders. In short, she acts out as a hysterical, scorned woman unable to overcome the emotional weakness of her sex. Convinced that Antony must have his "secret reasons" for marrying Octavia, Cleopatra rejects the notion that he might actually desire her. In her quest to know everything about her rival—the color of her hair, the sound of her voice, the range of her talents—she endeavors to regain her footing with Antony by identifying herself above all as a woman. An albeit jealous woman who is certain that her competition is "short, ugly and stupid," Cleopatra claims that she "won't be able to live until I have seen this woman."[59] In her fiery tirade against Octavia, Cleopatra reveals that Antony's betrayal is both political and personal. It is thus as both a dispossessed monarch and as a spurned woman that Bernhardt's Cleopatra confronts Rome and the Roman who deceived her.

For audiences who found Bernhardt's Cleopatra too self-possessed in the first acts, her declarations of womanly love in act 3 redeemed her. A critic writing for Le Figaro gushed, "At no time, in any role, was she a greater artist than in this act with the messenger." Through this interaction, he continued, Bernhardt conveyed "all that the woman's heart can express: the anguish of the abandoned lover, the fury of the betrayed woman, the curiosity to be informed about her rival, the way to jump, quickly from one explosion to the other, the way in which she seems to want to crush this cursed rival under her feet . . .

all the various sensations that can shake a woman's . . . heart, were rendered by Sarah Bernhardt with incomparable mastery." Lauding Bernhardt as the "greatest artist . . . of our time," unrivaled in the world even by her predecessor Rachel, the critic joined the audience in a standing ovation.[60] If the queen of Egypt was to be both powerful and compromised, as well as, in Antony's words, a "woman, true woman," it appeared to this critic that no actress performed the role more effectively than Bernhardt. It is thus at the moment of Cleopatra's defeat, when she has been reduced to a state of dependent womanhood, that Bernhardt shines for the *Figaro* journalist. It is at this moment as well that the actress receives a standing ovation from her audience. Whether they rose to their feet because Sardou restored the balance of power between men and women or because the thespian so convincingly played the "true woman," however, is unclear.

Determined to recover her position and to reclaim her man, Bernhardt's Cleopatra rallies as the fourth act opens. Rather than publicly challenge Antony, she has herself clandestinely delivered to his private quarters, concealed in a rolled-up carpet. Lying in wait in her secret refuge, Cleopatra overhears Antony and Octavia discussing their relationship. To assure his new wife of his honorable intentions, Antony pulls Octavia onto his lap. This move elicits "a more obvious reaction of rage by Cleopatra," highlighting the competition between the two women.[61] Explaining that a fleet is likely en route from Alexandria, Antony implies that the queen might soon appear in Actium. This revelation stokes Octavia's own feminine insecurity, and she confesses that she has wondered if Antony has been "thinking of her" when lost in his thoughts. She then confides that she fears that Cleopatra "is so powerful—even from afar!"

For Octavia, Cleopatra is a threat not only because she is a woman but also because she is Other: "They say she's a sorceress." To allay her concern, Antony reasons that it is Cleopatra who should be jealous. "Your radiant youth, the innocent charm of your chaste bearing, your limpid eyes," he reassures her, "they are your enchantments—more powerful than hers." Through this comment, Antony links Octavia's power to conventional womanhood; it is her "youth" and her (unmodified) "charm," traits associated with the true woman of the nineteenth century, that he finds appealing. Still unaware of Cleopatra's presence, Antony continues his conversation with his Roman wife before releasing her to confer with his generals. He immediately announces to them his intention to return to Egypt, not to reestablish ties with Cleopatra but to claim the territory for Rome.

At this moment Bernhardt's Cleopatra emerges. A shocked Antony orders his men to leave his chamber, and a heated argument ensues in which Antony chides Cleopatra for her intrusion. Her retort shifts focus onto his greater betrayal. "This man who left me, swearing of his love to men and gods!" she passionately exclaims. "And the first chance, arriving in Rome he marries another! Who disowns me, who insults me before his friends, his wife, the entire world." Torn between his need for Cleopatra and his political ambition, Antony seethes: "Yes, I hate you, sorceress, who have so well mixed your poisons into my flesh and in my soul that I can no longer tear you out! . . . I thought myself freed and forever escaped from your fatal love. But there you are, with that voice which bewitches me, with looks that burn me."[62] As Antony confesses his own jealousy as well as his inability to free himself from the Eastern "sorceress" who has burned him by mixing poisons into his flesh and soul, Cleopatra embraces her otherness, recognizing it as the source of her sexual allure and, by extension, her political power.

By the end of the act, she convinces the Roman to break his bond with Octavia and to declare war on his brother-in-law. Whether a misguided mission or the result of Cleopatra's cunning calculation, Antony's subsequent invasion of Actium proves disastrous when he follows her advice to invade at sea. During the battle, Cleopatra inexplicably recalls her fleet, leaving Antony with no choice but to retreat. In the final act, the pair return to Egypt, divided by the politics of state only to be reconciled once again by the passion of the flesh. In the afterglow of military defeat and amid great uncertainty as to what will become of the now crumbled political alliance between Rome and Egypt, Antony turns his rage on Cleopatra, declaring that her withdrawal belied her "woman's weakness." Attributing Cleopatra's decision to female jealousy, Antony accuses her of having "no horror of yourself, sorceress, at the thought of so many brave dead men" sacrificed to the "to mad chimeras of your stupid and ferocious jealousy." Though insulted by his allegations, Cleopatra counters that she acted prudently as a savvy political leader and not irrationally as a feeble-minded woman. Octavian had unexpectedly bested them at sea, and therefore they had no choice but to return to Alexandria, where, fortified by Cleopatra's militia and "on the African soil," victory would be assured.[63]

Besieged by the enemy and threatened by a mutiny from within, Cleopatra and Antony launch their final offensive. Once Octavian and his men infiltrate her fortress, Cleopatra fakes her own death, anticipating that she will later reconvene with Antony. Yet her ruse works too well; believing her dead, Antony is so overcome with grief that he mortally wounds himself. Upon learning her lover's fate, Cleopatra commits suicide by asp, holding a poisonous snake to her breast. "All the public wants is to see the asp bite Sarah," a critic for the *Nation* recounted. "The asp is a live serpent, and we have heard much about its education; the papers have been full of it. On the whole, it must be confessed that we have been a little disappointed; the serpent is very small, Sarah merely puts him in a sort of pocket which is inside her gown." And, although the gifted actress "knows how to die," the observer lamented that "we don't know what has become of the serpent." By this point, "it is late, very late; we feel that Sarah requires some rest, as we do ourselves, though she has been lying on luxurious beds of every shape, during five acts. We must leave her," he concludes. "We have heard enough vague, indistinct Arabic melodies, our eyes have been dazzled enough with colors in motion, we are drunk with sensations—and we have not preserved a thought."[64]

In the cultural imaginary of the fin de siècle, the venomous serpent signified the perilously seductive power of the femme fatale. Although less spectacular than audiences might have hoped, Sardou's living reptile distinguished his production, and it became synonymous with Bernhardt's Cleopatra. In her hands, the serpent, as sinewy in form and as crafty in character as the actress herself, elicited parallels between herself and Eve. Like the original temptress, Bernhardt's Cleopatra precipitated man's downfall, making her temptation of Antony a threat not only to Christian manhood but also to Western civilization. Cast in this doubly dangerous role, Bernhardt tantalized audiences with her own "serpentine movement" and "pantomimic undulations," replicating the serpent's somatic sensuality and encouraging audiences to connect Cleopatra's power with Bernhardt's celebrity.[65]

The notorious "S curve" of her thin body, noted for its lack of confining corset, enabled a flexible spine and connoted a malleable morality that came to exemplify the thespian's artistic versatility. The suicide scene was parodied in the artistic caricatures of André Gill and spoofed onstage by the cabaret performer Yvette Guilbert, whose irreverent song, "Le Petit serpent de Sarah," pitied the unfortunate asp who could not find enough flesh on Bernhardt's breast in which to sink his teeth. Detractors who drew facile parallels between the actor's serpentine body and the toxic femme fatale suggested that both were rooted in an especially noxious Jewish femininity.[66] Although he did not take his assessment quite that far, an observer for the *New York Times* commented, "Good folk regarded her art as something forbidden, an alien evil. Young people did not tell their parents when they went to see her. . . . That scene in which the Serpent of Old Nile drew her coils round the throne of Marc Antony, circling ever nearer with the venom of her wiles, was a revelation of things scarcely to be whispered."[67]

No less impressed by the venom of Bernhardt's wiles, some reviewers were certainly more biting in their critiques of Sardou's latest production. After attending the 1892 London performance, *Black and White* contributor Hafiz disparaged the play as exemplary of "Sardou's latest manner." "It is as valueless as *Thermidor*," he complained, referencing the playwright's 1891 four-act drama about the revolt of July 1794. "It is like *Thermidor*, splashy and claptrap."[68] In his lengthy contribution to the *Illustrated Review*, Gilbert Augustin-Thierry bemoaned that, given the modern era's "more complete knowledge of Roman life," in the play one hoped that the "mysteries of Egypt might finally be revealed." But, alas, in Sardou's drama that "has not happened." Sardou missed the opportunity to reveal the secrets of the ancient East and "emasculated" one of the greatest playwrights of the West, devaluing Shakespeare's genius and gutting his text until the story itself was reduced to a mere "pretext for decorations." The accusation that Sardou has in some way "emasculated" Shakespeare with his version of Cleopatra is telling. By keeping Egypt shrouded in mystery, Sardou's Cleopatra retains the mystique of the femme Orientale and continues to threaten Western masculinity. Chastising Sardou for pandering to the masses and for peddling the play for export and profit, Augustin-Thierry dismissed the production as a vacuous, commercial spectacle, a vehicle worthy of a Barnum but perhaps not a Bernhardt.[69] To that point, he asserted that the play's only redeeming quality was the leading lady's skillful performance. "The attraction of such a show was, first and foremost, Sarah Bernhardt," he wrote. "She has shown herself, as usual, a remarkable actress, intelligently composing that role of a forty-year-old lover who still knows how to frighten, retain and lose her lover forever. Cleopatra will be among the good creations of this acclaimed artist."[70] On this account, Hafiz agreed with his French counterpart. If there was one highlight in the production, it was "the acting of Sarah Bernhardt," whose "representation of 'Great Egypt'" marked another "triumph in her long roll of triumphs."[71]

Other critics were even more generous in their praise of Bernhardt's Cleopatra. Writing for *L'Écho de Paris,* Henry Bauer maintained that Bernhardt possessed the "grace and majesty of an ancient goddess statue, this Cleopatra who seemed radiant divinity among men; she restores the great seductress, the adorable enchantress proclaiming the Triumph of women, by turns seductive, pretty, terrible and moving. She made the character as only a supremely intelligent artist, having seen and understood the ancient, can create such a figure."[72] *Le Figaro* commented on Bernhardt's ability to be both vulnerable and irrepressible, noting that she delivered her early lines "like a frightened schoolgirl who dares to formulate a council with authority" but that by the second act she exuded "all that the heart of the woman can express: the anguish of the abandoned lover, the fury of the woman betrayed."[73]

The press not only lauded Bernhardt's talents but also suggested that she was the actress most suited to the role. To the feminist journalist Séverine, Bernhardt "could embody the most diverse possible of heroines," and "in her travels across two worlds, [she] left in her wake the luminous, imperishable trace of French art."[74] Commenting on Bernhardt's well-deserved standing ovation at the end of the third act, a *Figaro* journalist proclaimed, "I have long believed that this rare comedienne is not just a great artist, but the great artist, the only truly worthy of the name of our time, one that is unrivaled in the world."[75] Even as late as 1896, novelists Paul and Victor Margueritte proposed that Bernhardt's success in the role derived from her particular skill as a gifted dissembler: "She has managed to efface herself, to disappear in the reconstruction of great legendary figures. She is impersonal. Or rather she is the personage herself: Lady MacBeth, Cleopatra, Theodora. Incredible mirage!"[76]

Despite her fans' pronouncements, Bernhardt did not actually *become* Cleopatra; she *played* her. In so doing, she provided a "retrospective identification" of the queen, not a revivification of her. Scholars, poets, and playwrights had so often reworked and retold the queen's story that Bernhardt could offer audiences an inexact reverberation of the original. The publicity image for her American tour in 1898 exemplifies the many ways audiences envisioned Bernhardt's Cleopatra (figure 6). A collection of five vignettes, the image shows Bernhardt's Cleopatra twice seated on her throne—in the center looking forward at the viewer and on the left in profile. The right profile

FIG. 6. Publicity image, Bernhardt's tour of America, February 1898.

depicts a seemingly disembodied, sculpted figure looming over a crumpled female body, likely the deceased mortal body of the queen herself. And, at the top, Bernhardt's Cleopatra appears majestic, exercising her authority first (on the left) over her subjects (indicated by the figure kneeling at her feet) and second, emerging through an otherworldly portal. Unlike the previous publicity image (figure 5), that showcased Bernhardt's figure, face, and wardrobe, this one almost obscures the personality of the actress completely, making it appear as though she and the empress have blended into one another. Not only does this publicity image combine the figures of Bernhardt and Cleopatra; it also, as Lucy Hughes-Hallett has explained, demonstrates how Cleopatra provides a "mirror rather than a portrait" to later generations. "Her image," she explains, "has passed through as many changes as it has had spectators, for those who have tried to see her, to reimagine and reproduce her image, have instead seen and displayed themselves in her."[77]

From our perspective, Bernhardt's performance reinforces a linear chronology in which the historic Cleopatra signifies an antecedent (the ancient world) and the historic Bernhardt a descendent (the modern world). Yet the play itself put the ancient and modern in dialogue, inviting the past and present to comingle in suspended historical time. Through the fantasy of exceptional womanhood that framed both Cleopatra and Bernhardt's celebrity, the performance entangled the mythical actress and the mythical empress in perpetuity, perpetuating a series of "imagined repetitions and repetitions of imagined resemblances" in which Scott tells us, "the echo is a fantasy, the fantasy an echo."[78] As the astute *Figaro* reporter noted in 1890, "it is not Sarah Bernhardt who resembles Cleopatra, but on the contrary, Cleopatra who resembles Sarah Bernhardt."[79] This elision, premised on the infinite cycle of resemblances in which the mythic Bernhardt becomes Cleopatra, the mythic Cleopatra becomes Bernhardt, proposes a female-centric model of time that is synchronized rather than sequential. In preserving one illusion and generating another, Bernhardt's performance collapsed the distance not only between two women but also, as Séverine so astutely noted, between two worlds.

REVERBERATIONS

Bernhardt's seemingly preternatural ability to transcend time, place, and self, to appear to her various publics as a larger-than-life cosmic apparition, a shooting star that merged woman with actress, became the trademark of her celebrity. "There is the actress and then there is the woman," historian Léo Claretie averred in 1912. "Sarah is as famous as a woman as she is as an actress. . . . She has given the universe the spectacle of her existence as well as her roles."[80] Remarking on her Comédie-Française season in London, American novelist Henry James proclaimed that Bernhardt was very much a "child of her age—of her moment"; she was a "fantastically impertinent *victrix*" who pursued fame with an "intensity that has rarely been equaled." In their appraisals, Claretie and James articulated what the world was only beginning to ascertain. Bernhardt not only knew "how to profit by the idiosyncrasies of the time," but she also embodied the "the success of celebrity, pure and simple."[81]

Talented and charismatic, Bernhardt garnered fame by perfecting her craft. She earned superstar status, however, by relentlessly cultivating and packaging for mass consumption a fantasy of exceptional womanhood that excited the public. Trading on her indecipherable character, playing person against personality, and capitalizing on her outrageous offstage antics, she converted this fantasy into a profitable, even transcendent, celebrity brand.[82]

Indeed, Bernhardt's impenetrable illegibility was central to the fantasy of exceptional womanhood that underwrote her celebrity. On the one hand, Bernhardt posed a hybrid figure, a cultural amalgamation seemingly capable of reconciling incompatible nineteenth-century bourgeois attitudes governing sex, race, class, and gender with modern perspectives emerging on these issues. On the other hand, an unabashed provocateur, she aggravated the deeply entrenched anxieties of her era by demonstrating how a Jewish woman could take advantage of the commercial marketplace to pursue her personal pleasures, to build her wealth, and to conquer the French public. It was by synthesizing and deconstructing prevailing cultural norms that Bernhardt harnessed her star power. Precisely because she could portray both a seductive, Egyptian Cleopatra *and* a chaste, French Jeanne d'Arc, because she could compellingly embody both Hamlet *and* Ophelia, because she could effortlessly project Theodora's powerful feminism *as well as* enact Roxanne's sweet sentimentality, Bernhardt defied categorization. Through these performances, moreover, she exposed as arbitrary the complicated identity politics of her age.

It was not only in the theater but also in her private life (which, admittedly she turned into its own spectacular stage show) that Bernhardt challenged convention to curate her unique brand of celebrity. Engaged in a ceaseless double game, conflating her personal life with her theatrical roles, Bernhardt ensured her own commercial success and established a template for creating the modern mass media star.[83] Bernhardt, of course, was not the first actress to use the media and the stage to fabricate her star image. However, she manipulated these venues more effectively than her predecessors, and she benefited from an opportune historical moment: the rise of the mass market, the increased circulation of print media, and shifting attitudes regarding woman's social visibility, which together amplified her cultural impact and enabled her to set a standard against which other female celebrities would be measured.[84]

As evidenced in her memoir, from an early age Bernhardt knew how to attract attention. Whether engaging in daredevil escapades, throwing ear-shattering tantrums, or melodramatically melting into a fit of hysterics, she learned well how to make a spectacle of herself. As she matured, she transferred this expertise to her professional life. Onstage she was a gifted chameleon, a talented thespian, and an astonishing chimera. Offstage she was a perplexingly novel female curiosity, an unmatched superhuman force of nature, an egotistical, flamboyant personality, a tireless saleswoman and publicity hound, and, ultimately, the creator and purveyor of her own cultural mythology. Of course, Bernhardt never missed an opportunity to attract public attention or to promote her eccentricity. By narrating her manufactured life story to reporters, she offered the public behind-the-scenes entrée both backstage and into her private life. To this end, Bernhardt not only participated in contrived interviews, but she also used press agents and drama critics to plant her own media stories, directing exactly how she would be seen through the media.[85]

In addition to reportage on her life and art, Bernhardt ensured that her image was plastered all over the media, on the boulevards, and even in the private homes of French citizens. Alongside myriad newsprint-generated texts, Bernhardt's image appeared on thousands of *cartes de visite,* on art nouveau posters promoting productions and endorsing commercial products, and in countless portraits crafted by the period's most respected photographers and esteemed artists.[86] Monopolizing on the publicity value of these images, Bernhardt personally autographed and distributed some of them while others were peddled for sale at theaters and bookstores or reproduced in marketing materials. Photographs enabled Bernhardt not only to document her roles but also to conflate herself with the characters she played. By identifying so closely with the characters she portrayed, she participated in her own depersonation and challenged the spatial and temporal limitations imposed by the real world.

New York photographer Napoleon Sarony's series of photos for her performance in *Cleopatra* illustrate how Bernhardt visually conflated person and persona to manufacture her celebrity. Indeed, when looking at these images, viewers might wonder, Is it Bernhardt or Cleopatra that I see? Is this an ancient fantasy land or a modern theatrical set that has caught my attention? Sarony's trading cards, themselves very much a product of fin-de-siècle technology, became a vehicle for the mass distribution of Bernhardt's image. In these cards, like the one shown here (figure 7), Sarony captures Bernhardt's timeless sensuality by contextualizing her within a lexicon of competing aesthetic signs. Framed by a neo-Egyptian lens, the scene references but does not

FIG. 7. Napoleon Sarony performance trading card, 1891.

accurately portray the historical episode it pretends to represent. The chaise lounge upon which Bernhardt reclines, the animal skin rug upon which her devoted servant rests, and the art deco design of the jewelry worn by both women indicate just some of the ways that Bernhardt's Cleopatra was updated for contemporary audiences. That audiences could recognize these anachronistic elements and still celebrate the historical accuracy of Bernhardt's Cleopatra reveals how the fantasy of exceptional womanhood linking these women reverberated across time. Bernhardt was convincing as Cleopatra because the two shared a cultural illegibility that could be adapted and appropriated in ways that enabled viewers to recognize both figures regardless of how they were staged. In this way, Bernhardt's Cleopatra was not simply a woman of her time but a woman for all time; she was, in Henri Bauer's words, "a magnificent idol erected on ruins."[87]

What is even more interesting is how Bernhardt could so strongly identify with the characters that she played but still maintain a star image that somehow superseded them all. In this regard, Bernhardt was more than an actress. She was a cultural phenomenon, a self-possessed female artist who, through self-promotion and public display, rendered the female body visible in new and unsettling ways. Portraying womanhood itself as a process of becoming in which the individual constantly created and re-created a self, she refused to be typecast as a performer, she challenged the myth of the eternal feminine, and she multiplied the possibilities of female subjectivity. Through her innumerable self-fashioning campaigns, moreover, she modeled forms of womanhood that also threatened contemporary gender norms. Bernhardt's ubiquitous public visibility only amplified her message. If Bernhardt was any measure, then the female celebrity, it would seem, would play a critical role in redefining what it meant to be a modern woman.[88]

For Bernhardt, dramatic art was an essentially feminine art. In the *Art of Theater,* she explained that stage performance contained "the artifices which belong to the province of woman: the desire to please, facility to express emotions and hide defects, and the faculty of assimilation which is the real essence of woman." Acting showcased the female body, its suppleness, lyricism, and grace, and it necessarily engaged women's natural passions. Audiences, she maintained, demanded more from the actress than a pleasing face and a mechanical recitation of prose. Precisely because they were capable "of feeling strong passions, of being shaken by anger," women were more adept at "quitting their own personality to enter that of another being." "In our art," she concluded, "woman may more easily triumph . . . for the desire to . . . paint one's face and hide one's real feelings are qualities and defects that naturally belong more to woman than to man. Again, the grace of her body and the guile of her character render woman a being ten times more perfectible than man."[89]

In this assertion, Bernhardt resurrected tropes of the eternal feminine, exploiting the tension between nature and artifice that underwrote liberal ideologies of womanhood. She did so, however, not to reinscribe the gender binary but to subvert arguments deployed to support it. Woman's natural ability to dissemble, her desire to please, and her emotional instability made her especially suited to theater, and the theater would provide her access to the public stage. Rather than overtly contest the assumptions that women were naturally passive, passionless, and self-sacrificing, Bernhardt exposed the contradictions inherent in them. Onstage, a pleasing woman could be the proverbial "good wife," but she could also be seduced and even become a seductress in her own right. Predisposed toward sentimentality, women convincingly played at emotion; they alone were capable of replicating and affecting the broad spectrum of passions that animated human experience. Finally, because it was in a woman's nature to be selfless, the actress could more easily relinquish her personal ego to the character she played. Not only could she use the art of feminine artifice to credibly portray someone other than herself, but she could also, more importantly, make the illusion itself appear "natural."

Bernhardt reasoned that while an actor could not preserve her own ego if she "intended to make her characters live," she also could not appear natural to audiences if she could not inject the character she played with her own personality.[90] Bernhardt infused her characters with her own personality by contorting her body, modulating her voice, and exaggerating her facial expressions. Although other European and America actors practiced these same techniques, Bernhardt perfected them by making these gestures appear natural. Through her unexpected tactics (turning her back to her audiences) and corporeal hyperextensions (pulling faces, elongating her body), she enchanted and overpowered spectators, producing in them visceral, involuntary responses (chills, gasps, knee jerks). By literally and figuratively hitting a nerve with her audiences, Bernhardt seduced and subdued them, conquering them emotionally to bring them into her own fantasy world.[91] That she did all of this with her racially indecipherable woman's body only added to the overall effect.

Equally important to Bernhardt's seductive persona, and inextricably linked to her shape-shifting femininity, was her ambiguous racial identity. Although she attended convent school and converted to Catholicism, Bernhardt was, throughout her career and well after her life, identified with her Jewish origins. Bernhardt herself added to the debate, claiming to be Catholic one moment and Jewish the next. Regardless of how she self-identified, however, she could never fully transcend the cultural limitations that the public imposed on her Jewish, female body. Whether ridiculed for her sickly, degenerate, tubercular, thinness (anti-Semites considered Jews especially suspectable to this deteriorating disease), or fetishized for her sinewy form and exotic "dark type," Bernhardt represented the "exclusionary feminine," a disruptive, yet enchanting, countertype to the ideal.[92]

The Jewish woman's dual status as the dangerous yet alluring Other was as much a product of the fin de siècle as Bernhardt herself. Christian Europeans had regarded the Jew as Other for centuries. But by the nineteenth century, they conceived of Jewishness not only as a religious affiliation but also, and primarily, as a racial identity. In France, which had a stable but relatively small Jewish population, the influx of Jews into Paris following the Franco-Prussian War alongside a century of effective acculturation and assimilation—two developments that rendered Jews simultaneously more and less visible—excited anti-Semitic sentiment by playing on extant social anxieties.[93] For those malcontents desperate for scapegoats, Jews were blamed for everything from labor unrest and military defeat to depopulation and the dilution of the French blood.

Intent on eroding similarities between themselves and assimilated Jews, anti-Semites constructed racial stereotypes that positioned Jews firmly as racial hybrids. Jews, they asserted, carried markers of multiple races in their bodies, mannerisms, behaviors, and language. Belonging to no race in particular, they were loyal exclusively to themselves. Behind what could only be the mask of assimilation Jews undermined the cultures they infiltrated, weakening that race in the process. Their chameleon-like ability to appear to belong everywhere and to everyone, a trait often associated with Bernhardt regardless of the political perspective of the commentator, moreover, marked Jews as irrefutably and eternally Other, incapable of authentically integrating into European society.[94] Associated with both the Jew and the African, Bernhardt's Cleopatra was thus doubly Othered. Her racial ambiguity reinforced her cultural hybridity, and both of these features, according to anti-Semites and xenophobes, disqualified her from Frenchness.

In many ways, Bernhardt's Cleopatra reflected contemporary inclinations to reify the Other through racialized female stereotypes. As we have seen, she was particularly associated with the *belle juive*. Drawn from a common fund of Orientalist tropes that conflated Semitic qualities with blackness, this hypersexualized archetype stoked white male sexual desire at the same time that it, when aligned with the figure of the femme fatale, as in the case of Bernhardt's Cleopatra, signaled dangerous female sexuality.[95] In many ways, the *belle juive* acted as a cultural mediator between Europeans and Others. As an object of European male lust, she represented his desire to conquer non-European territories. Her submission (voluntary or not) to his sexual advances thus symbolized man's mastery over woman as well as the Westerner's superiority over his perceived racial and cultural inferiors. Yet because the European male himself submits to the *belle juive*'s irresistible charms, it is he, rather than the object of his lust, who contaminates European blood with the stain of the Other.[96] Because her threat was so insidious as to become untraceable in the gene pool, Bernhardt in the figures of both the *belle juive* and as Cleopatra played on the generalized fear of emasculation that plagued bourgeois France in the Third Republic. Moreover, by holding up a mirror to the West, calling out its own hypocrisy and challenging its claim to modernity and its pretense of an evolved civilization, Bernhardt's Cleopatra also forced theatergoers to see the ways in which the foreign Other was so very much *just like us.*

The *belle juive*'s racialized female body also offered an enticing yet troubling countertype to bourgeois European femininity. Indelibly marked by both their race and their gender, these women could remain relegated to the social periphery, segregated from mainstream French society, and easily associated with their non-European counterparts. As eroticized objects of European male desire, however, performers like Bernhardt also embodied for detractors, the perils and for proponents, the possibilities, of assimilation. A seductive, racially ambiguous Afro-Mediterranean queen who, through her political acumen and sexual allure, assimilates to Roman culture while preserving her own, Bernhardt's Cleopatra drew on contemporary stereotypes of the *belle juive* to make her character legible to French audiences. Indeed, Bernhardt's Cleopatra intentionally evoked the stereotype of the *belle juive* to challenge arbitrary notions of racial difference.[97] Whether accentuating her thinness, engaging in shameless self-promotion, or flaunting her desire for publicity, she exaggerated racial stereotypes and caricatured tropes of womanliness to construct a persona that defied classification.[98] As a cultural broker, Bernhardt in the figure of the *belle juive* playing Cleopatra not only mediated between fact and fantasy, but she also exposed the Other's centrality to constructions of the French national self.[99]

Bernhardt's manipulation of stereotype, her ability to present artifice as nature and vice versa, and her skill at seducing her audience won her global adoration. At the same time, however, these qualities marked her as public enemy number one for the anti-Semitic and nationalist Right. Engaging a particular set of racist and misogynist fantasies, these malcontents linked Bernhardt to a contrived version of Jewish womanhood that not only indemnified her racial otherness but also marked her as a sexual deviant, an unredeemable threat to the status quo.[100] Although often little invested in the republic itself, these groups demonized Bernhardt, blaming her for its internal demise. They also evoked her as a cautionary tale: if French men and women could be so enchanted with the actress as to be overcome with chills, how would they fare in the face of real enemies, foreign invaders whose aims stretched beyond the merely cultural and commercial? In this context, Bernhardt's body performed double duty: it signified sexual and racial difference even as it made claims of sameness; it demarcated boundaries between us and Other at the same time that it exposed the permeability of such artificially constructed barriers; and it revealed how a person who could appear *just like us* was also *not quite* like us.[101]

On March 28, 1923, the front page of the London *Times* announced, "There is but one sentence today on the lips of Paris—Bernhardt is dead."[102] For several days beforehand, reverent crowds, concerned with the star's health, congregated outside her home on the Boulevard Péreire in Paris's Seventeenth Arrondissement. News of Bernhardt's passing finally arrived at eight o'clock on the evening of March 26. For the next three days, legions of fans, friends, and curious onlookers filed past her coffin. Thousands of mourners participated in the funeral procession from the actress's home to the Church of Saint François de Sales. Many of them then accompanied Bernhardt to her final resting place in Père-Lachaise Cemetery. Although she was not given a state funeral, she was displayed in her coffin with her Legion of Honor medal across her breast.[103] If, as *Le Figaro* had once observed, tourists came to Paris to see only the Eiffel Tower and Sarah Bernhardt, in this final performance Bernhardt left the city, its residents, and its sightseers with one befittingly spectacular farewell.[104]

The press memorialized her passing by speculating on her inevitable afterlife. *New York Telegram* correspondent Fanny Fair called Bernhardt a "strange being [whose living body] had ceased to be governed by the hampering laws of the flesh." For someone who appeared in life as "something supernatural," death alone, Fair waxed, could not provoke a final curtain call.[105] "For beings like Sarah," Maurice Rostand declared in his 1950 memoir of her life, "death is not only an end, it's a beginning as well. The life may be interrupted, but the legend goes on. Sarah has not been forgotten, she has not been replaced. . . .

Her mysterious throne remains empty."[106] In life and death Bernhardt was, in the words one biographer, "a famous monument who people came to see." She was a relic of another era, a national treasure, a cultural landmark, and a great woman of France.[107]

In his opening tribute to Bernhardt for a special issue of *Le Théâtre et Comœdia Illustré* devoted to her in June 1926, Robert de Flers of the Académie Française professed that even before her death, "Sarah Bernhardt already belonged to legend." For Flers, Bernhardt was a mystery, an actress impossible to see "apart from the characters she impersonated," who "sacrificed her individuality . . . so as to infuse them [her characters] with fuller life." The great miracle of Bernhardt's sacrifice, he went on to explain, was that through these continuous metamorphoses she "every time arose more completely, more wonderfully herself." Characterizing Bernhardt's fame as "unchanging and unique," Flers acknowledged that her "popularity extends all over the world, and both our literary inheritance and our country itself have benefited by it." In light of her magnificent contributions, he was incensed that the French "Government thought it unadvisable to have national obsequies for the great tragic actress." Where the national government failed, however, Paris persevered. "It is only fair that a supreme tribute should be paid to the memory of one who," according to Jules Lemaître, "will always remain 'one of the most gracious apparitions that ever flitted over the changing face of our material world, to be a solace onto men.'"[108]

As chroniclers wrote Bernhardt into legend, perpetuating a mythography that she herself created, they ensured that she live forever among the immortals who were gone but not forgotten. Although actors, artists, and other accomplished persons were celebrated after death, the level of devotion shown to Bernhardt was unprecedented. Bernhardt has lived on in the films, art, literature, and merchandise produced during her lifetime as well as in the vast array of articles, biographies, biopics, websites, fan pages, exhibitions, conference papers, and academic works devoted to her since. Her image would appear on a commemorative postage stamp, her name on a Paris street sign, her star on Hollywood's fabled Walk of Fame, and her grave would become a pilgrimage site. She achieved this status because she was a talented performer but also because she was a skilled self-promoter, a storyteller who narrated her achievements through a fantasy of exceptional womanhood that has resonated across time. This fantasy, rooted in the star's cultural illegibility, her racial and sexual ambiguity, and her gender fluidity enabled Bernhardt to be all things to all people. Love her or hate her, everyone knew her, and everyone held an opinion about her. As a fantasy figure, moreover, Bernhardt stoked the imagination, offering audiences a model of womanhood that was both timely and timeless.

Spinning her own fantasy of exceptional womanhood, Bernhardt not only reverberated as Cleopatra's echo, but she also previewed and provided a prototype for the modern female celebrity. She was certainly not the first female actress to gain notoriety; however, she helped turn a once precarious form of woman's work into a glamorous female profession. Historically poorly compensated for their labor, actresses paid for their own costumes, worked long hours, and clandestinely supplemented their meager wages with sex work to survive. Whereas a few select actresses managed to negotiate additional fees for rehearsals or extra performances, most of them could not. In addition to these economic hardships, they were upheld as social pariahs, criticized for their sexual libertinism, blamed for the moral decay of the nation.[109] Bernhardt changed all of this. She set her own wage, ran her own theater, turned to sex for publicity rather than payment, promoted acting as a feminine art, and she became a beloved symbol of France.

Bernhardt accomplished these feats by taking advantage of changes underway within the profession as well as within French society. By the middle of the nineteenth century, troupes were supplanted by a star system that privileged individual performers. Women entered the theater not only on its stage but also in its balconies, boxes, and aisles. As women equaled and sometimes outnumbered men in attendance, the actress modeled fashionable beauty even as she continued to stoke male sexual desire. Moreover, by revealing the secrets of her private life in the press, she created common ground between herself and her female audience, expanding the boundaries of social acceptability and redefining the limits of moral probity. Actresses remained public women in the literal sense; however, by presenting private life as performance in the commercial media, Bernhardt infiltrated the domestic sphere and metaphorically invited otherwise private women onto the public stage.[110]

Thus, Bernhardt's star power resided in her uncanny ability to present herself simultaneously as an untouchable force of nature as well as an accessible, intimate stranger. By harnessing the transformative power of the media, she inundated the public with her image, her life stories, and her opinions, and she fed its desire to access the private lives of popular figures. Bernhardt knew that celebrity did not exist without an audience; therefore, she transformed her entire life into spectacle. To this end, she masked her person with her persona, and she blurred lines between fact and fiction, sameness and difference. The power of Bernhardt's celebrity ultimately resided in the star's cultural illegibility, in her ability to embody the Other and somehow appear *just like us.*

The fantasy of exceptional womanhood that circumscribed Bernhardt's celebrity, moreover, echoed the past and foretold the future. Embodying both the artistry of the stage and its increasing commercialization, blending formal technique with experimental forms, transforming her private life into one of many public stages on which to showcase her extravagant personality, Bernhardt marked her moment at the same time that she anticipated the next.[111] Ultimately, Bernhardt's blending of styles and forms, her collapsing of boundaries between public and private, and her capacity to evoke debate regarding the true nature of womanhood and of Frenchness, would reverberate in the mimetic pantomimes and frenetic dancing as well as in the salacious scandals and the stunning successes of two twentieth-century celebrities who were themselves also linked to Cleopatra: Colette and Josephine Baker.

3

Colette

It is almost impossible to explain, to respectable readers, how . . .
the exhibition of the Marquise de Belbeuf, in drag, onstage alongside
Mme. Colette Willy . . . caused such a revolting scandal. . . . M. Willy,
the husband, was seated upfront in the proscenium, an amused and
complacent spectator of a pantomime, which could have passed for a
reproduction of too real scenes from the intimate life of these three
characters, creating a spectacle of such audacious shamelessness
that the whole audience rose up against them.

—FÉLICIEN PASCAL, *L'Éclair de Montpellier,* January 7, 1907

In his "Chronique parisienne" column for *L'Éclair,* a regional daily broadly
distributed throughout southern France that was known for its pro-Catholic
perspective and royalist sympathies, Félicien Pascal railed against the dissolute depravity of the contemporary Parisian theater. The centerpiece of his
broader critique, Pascal's scathing review of the one-act pantomime *Rêve
d'Égypte,* identified the many ways that the theater was eroding French morals.
Starring the Marquise de Belbeuf (Missy) and Colette Willy, the performance
not only provoked a public scandal but also actually incited physical violence
when it opened at the Moulin Rouge on January 3, 1907. In his indignation,
Pascal only insinuated the cause for the eruption, the notorious kiss that
transpired between the two women onstage. Focusing his attention on the
spectators' reactions to it, Pascal was careful not to offend the sensibilities of
his "respectable readers," even as he elucidated his concerns about the class
and gender inversions unfolding before him. To this end, he chastised the aris-

tocratic Missy for dressing and acting as a man, calling her a "great lady gone bad." He then rebuked the Willys, not only for the wife's onstage promiscuity but also for the husband's offstage voyeurism—for their "too real," too public, too erotic, too commercial, "English no doubt," subversion of middle-class conventions. That the audience, mortified by such "audacious shamelessness . . . rose up against" both the perverse performers and their nefarious impresario seemed to reassure the distressed journalist (and perhaps his readers) that "there is still some filth that the public does not want to put up with and to which it knows how to do justice."[1]

Whereas *Rêve d'Égypte* marked the marquise's second public theatrical performance, it was but one of many in her costar's expanding professional repertoire. After launching her stage career a year earlier, Colette performed in several pantomimes and had even executed her first speaking role in a racy one-act production written by her husband, Willy.[2] By the time that *Rêve d'Égypte* opened, Colette had engaged in provocative, gender-bending recitals for both public and private audiences, and, although new to the theatrical stage, the marquise's personal performances of impropriety on the public stage were legendary. Why, then, should French audiences find this production particularly scandalous? What was it about the fifteen-minute silent performance that so concerned, so inflamed, theatergoers that they were moved to physical violence? And why is it significant that the spectre of Cleopatra, implied in the pantomime's title, *Dream of Egypt,* should find her echo in this way, at this moment, in the crowded theater of the Moulin Rouge?

By the time the performance opened, Colette, Willy, and the marquise were well acquainted with public scandal. Common fixtures of bohemian Paris at the turn of the century, Willy, an established publisher and familiar man about town, and his provincial young bride were skyrocketed to stardom with the publication of the *Claudines,* a series of wildly popular novels that introduced the world to both the modern teenager and to the writer who would become, simply, Colette. As Claudine became a household name, however, Colette and Willy's household fell apart. Willy took up residence with his mistress, Meg (another stage performer, whom he would later marry), and Colette moved in with the divorcée transvestite Missy, the Marquise de Belbeuf. Ten years Colette's senior and a titled aristocrat (Napoleon III was her illegitimate half brother), Missy openly flouted social convention, dressing in the finest men's suits from England, pursuing women for sexual relationships, and engaging in the recreational drug culture of the age. In light of these antics, her decision to perform onstage alongside her real-life female paramour, a woman herself notorious for challenging norms of gender and class, should not have raised many eyebrows. And yet, it did.

To understand why a one-act pantomime performed in one of the city's most hedonistic entertainment venues would cause such an outrage, we need first to understand how Colette animated her own fantasy of exceptional womanhood. Like Bernhardt before her, Colette capitalized on opportunities opened up to women onstage and in the media at the fin de siècle. Through her skillful role-playing, both onstage and off—appearing publicly in drag, personifying characters from her own stories, posing as a devoted wife or mistress, acting the part of the intellectual one moment, the ingenue the next—she incessantly invited misidentifications. She was an esteemed author, a popular stage performer, an intrepid journalist, an insightful arts critic, a part-time commercial jingle writer, an ad hoc advice columnist, and a risk-taking entrepreneur. She was also an antifeminist bourgeois wife turned divorcée turned bourgeois wife, a reluctant mother to a wayward daughter and several corruptible stepchildren, a cosmopolitan Parisian who yearned for the countryside, an observer of human nature who favored animals to people, and an international celebrity who only ever felt at home in France.

Colette played all of these roles concurrently and consecutively, and she did so to author her own cultural illegibility. Unlike the other women in this book who were differentiated from the French status quo because of their race, religion, or nationality, Colette's identity as a middle-class provincial from the Yonne secured her place within it. It would be from this privileged position that Colette would invent and enact her fantasy of exceptional womanhood. A daughter of the republican bourgeoisie who held many of the opinions and values of that milieu, Colette, as her semi-autobiographical writings make clear, was never the Other. In fact, because her contemporaries regarded her as one of them, she was free, as we will see, to play up her "Black" roots, to express or to deny her sexual desire for other women, and to adopt or abandon the trappings of femininity as it suited her. It was thus not as the Other but through her unremitting masquerade of it that Colette created her celebrity persona. Through an intricate game of hide-and-seek, Colette played with her public, turning the fact of her identity into a question. In the process, she displayed the myriad ways that race, sexuality, and femininity could be constructed, performed, and denaturalized.

Drawing on her fictional autobiographies, media coverage of her performance in *Rêve d'Égypte,* and analysis of the ways in which she complicated convention to reveal sameness and difference as two sides of the same coin, this chapter examines how, in both her life and her work, Colette produced a fantasy of exceptional womanhood that revealed cultural illegibility itself as a fabrication. Colette was first and foremost a writer, a storyteller. In light of this fact, the chapter opens by examining the spellbinding autobiographical fictions through which she narrated the self. Beginning here undoubtedly moves us beyond that prewar moment when she more explicitly echoed Cleopatra on the stage of the Moulin Rouge. However, the implications of that performance can be more easily understood when considered within the broader context of both Colette's biography and her collective creative work. In the *Rêve d'Égypte* episode, Colette insighted scandal by *posing* as the Other, a strategy she would deploy and perfect in her autofiction. Onstage she navigated the prickly politics of social convention, disarming the status quo by enacting the sexually deviant, racially indeterminate, and literally not quite human Other. In this way, her playacting exposed the arbitrariness of culturally constructed categories anchored in difference. Read within the context of the numerous fictionalized "true stories" through which Colette narrated her life, moreover, the performance indelibly collapsed distinctions between reality and fantasy. In her shameless audacity to claim the Other as the self, an uncannily conventional Colette challenged social mores even as she appeared to uphold them. Circumscribed by a fantasy of exceptional womanhood in which one's hypervisibility was shrouded in a manufactured cultural illegibility, Colette flipped the script of female celebrity, creating distance from a public who could so easily see her as *just like us.*

INVENTING COLETTE

As in the case of Bernhardt, Colette has fascinated journalists, biographers, and scholars. Biographies published during her lifetime were generally authored either by people who knew her or by those eager to venerate her. To this end, Willy's thinly disguised revenge novels, *Sidonie: or The Perverted Peas-*

ant and *Les Imprudences de Peggy,* which brutally caricatured Colette, skewered her work, and advanced wild accusations intended to damage her in the couple's divorce proceedings, contrasted sharply with the works of literary historian Jean Larnac and Colette's protégé Claude Chauvière, who upheld her as a literary genius and generous mentor.[3] Despite their agendas, however, biographers had their work cut out for them when they attempted to chronicle Colette's life. Whereas Bernhardt contributed to press stories and even penned a few creative works as well as an acting manual and a memoir of her own, Colette produced hundreds of texts—advice columns, news reportage, music criticism, advertisements, novels, novellas, memoirs, essays, and published letters—all of which revealed and concealed facets of her identity. The task of recounting Colette's life is all the more daunting because many of her novels pose as autobiographies and many of her autobiographical writings masquerade as fiction. Conflating real-life personages with invented characters, her texts coquettishly obfuscate as much as they reveal the woman behind them.

Nevertheless, biographers have agreed upon certain facts regarding Colette's life. The youngest of four children, (two brothers, Achille and Léo, and a half sister, Juliette) Sidonie-Gabrielle Colette was born in the village of Saint-Sauveur-en-Puisaye, in the Yonne department in Bourgogne-Franche-Comté in north-central France, on January 28, 1873. She was named after her mother, Adèle Eugénie Sidonie ("Sido") Colette, a forward-thinking atheist who carried on an affair with Colette's father while still married to her abusive, alcoholic first husband. Gabrielle, or Gabri, as she was called in her childhood, also bore the surname of her father, Sido's second husband, Jules Colette. A former captain in the Zouaves, Jules was a dislocated southerner who precariously supported his family as a tax collector and amateur statesman. Gabri enjoyed criticizing literature or attending local debates with her father, who referred to her frequently as his "Bel-Gazou," a Provençale phrase meaning "lovely babble."[4] A staunch republican who dabbled in village governance, the "Captain," as Colette called him, delivered public lectures on a variety of educational topics and spent his leisure hours contemplating poetry and science. Upon his death, his family found dozens of empty notebooks disguised as his life work. Nothing more than blank pages collected in extravagantly bound volumes, these journals revealed both the intellectual impotence and the unrealized ambitions of a father who would, according to Colette, inspire his daughter to write.

At the age of sixteen, Gabrielle met Willy Gauthier-Villars, a notable Parisian writer, reviewer, and publisher fourteen years her senior. Born into an ultra-Catholic haute bourgeois family, Willy's pro-military right-wing nationalist leanings, his fear of "the people," and his abhorrence of foreigners and Jews did not seem to gel with the Colettes' agnostic republicanism. Although Willy earned a law degree, he never practiced the profession, preferring instead to make his name in the media.[5] Relying on a stable of lesser-known and up-and-coming ghostwriters to co-author his publications, Willy turned his name into a literary brand. Whether prosecuted for literary pornography in public show trials or caricatured in the press for provoking scandal, Willy reveled in the fin-de-siècle spotlight. Like his notorious contemporaries Oscar Wilde and P. T. Barnum, he believed that *all* publicity was good publicity.

On May 15, 1893, Sidonie-Gabrielle Colette married this larger-than-life impresario, hitching her metaphorical wagon and her very real future to a philandering spendthrift, a literary charlatan whose mediocre talent was overshadowed by his oversized ego. As Colette settled into married life, like many other middle-class wives, she maintained the household ledger, supervised a maid and a cook, responded to Willy's correspondence, and endured a life of relative isolation within the capital city. Colette was rescued from this ennui by the couple's need for money, which led to their professional collaboration. Recognizing his spouse's raw talent, Willy employed Colette to author six articles of music criticism for Maurice Barrès's review *La Cocarde*. Shortly thereafter, the pair serialized what would become Colette's first bestselling novel, *Claudine à l'école*. Followed by three sequels, featured in countless stage productions, and supplemented with tie-in commodities, publicity photos, postcards, and eventually films, *Claudine* would launch the duo to superstardom.[6]

Between 1901 and 1906, Colette and Willy coauthored a book a year. They earned enough money to pay off some debts and even to purchase a ramshackle country house in Besançon. Tucked away in her eighteenth-century hunting lodge, Colette practiced gymnastics daily and cultivated a garden of her own, finding tranquility by burying her writer's hands in the upturned soil of her *patrie*. Amid all of this, she tolerated her husband's publicity stunts as well as his infidelity. Impersonating the good bourgeois wife, Colette received only heartache and a sexually transmitted disease in return. To add insult to injury, Willy eventually sold the copyrights to the *Claudines,* keeping all the royalties for himself, robbing Colette of both her financial share and her literary patrimony. The couple separated in 1905 and formally divorced in 1910.

At this juncture, the thirty-something Colette entered vagabondage. She launched a stage career, initiated a same-sex love affair with the Marquise de Belbeuf, worked as a suburban real estate broker, and authored three important works of fiction: *La Retraite sentimentale* (1907) *Les Vrille de la vigne* (1908); and *La Vagabonde* (1910). In 1910, she signed on to write a semi-monthly literary column for *Le Matin,* the French daily with the second-largest circulation in Europe. At *Le Matin,* she tackled controversial topics such as domestic violence and the plight of the unemployed, and she became one of the first women to report from the front during the Great War. She also met the man who would become her second husband, Henry Bertrand, baron de Jouvenel des Ursins.

Three years her junior, "Sidi," as she called Jouvenel, was a handsome, established *Le Matin* journalist with lofty political ambitions. Unlike the conservative Gauthier-Villars, Jouvenel was an avid Dreyfusard, an outspoken republican whose leftist politics diverged dramatically from the reactionary anti-Semitism espoused by his parents' generation. Their union was passionate but tumultuous, and Colette found herself again confronted with a lover's betrayal. Tethered to him financially and reeling from the recent death of her beloved mother, she conceived her only biological child with Jouvenel in the fall of 1912. On December 19, the pair married in a civil ceremony. On July 3, 1913, after "thirty hours with no relief, chloroform and forceps," they welcomed a daughter, "a little Rat," Colette Renée de Jouvenel, whom she nicknamed "Bel-Gazou."[7]

The Great War disrupted both her marriage (Jouvenel joined the infantry as a sergeant and was sent to the front) and her daily life. At first, the new mother remained in Paris, dividing tasks among friends and temporarily volunteering as a night nurse at the Lycée Janson-de-Sailly. After acquiring falsified papers, she spent the remainder of 1914 and half of 1915 in Verdun, tending her husband, acclimating herself to daily bombing raids, and taking nightly hygienic walks into the damaged villages of eastern France. In the summer of 1915, she traveled to Rome as a war correspondent for *Le Matin.* After the armistice, Jouvenel returned to his job at the paper, and Colette joined his staff full-time as literary editor. Although reunited in the newsroom, the couple's marriage was unraveling. Jouvenel continued his affairs, and Colette initiated her own with his sixteen-year-old son, Bertrand. Amid this personal turmoil,

Colette retreated into her work. Indeed, the postwar period proved one of the author's most productive, and it brought her national recognition on September 25, 1920, when the republic recognized her with its highest accolade, the Legion of Honor.[8]

Officially divorced from Jouvenel in 1924, she sold her beloved home at Rozven and purchased a farmhouse near Saint-Tropez. She bought an expensive bulldog named Souci, underwent a rudimentary face-lift, submitted to corrective dental work, and created what would become her signature look by perming and coloring mauve her now short hair. She also published some of her most poignant and critically acclaimed works: *La Fin de Chéri* (1926), *La Naissance du jour* (1928), and *Sido* (1929). She contributed to the celebrity magazines *Gil Blas* and *Fantasio* while providing two weekly columns on a range of topics from fashion and food to gardening and motherhood to the dailies *Le Journal* and *Paris Soir*.[9] In 1926 alone, she played Renée Néré (the heroine of *La Vagabonde*) in Brussels, toured sixteen casinos with *Chéri*, lectured on her musical hall experiences in at least six different cities, and even found time to become the personal guest of the pasha of Marrakesh while traveling in Morocco.[10]

Amid all of this, the fifty-two-year-old Colette found love again with a fashionable, well-spoken pearl salesman seventeen years her junior. Maurice Goudeket, Colette's latest and last paramour, became her third husband in 1935. Unlike Willy and Jouvenel, whose lineage linked them closely to their *patrie*, Goudeket was born to a French mother and Dutch father. As a Jew of mixed nationality, moreover, he only earned French citizenship through his army service during the Great War. Colette, who had more than once been accused of holding anti-Semitic opinions—she had contributed to the rabidly nationalist Maurice Barrès review *La Cocarde*, she remained publicly neutral regarding Dreyfus, and her good friend Renée Hammond called her a "born anti-Semite" in her 1945 journal—seemingly overlooked this aspect of her partner's pedigree.[11] Goudeket, for his part, devoted himself entirely to Colette. When Colette began regular blood transfusions to improve her vision and vitality; when she decided, despite suffering from a severely arthritic hip, to launch her own beauty business as the world devolved into global economic depression; and when she sacrificed her reputation to hawk Lucky Strike cigarettes, Ford motor cars, or Perrier water, Goudeket stood by her side.[12] He was there as she authored three of her most introspective works, *Le Pur et l'impur*

(1932), *La Chatte* (1933) and *Duo* (1934), and he was there as she peddled life-style advice in *Femina, Vogue, Votre Beauté,* and *Marie-Claire.*[13] He was there in March 1935 when she was elected to the Belgian Royal Academy and when she was voted the most popular French writer of the period. He was there in February 1939 when her favorite cat succumbed to cancer and when she had to have to have Souci euthanized. And he was there throughout the 1930s, as she published her fiction in the well-paying pro-Nazi literary weekly *Gringoire.*

When France fell to invading German forces in the spring of 1940, Colette and Goudeket hunkered down in Paris. Colette's writing during the Occupation, as it had during the Great War, skirted all talk of controversial contemporary issues. In her private letters as well as in her public interviews, Colette rarely, if ever, mentioned national politics and seldom referenced the deprivations engendered by wartime conditions. Biographers have speculated that because of her husband's ambiguous status as well as her persistent arthritis, which limited her personal mobility, she elected to lay low during the Occupation. Despite her regular contributions to the pro-Vichy and pro-Nazi press, her good relationships with Occupation editors, and her belief that Maurice was a "Jew who doesn't know he's one," Colette could not "lay low" enough to prevent Goudeket's six-week interment in a Compiègne camp.[14] Although conditions there were less harsh than in other detention centers, the ordeal, and Colette's crafty negotiations to ensure her husband's well-being, exposed a vulnerability that she had never before experienced. Linked to her Jewish husband, perhaps for the first time in her life, Colette found her Frenchness called into question.

Neither the Occupation of her country nor the crumbling of the republic upon which it had been built prevented Colette from writing. In addition to revising *Le Pur et l'impur* and *Belle saisons,* she produced five new books during the war years, *Julie de Carneilhan* (1941), *Le Képi* (1943), *Gigi* (1944), *Paris de ma fenêtre* (1944), and *l'Étoile Vesper* (1947), and she began work on *Le Fanal bleu,* which appeared in print in 1949. Published under the Occupation government, these books carried the Nazi stamp, were vetted by Third Reich censors, and have led some to view Colette as, at best, a Nazi sympathizer—at worst, a collaborator. The charge, whether accurate or not, did not seem without merit. Colette serialized her novel *Julie de Carneilhan* (1941) in *Gringoire* before permitting Fayard to publish it in book form, complete with advertisements for works authored by Hitler. She also wrote articles for Charles Maurras's extreme right-wing *Candide,* authored a dictée for French schoolchildren on the theme of solidarity in the Vichyite *Le Semaine,* sold an article to *Combats,* the journal of the Vichy militia, and serialized her novel *Gigi* (1944) in the pro-Vichy tract *Present.*[15]

Perhaps it was self-preservation, as much as any sense of loyalty to Vichy or to the Nazis, that enabled her to justify her actions during the war. Colette had always, after all, presented herself as apolitical. She was simply, in her public portrayal of herself, a provincial French woman. As with so many of her countrymen and women, Colette's cooperation with the Occupation government was overlooked once the war ended in 1945. As France began the complicated work of national recovery and as a new republic, its politicians, its scholars, its historians, and its storytellers began weaving together a narrative tapestry of universal resistance that could cover over four years of collective guilt and cloak personal shame—Colette became the second woman elected to the country's most prestigious literary society, the Académie Goncourt. She became its president in 1949, and when she passed away on August 7, 1954, she received the first state funeral the republic ever gave a woman. Her coffin was patriotically draped in the tricolor. More than six thousand Parisians and tourists, most of them female, flooded the streets to mourn France's greatest woman's writer.

In their efforts to cobble her life story together, biographers have relied on both the archival record and on Colette's own capricious autobiographical narrations. Yet, as literary scholar Jerry Flieger explains, Colette's lyrical impressionist memoirs, (*Le Fanal bleu, L'Étoile vesper,* and *Le Voyage égoïste*), and popular autobiographical fictions (*La Vagabonde, Chéri,* and the *Claudines*) parade as confessional texts that presume intimacy without actually divulging biographical information.[16] Colette seemingly reconciles this dilemma in her fictional autobiographies, *La Maison de Claudine* (1922), *Sido* (1929), and *La Naissance du jour* (1928), by identifying the author *as* narrator. Yet these texts, too, are part of the author's pose. "Is anyone imagining as he reads me," she quips in *La Naissance du jour* "that I am portraying myself? Have patience: this is merely my model."[17]

Although Colette first considered writing her memoirs in 1913, before she was yet forty years old, she postponed the endeavor, unconvinced that she had fully mined reality for her fiction. After the Great War, the birth of her daughter, and the deaths of both of her parents, Colette serialized thirty self-reflective vignettes and published them in various Parisian dailies. In 1922, these reflections were collected under the title *La Maison de Claudine,* a transparent reference to the fictive prewar protagonist who first brought Colette fame.[18] In *Sido,* the companion piece to *La Maison de Claudine,* Colette replaces her fictional avatar with "the personage who, little by little, has dominated all the rest of my work."[19] Yet the textual Sido, much like Claudine in the previous text, is not a real person; she is a Colette creation. As her mirrors as well as her masks, Claudine and Sido enable and enhance the author's self-performance. Rather than provide a retrospective on her lived experiences, these works provide the material through which Colette articulates the self and illustrate how deeply that self is implicated in the French *patrie.* As "fictional" autobiographies, however, they also permit the writer the space to dramatize and to Other that self, to create "Colette," the celebrity.

In *La Maison de Claudine* and its companion *Sido,* Colette portrays her provincial young ladyhood as part pastoral idyll, part fairy-tale. "Both house and garden are living still, I know," she asserts on the first page of *La Maison de Claudine,* "but what of that, if the magic has deserted them? If the secret is lost that opened to me a whole world . . . a world of which I have ceased to be worthy?" The bucolic setting of the Yonne provides a backdrop for the mischievous play of the sometimes restless, often too curious and too quiet "savages," who belong to Sido's house. Focusing on the flora and fauna that surrounded an otherwise "somber" dwelling, delighting in the birthing of kittens, the flutter of butterflies, and the security of dogs who always followed one home, Colette romanticizes her days as an "urchin-like tomboy" who, alongside the other isolated children of the countryside, daydreamed about worlds far away from their mother's house.[20] Through these ideations, Colette connects herself to her countrymen, the other boys and girls of her village. At the same time, comparing herself to nature's other creatures, and locating the stories themselves within her "mother's house," perhaps itself a thinly disguised metaphor for the *patrie,* she roots herself firmly in the soil of France.

Importantly, Colette inherits her magical *amour de la patrie* from her mother. A potent maternal figure whose steady hand and pragmatism temper the child, Sido also appears in the text as a transcendental mirage, an enchanting earth mother, whose "placid, radiant garden-face" lit up the countryside. Colette remembers how this mythical mother-goddess tamed the wild countryside but also enjoyed biannual excursions to the capital city. She returned home from these adventures loaded down with "chocolate bars, exotic foods, remnants of material, but above all with violet essences and theater programs." Despite her taste for the capital city's luxuries, however, Colette's Sido never mistakes Paris for France. Sido confides that it "makes me laugh to see how proud of living in Paris all Parisians are; the real ones seem to think the mere fact ennobles them and the others imagine they've gone up in the world." She later cautions her adult daughter, "As for you, you give yourself airs just because you have married a Parisian. . . . Your true-born Parisians haven't so much character in their faces. You might say that Paris de-faces them!"[21] On her own first trip to Paris, Colette was mesmerized by the city's theaters, museums, and shopping venues. Yet, she, too, returned home with "memories of finery and greediness, mixed with hopes, regrets, and feelings of scorn, as innocent and awkward as myself, the surprise and the melancholy aversion aroused in me by what I called houses without animals."[22] Like her mother, it would seem, Colette acknowledged that one might reside in Paris, but one did not *live* there. Paris was the nerve center of France, the seat of government, and the nation's economic engine, but it was devoid of the magic found in the provinces. By portraying Paris as artificial, as antithetical to the countryside, she called into question the city's claim on Frenchness. If the real France was to be found outside of the capital city, then Colette, through her provincial young ladyhood, had a genuine claim on the *patrie.*

When Colette compiled the stories for *La Maison de Claudine,* just after the Great War, she had resided in both Paris and the countryside, she was still married to Jouvenel, and she was playing mother to three children—stepchildren Bertrand, eighteen, and Renaud, fifteen; and her daughter, Bel-Gazou, aged eight. By the time that *Sido* appeared in print, she had divorced Jouvenel, ended her affair with his son, and taken up with the man who would become her third husband. Through all of this, and even as she gestures to the almost sacred relationship that she enjoyed with her own mother, Colette struggled to connect with her estranged daughter. Like Sido, the textual Bel-Gazou was a Colette creation, an echo of the self not unlike the fictional characters who animated her prose. "I know that to her faithful nurse, Bel-Gazou is alternately the center of the universe, a consummate masterpiece, a possessed monster from whom the devil must hourly be exorcised, a champion runner, a dizzy abyss of perversity, a *dear little one* and a baby rabbit," she explains. "But who will tell me how my daughter appears to herself?"[23] Viewed through the eyes of her "faithful nurse," Bel-Gazou is a "masterpiece," a "dizzy abyss of perversity," and a "baby rabbit." By focusing on how her nurse, an outsider, sees her, Colette concedes how one's visibility, how she appears to others, circumscribes female identity. In many ways, the textual Bel-Gazou, like the textual Sido, exists as an "idealized double" for Colette. An illegible repetition of names, the daughter, like the mother, comes into focus through the eyes of others; she appears in fragments, and she is fragmented. As kaleidoscopic replications of Colette's multifaceted self, Sido and Bel-Gazou amplified the narrator's exceptionalism. By positioning her firmly within the nuclear family, however, they also demonstrated the fundamental ways that Colette was just like the public so eager to know her.[24]

Between the publication of *La Maison de Claudine* and the début of *Sido*, Colette released *La Naissance du jour*. Another hybrid text that mingled historical figures with imagined characters, *La Naissance du jour* poses as a conversation between Colette and her deceased mother. The book opens with Colette's response to a letter from Sido, which is withheld from the reader. "Now that little by little I am beginning to age, and little by little taking on her likeness in the mirror," Colette wonders whether her mother, "if she were to return . . . would recognize me for her daughter. She might if she came back at the break of day and found me up and alert in a sleeping world, awake as she used to be, and I often am, before everyone."[25] Wide awake in a world that sleeps, Colette encounters the break of day, the *naissance,* as a new dawn but also as a new beginning, a day lived in the absence of the mother, an occasion for the metaphorical birthing of a new self. In this respect, *La Naissance du jour* reads as both a creation myth and as a search for origins. "My mother climbed too, mounting ceaselessly up the ladder of the hours, trying to possess the beginning of the beginning," Colette expounds. "I know what that particular intoxication is like."[26] By waking early in a dormant world, mother and daughter, as Colette writes them into being, discover an undisturbed, pristine Eden, a garden in which the self evolves in communion with nature. "To lift and penetrate and tear apart the soil is a labor—a pleasure—always accompanied by an exaltation that no unprofitable exercise can provide," she muses. Attentive to the swirling of finches overhead and the meanderings of the cat and dog at her feet, Colette explains how, "when you open up the earth . . . you always feel like the first man, the master, the husband with no rivals. The earth you open up no longer has any past—only a future."[27]

Born of the soil, Colette presents herself in these passages as a natural child of the land. Frenchness for her is a birthright as much as a rite of passage. Yet by characterizing herself and Sido as the land's masculine cultivators—the "first man, the master, the husband with no rivals"—she upholds the notion that national belonging is fundamentally male. In this way, she reiterates the gender politics espoused within the liberal bourgeois order and reasserts the necessity of sex complementarity to the survival of the *patrie.* For a brief moment, in suggesting that she and Sido might usurp the male role, whether through birth or cultivation, and by claiming that it is the future not the past that matters, she troubles this binary by implying a new prominence for French women. Despite her desire to begin anew, however, the future before her is irrevocably circumscribed by the past. Lurking in the shadows of Colette's ruminations are images of the real and the fictional Sido as well as the figures of Colette's many daughters—Bel-Gazou, Claudine, Renée (*La Vagabonde*), and Léa (*Chéri*). Colette nurtures this elision between herself and these alter egos, acknowledging how in her fiction, "I call myself Renée Néré, or else, prophetically, I introduced a Léa." Although she has "no objection to putting into the hands of the public, in print, rearranged fragments of my emotional life," she reserves the right to "tie up tight in the same sack, strictly private, all that concerns a *preference* for animals and—it's a question of partiality too—the child whom I brought into the world." But of which child does Colette speak here? It appears that she means Bel-Gazou, that urchin who reminds the absent mother of her younger self. However, Colette goes on to declare, "Once upon a time I took myself to make a girl of fourteen or fifteen the heroine of a novel. May I be forgiven, for I did not then know what I was doing."[28] The author's inability to separate out her "daughters" and to distinguish herself from them suggests that the female self, as Colette sees it, is both an intergenerational tapestry of familial bloodlines and an act of imagination, a "once upon a time," that is death-defyingly timeless.

Unsurprisingly, the theme of rebirth echoes throughout *La Naissance du jour.* Colette, finding herself "not dependent on a man's love for the first time since [she] was sixteen," proclaims that she is ready to "make a clean sweep, to build up once more, to be born again has never been too much for me." Colette makes this "clean sweep" by breaking ties with others to claim her own name. "So, it came about that both legally and familiarly, as well as in my books," she proclaimed, that "I now have only one name [Colette], which is my own. Did it take only thirty years of my life to reach that point, or rather to get back to it?"[29] By the time that she penned *La Naissance du jour,* Colette had passed through many names. In her childhood, Gabri, Sidonie-Gabrielle; Bel-Gazou; after her first marriage, she dropped her mother's name and acquired the family name to become Colette Willy and then Colette de Jouvenel, adopting the surname of her second husband. In all of these iterations, Colette existed only in relation to others—the mother, the father, the husband. In this capacity, she was as much the object as the subject of her name; it possessed her as much as she possessed it. Importantly, it is only after her parents have died, that she has divorced two husbands, and that she has established herself as one of France's most celebrated writers that she breaks with her maiden names, her married names, and her pen names to establish herself simply and definitively as "Colette."[30] Through the process of naming the self and giving that self a single name, Colette ultimately created a celebrity brand that would belong not only to the individual who invented it but also to the public that consumed it and the nation that commemorated it. Through the process of naming the self, Colette created her own posterity.

As the example of naming demonstrates, Colette's fantasy of exceptional womanhood was anchored in a self-manufactured cultural illegibility. In her autobiographical texts, she rooted herself firmly in the *patrie,* proclaiming her generational inheritance, portraying Frenchness as her birthright. Despite her complicated relationship to the republic, especially during the Occupation, Colette could be venerated upon her death because her Frenchness was assumed. As a provincial, Catholic, middle-class woman, Colette appeared to her contemporaries to be *just like us.* Colette further reinforced her claim to Frenchness by playing the role of the respectable bourgeois. Not only was she a wife and mother, but she was also a woman who knew her place in the polity. An antifeminist who maintained that women did not belong in politics, she embraced the rhetoric of gender complementarity that underwrote republican citizenship.

Although she hid behind avatars and subverted literary convention in her autobiographical fiction, in many ways, the genre enabled Colette to re-affirm her position in the *patrie.* It was precisely because Colette presented as quintessentially French, moreover, that she got away with transgressing social conventions. Carrying on extramarital affairs, divorcing twice, seducing her stepson, taking female lovers, performing onstage in the popular music halls but also in the seedy café-concerts of Europe, and pursuing careers in journalism, business, and of course writing, she was decidedly not like everybody else. Through these activities Colette challenged social norms, but she also adopted the valence of otherness to author her own fantasy of exceptional womanhood. In her beguiling autobiographical texts, in her professional pursuits, and in her stage appearances, contemporaries read Colette's cultural illegibility as performance, as part of the act. In so doing, and as her performance in *Rêve d'Égypte* illustrates, they minimized her threat to the status quo even as they authorized her subversion of it.

CLEOPATRA'S KISS: FIFTEEN MINUTES OF INFAMY

As a stage performer, Colette frequently relied upon the unproblematic presumption of her white, middle-class French womanhood to shuffle categories of race, class, gender, and nationality. Throughout her theatrical career, she added credibility to her work by correlating the physical labor of stage performance with middle-class domesticity. In the process, she elevated working-class wage labor and legitimized middle-class feminine work. Bringing respectability to both forms of women's work, moreover, she compensated for her own social transgressions and portrayed her controversial profession as an acceptable female *métier,* a skilled trade rooted in male-coded republican values of hard work and craftsmanship.[31]

Colette's philosophy not only shaped her work ethic but also influenced how audiences received her. She frequently performed in drag, as a racially ambiguous, class-indeterminate, or foreign Other, and she enacted same-sex romance scenarios. Audiences often applauded these performances. They were less receptive, however, to *Rêve d'Égypte* when it opened in 1907. Perhaps this performance elicited such a heated response because her costar was an openly homosexual aristocrat; perhaps because the two women were lovers in real life; or perhaps because, in this performance, she dared to jumble all of the identity categories through which her audience understood Frenchness. In any case, the quintessentially French bourgeois wife Colette Willy ruffled feathers that opening night when she appeared alongside her female paramour semi-nude in the guise of a mummified Egyptian queen.

After dabbling in amateur performance—appearing primarily in improvised parlor farces or as part of Willy's suggestive ménage-à-trois Claudine tableaux, it was only in 1905 that Colette turned to acting as a profession. That year, she began training with the talented mime Georges Wague, and it was with him that she made her professional début at the Théâtre des Mathurins on February 6, 1906.[32] Between 1906 and 1913, Colette and Wague headlined hundreds of productions across France, Belgium, and Switzerland, staging the salacious (and literal) bodice-ripper *La Chair* (*The Flesh*) more than three hundred times.[33] During this period, Colette also appeared in Willy's adaptation of *Claudine à Paris,* and she took on her first speaking role as a male gigolo in Willy's one-act *Aux innocents les mains plaines.* Not long thereafter, Colette staged adaptations of her own works, *En comrades, La Vagabonde,* and *Chéri.*[34]

It was thus in December 1906, in the early days of her stage career, that the Moulin Rouge engaged Colette and Missy to perform a romantic pantomime, *La Romanichelle.* Although she loved the theater and she indulged Colette in private performances, Missy was reluctant to take the stage. She agreed to perform alongside her mistress on the condition that she retain her amateur status and that the theater bill her under the anagram Yssim.[35] Her trepidation about joining the theater was not unfounded, it would seem, as, having caught wind of the performance on the eve of its opening night, an acerbic *Fantasio* contributor, who hid behind the fictious pen name "M. Vitriol," took advantage of the occasion to publicly malign the marquise. In his scathing commentary, M. Vitriol attacked every aspect of Missy's character. Divulging scandals from her youth, exposing her battles with depression, and mocking the trapezes installed in her *garçonnière* "love chambers," the malevolent commentator ridiculed the "desexed creature with a bloated face of soft plaster" who had fallen so low as to appear in "a pantomime with a girlfriend . . . who's already famous."[36]

Notwithstanding the *Fantasio* contributor's caustic character assassination of the production's costar, the show went on, as scheduled, on December 16. When Colette and Missy took the stage, the former seductively costumed as a licentious gypsy, the latter adorned in trousers and waistcoat, personifying the infatuated bourgeois artist, they played to a sold-out crowd.[37] As the pantomime unfolded, the audience hooted and hollered, it moaned and it wailed, it boorishly cried out, "Go to it, old Yssim! Take her!"[38] It did all of this and yet it did not entirely bring down the house. Paris would have to wait another three weeks for *that* to happen.

Despite having had her name and imperfect reputation maligned in *Fan-*

tasio, Missy agreed to join Colette onstage the following January. Bringing "together two personalities of somewhat scandalous notoriety . . . whose eccentricities have for quite some time fueled the chronicles," *Rêve d'Égypte,* another one-act pantomime, written by Willy, Wague, and Vuillermoz and set to music by Édouard Mathé, enacted the revivification of a mummified Egyptian queen.[39] Patrons filtered into the overcrowded Moulin Rouge, curious to witness what new scandal these "eccentric personalities" might perpetrate. The opening act transpired in relative calm, followed by applause that led into a typically noisy intermission. The second act, set in the lobby of a morning newspaper, announced the upcoming pantomime starring "a marquise that everyone will recognize under the pseudonym of Yssim," caused a bit more of a stir, as spectators began to vocalize their mounting anticipation. When the curtain rose for the main act at 10:45 p.m., muffled groans and sundry whistles almost immediately gave way to a torrent of vulgar invectives. By 10:46, the frenzied audience had transformed itself into a riotous mob.

Set in an Egyptologist's cluttered study and focused on a middle-aged scholar who thinks his collections have come to life, the pantomime's plot should not have elicited such a fervid response. What excited audiences was that both the mummified queen and her liberator were played by women. Outfitted in a velvet suit and tie from her personal wardrobe, the crowd recognized, according to *Figaro* journalist and playwright Alfred Delilia, "the ex-Mme. de Belbeuf." In response to this discovery, "whistles arose from all corners, the cries r[a]ng out, the howls [we]re heard continuously." Amid the audience tumult, "the noise redoubled when Colette Willy, came to life in her sarcophagus." Escaping her entombment, Colette's Egyptian queen began dancing provocatively, encouraging her liberator to continue *his* task of tearing off the transparent strips of cloth that had bound her.[40] Completely unwrapped, the newly unencumbered Colette—clad in a golden breastplate, a diaphanous calf-length skirt, bangled arm bracelets featuring entwined snakes (a possible allusion to Cleopatra and a hallmark of the femme fatale), and a striking, jeweled head piece and collar—boldly rewarded her emancipator with a passionate kiss (figure 8).

There are many reasons that such a scene resonated with its Paris audience. A work of fiction, it could easily be dismissed as nothing more an imaginative exercise, a harmless fantasy. Or it could be interpreted more literally as a reenactment of the imperialist fantasy in which the civilized Westerner

"awakens" the colonial Other. What so upset theatergoers, of course, was not the content of the pantomime itself but the women who performed it. In the lead role as the Egyptologist, Missy perverted a masculinist conquest fantasy—one that was both political and sexual—by assuming and asserting that women might entertain and act upon the same fantasy. For many in the audience, imperial power was white and Western, but it was also undeniably masculine. Missy may have been a French-born aristocrat, but she was not, despite her best efforts at self-fashioning, a man. As the liberating Egyptologist, Missy usurped male privilege at the same time that she troubled the narratives of colonial conquest central to France's imperial mission.

Although this challenge to male prerogative might have been enough on its own to irritate theatergoers, it was the real-life, cross-class romantic relationship between the two women on stage that really riled them. Even before the performance reached its climax, spectators physically assaulted the duo.

Audience members hurled candy tins and coins at them, littered the stage with half-eaten, rotting produce, and forced the pair to dodge projectile seat cushions. Amid nasty catcalls, the obnoxious ringing of shrill noisemakers, and a coordinated chanting so loud as to drown out the forty-piece orchestra, Colette and Missy completed the performance.[41] The flabbergasted *L'Intransigeant* reporter Henri Rochefort reflected the next day, "If the characters of the play remained silent, the spectators, who crowded the room, took charge of the dialogue. The barking of dogs, the whistles . . . , the growling of invective, the eruption of slang so offensive that its meaning sometimes escaped me, everything contributed to give this solemnity an unprecedented brilliance." Notably, it was not the necrophilic aspect of the performance but its gender and class inversions that so outraged Rochefort. The "great-granddaughter of the Empress Joséphine," he railed, "from whom she is descended through women—only women—played . . . in the company of the absurd Colette Willy, a pantomime which interested me enormously, although I didn't entirely understand it."[42] Rochefort was not alone in his indignation. Other critics derided Colette as a disgraced bourgeoise, a class traitor, and a vulgar publicity hound who, despite her moral upbringing and literary aptitude, pandered to the public in ways "reserved for women of no talent."[43]

The real show, the performance that would become the talk of Paris in the days ahead, thus unfolded not on the stage of the Moulin Rouge that fateful night but in its raucous galleries and boisterous boxes. When the curtain fell sometime around eleven, the agitated crowd shifted its attention from the stage, to shout insults, throw fists, and fling objects at Willy and Meg, who had witnessed the spectacle from their seats at the front of the auditorium. Indeed, the throng chased the headliner's estranged husband and his mistress through the theater aisles, taunting the latter with lewd barbs and verbally abusing the former, shouting down the "cuckold" whose woman had so publicly disgraced him. Willy fought off his increasingly violent assailants, weaponizing his cane against them, while his feisty companion punched and clawed her way through the chaotic free-for-all. It was only with the assistance of a handful of friends and a police escort that the couple finally escaped the "pack of rabid beasts."[44] Calm was "reestablished . . . in front of a half-empty room," terminating the "deplorable exhibition, which, we hope," Delilia concluded, "will have no tomorrow."[45]

In less than half an hour, the *Dream of Egypt* became a Parisian nightmare. And yet, even this unpredictable outcome should not have altogether surprised theatergoers, theater managers, or the performers themselves. Just as with *La Romanichelle, Rêve d'Égypte* incited controversy days before opening night. Despite the thrashing that Missy took in the press after her stage début and notwithstanding her desire to remain an amateur, Moulin Rouge managers, eager to claim a hefty return on their steep investment, relentlessly promoted *Rêve d'Égypte*, using the Morny name and coat of arms on its colorful poster advertisements. They strategically placed these posters outside of the theater entrance, which had the effect of not only announcing the event but of also annoying Missy's brother, her ex-husband, and others, who wanted neither their aristocratic names associated with the theater nor their patrimony peddled for sale as a vulgar object of commerce. To make matters worse, rather than contest the Moulin Rouge's cheeky publicity strategy, Missy, Colette, and Willy actively abetted it.[46] They spread rumors in the press and participated in suggestive interviews, playing up their roles offstage to preview what would transpire onstage. And, perhaps most crucially, they scoffed at the Mornys' feigned aristocratic outrage.[47] Defending her theater-loving mistress as "an independent woman," Colette told *Le Journal* that "it would be ridiculous if the fact of belonging to the nobility prevented a woman from doing what she wanted!"[48]

What the theater managers, Colette, and Missy may have anticipated, but could not have known, however, was that elite patrons would purchase no fewer than 150 seats for opening night. Adorned in elegant eveningwear and outfitted in the most fashionable gowns, *tout-Paris* packed the theater.[49] "Everybody who is anybody was there," recounted *Gil Blas* observer Pierre Mortier, "the blue-bloods and the big names."[50] Yet the bluebloods and the big names were not the only spectators in attendance. Tickets had also gone to Jockey Club cronies, moralizing hecklers, and indiscriminate hoodlums, many of whom, compensated for their services, proved perfectly delighted to cause a scene.[51] In a postproduction interview conducted by *Semaine Parisienne*, an indignant Colette admitted that she had been "a bit disgusted by the cowardice of all these people who . . . showered me with insults. . . . [I]f I didn't get a footstool thrown smack in my face, it's only because I dodged it in time. Very attractive, don't you think?"[52]

Following the January 3 mêlée, Missy's relatives, claiming that the theater used the family name and the coat of arms without its permission, demanded that the prefect of police shut the show down. Despite police intervention, however, theater managers began preparations for the second performance, scheduled for the night of January 4. Just as they had the previous evening, onlookers crowded into the auditorium, eager to witness the latest spectacle to enflame Paris. Much to their disappointment, however, they would not see the *Rêve d'Égypte*—at least not in its original incarnation. Minutes before the curtain went up, a producer informed the audience that, by order of the police, the *Rêve d'Égypte* would now be called *Songe d'Orient,* and Georges Wague rather than the Marquise de Belbeuf would play the archeologist. Annoyed by this turn of events, audience members once more cried out, this time demanding to see Missy.[53]

In the weeks following the performance, scandal continued to plague Missy, the Gauthier-Villars, and the Moulin Rouge. Claiming a breach of contract for using the family crest without her consent, Missy sued the theater, demanding a thousand francs in restitution. The January 3 uproar and her family's subsequent cutting off of her income, she claimed, might have been avoided altogether had managers not plastered her family coat of arms on publicity materials. In a somewhat pathetic but nonetheless calculated effort to absolve himself from responsibility for the ruckus, Willy attempted to shift public focus onto his deteriorating relationship with his estranged wife. On January 4, the cavalier publisher marched into the press room at *Le Temps* to officially proclaim his divorce from Madame Willy. Biographers speculate that he did so to maintain his regular income as a music critic for *L'Écho de Paris,* a journal that had vociferously condemned the incident. Facing hard financial times once more, Willy sought to disentangle himself from Colette, leaving her to fend for herself. Willy's headline for *Le Temps* not only formally announced the dissolution of the couple's marriage but also incited a media storm around the pair's tempestuous divorce proceedings that would play out publicly over the next three years. In the months following the press release, husband and wife squabbled over property, accused one another of numerous indiscretions, and wrote scathing farewell letters to each other. They made their private life public and callously aired their dirty laundry in the daily press.[54]

Although the law of July 27, 1884 (also known as the Naquet law), legally reestablished divorce in France, it did not erase the social stigma around the practice, nor did it suppress debates regarding its moral, economic, demographic, and political consequences.[55] Indeed, the French had hotly contested divorce since it was first legalized on September 20, 1792. Legislators abolished it completely in 1816, and they voted down numerous bills in the 1830s and in 1848 that might have reinstated it in some form. Passed under the relatively young Third Republic, the somewhat conservative Naquet law defined marriage as a civil, rather than religious, contract, and it empowered the state, granting courts the discretion to adjudicate marital dissolutions. However, it enabled individuals to petition for divorce only on the grounds of adultery, cruelty, or abuse resulting in grave bodily injury, slander, or conviction of a serious crime. While abuse and criminality might not be tolerated, adultery was a moveable feast, especially given arguments that extramarital affairs did not automatically discount a husband's moral fitness for nor disqualify him from conjugal life. Slander could also be tricky, as it needed to be indisputably demonstrated in a court of law. By so narrowly defining the legitimate causes for filing for a termination of marriage, the law reinstated a republican ideology that valued the individual's (male's) political rights even as it sought to maintain the integrity of French families.[56]

The limitations placed on divorce under the Third Republic notwithstanding, the Gauthier-Villars were not the only couple to petition for it. As Edward Berenson has documented, French "courts had dissolved some 5,000 marriages in 1887 and 10,000 in 1903, growing to nearly 17,000 in 1912. Even more troubling than actual divorces was the annual number of requests for divorce: 4,600 in 1885, 19,000 in 1912—more than a four-fold increase in less than three decades."[57] Willy, who could prove neither criminal conviction nor cruelty and who was himself guilty of adultery, filed, claiming that his partner had "deserted" the marriage. Colette countersued on the grounds that her adulterous husband had been cohabiting with his mistress, Meg.[58] As a bourgeois male, Willy could evoke desertion as reason enough to dissolve the union; however, Colette, as a middle-class woman, could not make a case based on adultery alone. She had to prove that her partner installed another woman in the (presumably) familial domicile. In this way, the Gauthier-Villars divorce was in no way unique: the burden of proof placed upon women was higher than that placed upon men when attempting to dissolve a marriage. The burden was so high, in part, because republican legislators regarded marriage as a union between families, not individuals, and they viewed married life, especially middle-class married life, as the bedrock of sociopolitical stability. Thus, restrictions written into the law were intended to preserve male privilege by maintaining the sanctity of the patriarchal family.[59]

As the number of petitions for divorce increased across this period, so too did the attention that dissolute marriages attracted in the press. In 1908 alone, the widely circulated daily *Le Matin* apportioned its front page, usually reserved for international news and political coverage, to a debate about the "crisis of marriage." Editors allocated space for three positions—those for, those against, and those who supported a *union libre.* Coupled with the already popular *fait divers* section of the paper, which was devoted exclusively to human interest stories, *Le Matin* elevated the divorce debate to the front page of national consciousness, literally blending the public and the private, and metaphorically elevating the personal to the political.[60]

Given recent interest in the issue and the media's willingness to publish personal narratives alongside general reportage as "news," it is not altogether surprising that the publicity-driven Gauthier-Villars would play out their divorce in the press.[61] Both parties benefited from the visibility the media afforded them—Colette garnered attention for her theatrical productions and new publications, Willy for his continued influence in the world of publishing. The press provided the embattled couple an inexpensive, wide-reaching public forum for publicizing its domestic drama, and it did so because feuding spouses generated reader interest as well as revenue.[62] As ordinary people were increasingly eager to access the juicy details of the public figure's private life, newspapers obliged, providing space for both Willy and Colette to accuse each other of heinous crimes, to reveal cruelties done to them, and to portray themselves as sympathetic victims, fallible human beings caught up, like so many of their contemporaries, in the unpredictable vortex of modern marriage.

Whereas the Morny family drama subverted entrenched class hierarchies by challenging the preservation of aristocratic privilege and the Gauthier-Villars divorce saga undermined the sanctity of bourgeois marriage, the act that immediately preceded these public spectacles, the onstage kiss (and the real-life relationship it signified) between Colette and Missy, engaged current debates around female sexuality, public obscenity, and national morality. In the first decade of the twentieth century, female homosexuality was widely debated. Some embraced it as a healthy form of sexual expression, some dismissed it as a passing phase, a juvenile proclivity that young girls would outgrow in their maturity, and some merely fetishized it as an erotic turn-on.

Others, however, demonized it as a form of sexual deviance; they regarded it as an unnatural aberration, cited it as a factor in national population decline, and identified it as a particularly insidious form of degeneration, a moral cancer infecting all levels of French society.[63]

Although themselves engaged in a long-term same-sex love affair, Missy and Colette expressed ambivalence, even disdain, for lesbianism. Missy had notoriously participated in orgies, overindulged in drugs, cropped her hair short, and ordered her men's suits from the best tailors in London and Paris, yet she proclaimed that she did not "like women who dress as men."[64] She was also critical of other homosexual women, most notably Natalie Barney, whom she disparaged for her Jewish ancestry and condemned for her wealth derived from trade. In this particular critique, Missy echoed sentiments shared by many men and women of her social class—anti-Semitism, snobbery against the nouveaux riches, and a discernible pro-French bias—as Barney was an American expatriate who made Paris her home as recently as 1902.

Colette, who would have a brief romantic entanglement with Barney, was a bit more sympathetic toward the poet. For many years, she participated in Barney's literary salons, she joined a variety of companions at the Barney home for interminable dinner parties, and she corresponded with the American transplant on a semi-regular basis. Despite her personal fondness for Barney, her passionate love for Missy, her numerous sexual liaisons with other women, and her pursuit of same-sex love as a theme in her literature, however, Colette claimed to find the world of Lesbos lacking. "There is no Gomorrah," she wrote in *Le Pur et l'impur*. "Puberty, boarding schools, solitude, prisons, snobbery . . . these are fallow breeding grounds, not rich enough to nurture and develop a widespread, established vice and its essential solidarity. . . . Sodom contemplates its frail imitation from on high."[65] Women who pursued other women, Colette continued, did not exhibit the same level of passion as their male counterparts; they could not sustain the same kind of visceral connection, nor could they experience the elusive "total fusion with the other," that she herself desired.

In light of these comments, should we read Colette's same-sex affairs merely as play—as yet another screen upon which she publicly projected her contrived rejection of bourgeois convention? Certainly, in her appraisal that there could be no Gomorrah to rival Sodom because women were incapable of producing the prolonged sexual feeling necessary to maintain it, she reiterated contemporary ideas regarding women's natural passionlessness and innate virtue. Yet this claim, which contradicted her own actions, conveniently provides Colette a mask for concealing her own (mis)deeds. By asserting that women are naturally incapable of sustaining same-sex partnerships, she undermines their validity, neutralizes their social threat, defends herself against accusations of unwomanliness, and distances herself from sexually deviant Others. As an author who continuously implores her readers not to mistake her writing for fact, however, we are ultimately left with more questions than answers concerning Colette's attitude toward woman's capacity for same-sex love.

So, what about that kiss then? Was it a political act intended to rally public support for the Sapphic cult, to legitimize cross-class same-sex love? Or was it merely a publicity stunt, a way to sell tickets and to keep one's name in the press? Just as divorce was no stranger to the Third Republic, neither was the public display of same-sex sexual desire. Same-sex encounters occurred regularly in the brothels and around the theaters of the notorious Place Pigalle, but they could also be witnessed in the bustling bohemian cafés of Montmartre, spied in the popular student *bals* of the Latin Quarter, or even, at a certain time each day, be observed in one of the most popular bourgeois playgrounds, the Bois de Bologne.[66] In addition to these public venues, same-sex encounters transpired in the private sitting rooms, boudoirs, carriages, and domestic gardens, as well as in the semi-public opium dens, urban urinals, and bathhouses located across the city.[67]

Of course, not everyone was pleased by the increased visibility of homosexual relationships on the streets and in the commercial venues of Paris. Citing this development as evidence of the nation's festering moral degeneracy, critics demanded that such practices, if they could not be curtailed altogether, at least remain hidden from public view. To this end, conservative newspapers like *L'Autorité* routinely printed antipornography tracts. The morals brigade censored literary works, closed down houses of ill-repute, and policed the behaviors of ordinary citizens. Purity campaigners pressured police to shutter offensive stage productions and agitated successfully enough that an office for theater inspectors was established in 1906. These inspectors monitored nudity and obscenity on the stage and hauled dozens of performers and theater managers into French courts on charges of public indecency.[68]

Colette and Missy's infamous kiss transpired amid these ferocious debates about French morality, public decency, the sanctity of bourgeois marriage, and the management of sexed bodies. That it did so not in the semi-secluded foliage off the beaten path of the *bois* or in a hidden corner of a profligate avant-garde café but on the stage of the Moulin Rouge in front of a diverse audience that included men and women from every social class as well as journalists who would publicize the performance across the country meant that the kiss elevated female same-sex desire, bringing it out of the shadows, making it visible on a national stage. What concerned critics most was not that the show featured one woman wearing men's clothing and another woman wearing close to nothing at all—although for some, this would have been enough to incite outrage and provoke demand that the show be closed—but that, by staging Colette's metaphorical sexual awakening, the mummy coming to life beneath Missy's suggestive gaze, the performance too closely replicated the couple's offstage relationship.[69] As the director of *Le Figaro,* Gaston Calmette, explained, "The scandal is not in the vehement protest of a disgusted public, but in the paradoxical exhibition they were presented with. If people don't understand that their peculiar relationships shouldn't be displayed in public, then it is right that Paris makes them hear it, even with an elementary tool like a whistle."[70] Calmette maintained that the crowd's obstreperous reaction was justified not simply because a kiss transpired on the stage at the Moulin Rouge but because the kiss signified a perverse offstage relationship between two women who should have known better. In its suggestion that women might possess sexual feeling, that they might pursue romantic love in the absence of men, the kiss teased a sexual inversion that rendered men impotent, irrelevant, and unnecessary. The kiss was so threatening, then, because the fantasy it projected was all too real.[71]

Although the relationship between Colette and Missy was quite real, the fact that the pair parodied it on the stage is nevertheless noteworthy. More significant is the fact that the pantomime featured Colette not in the role of the liberated New Woman or even in the guise of the cosmopolitan Parisienne but in the image of the femme Orientale. Long after the opening-night scandal subsided, the show went on as the *Song of the Orient,* and publicity photographs, like those taken by the esteemed celebrity photographer Léopold-Émile Reutlinger, highlighted the more exotic aspects of Colette's character

FIG. 9. Colette in *Rêve d'Égypte,* 1907, Moulin Rouge, *Album Reutlinger de portraits divers,* vol. 55.

(figure 9). In several photos, Reutlinger depicted the mummy's lyric movements, reminiscent of Salomé's infamous dance of the veils. In these images, he captures the elasticity of Colette's body not only through her supple poses but also by highlighting the delicate drapery of the diaphanous fabrics covering it. For Reutlinger, Colette's revivified mummy is sensual and seductive; she is fluid and flexible; she is indisputably feminine, and she is the ultimate femme fatale.

While so many of Reutlinger's photographs capture Colette in motion, dancing in that moment when she comes to life, one image in the series portrays her at rest. It is when she is posed as a sphinx—a position that she likely did not enact during the pantomime itself but rather performed for Reutlinger in his studio—that Colette most acutely embodies the male fantasy of

FIG. 10. Colette in *Rêve d'Égypte*, 1907, Moulin Rouge, *Album Reutlinger de portraits divers*, vol. 55.

the femme Orientale (figure 10). In Greek mythology, the merciless sphinx, a creature with a woman's head, a bird's wings, and a lion's body seduced men with riddles and devoured those who could not solve her puzzles. A fabled "man-eater," this hybrid organism shared much in common with the nightmarish nineteenth-century femme fatale who also emasculated and destroyed her prey. Yet in Egyptian mythology, the sphinx is male not female, he is benevolent rather than ruthless, and rather than call forth the forces of evil, he protects against them. A fusion of both the masculine and the feminine, Colette's sphinx, with its downward gaze and relaxed body settles both sexes into stable repose. She is supple and female, but she also appears submissive and supine. Resting on her elbows, she is vulnerable. The object of the camera, she is presented for the viewer's ocular enjoyment. In this way, her image neutralizes the femme Orientale's threat and restores her as a figure of male fantasy. Dancing, she is dangerous; reclining, she is but another odalisque subdued under the male gaze. At the same time, however, she is the subject as well as the object of the photograph. As such, it is upon her power which she rests, her story as much as that of her character's that creates the narrative through which she is framed. In her image, even in repose, the threat of the independent woman is softened but it is not entirely extinguished.

Colette appeared in these Reutlinger photographs alone—neither Missy nor Wague, the studio nor the Moulin Rouge, were anywhere in sight. And yet, it was that kiss rather than Colette's performance per se that enflamed debates across Paris. The question of onstage kissing was prescient enough in 1907 for the weekly *Paris-Théâtre* to survey a number of performers about it. Appearing on the front page of its January 18 edition under the headline "The Kiss on Stage: Should It Be Fake or Real?" the magazine published numerous participant responses. Among those who completed the questionnaire were Colette and Missy. "Dear Sir," Colette asserted, "my opinion about 'stage kissing' is clear—never fake it." On the same sheet of paper, just beneath Colette's entry, Missy added "in her aristocratic handwriting . . . 'My sentiments precisely!'"[72] Colette's attitude toward stage kissing, her insistence on equating love with pretense, and her proclivity for melding person with persona, in many ways echoed Bernhardt's incessant blurring of fact and fiction. Conflating performance with one's real life, both women perfected the art of the lie by adorning their most colorful falsehoods with the glittering accessories of truth.

Whereas Bernhardt's fantasy of exceptional womanhood was firmly rooted in her cultural illegibility, however, Colette's was circumscribed by the *appearance* of truth. These women both brokered their commercial success through an invented persona that conflated fact with fiction. They were astute self-promoters who used the media and the new opportunities available to French women at the end of the nineteenth century to carve out their own professional space and to pursue their own personal fulfilment. And both women dramatized their real lives, albeit in vastly different ways, to keep the public eye always upon them. Bernhardt relied almost exclusively on embodied performance (onstage and off) to brazenly challenge social norms, whereas Colette, through her feline pantomimes as well as through her ludic prose, launched a more subtle if equally subversive sensory infiltration of the status quo. If Bernhardt's exceptionalism resided in the ways that she distinguished herself from other women, then Colette's stemmed from all the ways that she and her characters appeared *just like us.*

Colette's aptitude for mimicking the trappings of middle-class womanhood is even more remarkable considering that she rarely acted like the typical bourgeoise. If convention dictated that a woman's destiny was to be a good wife and an even better mother, then, as a divorcée twice over and as a reluctant matriarch who ardently resisted the maternal yoke, Colette indubitably fell short. Colette's contemporaries routinely characterized the female body as a trivial, hypersexualized plaything, or they regarded it as a reproductive vessel whose function was to ensure the survival of nation and race. In so doing, they reinforced engrained notions of sex difference and justified an exclusionary liberal politics premised on gender complementarity. As a risqué pantomimer who performed in public scantily clad or completely nude, Colette seemed to embody the figure of the pleasing female, the specular object invented entirely for man's amusement. At the same time, however, as a white, middle-class woman who publicly revealed her body to paying spectators, she also perverted this fantasy, calling attention to the hypocritical ways in which men esteemed certain female bodies while they devalued others. Moreover, when she appeared onstage in drag, cloaked in the sartorial signifiers of masculinity, she troubled distinctions of sex difference loosely premised on the biological fact of anatomical bodies. Her admonishments against the cult of Lesbos notwithstanding, in both her fiction and in her figure, Colette portrayed gender as performative, sexuality as fluid, race as arbitrary, and carnal passion as a human right.

Although guilty of acting out in numerous ways, of persistently pushing the bounds of moral probity and of upending notions of social acceptability, Colette never fully escaped her bourgeois, provincial upbringing. In this regard, she embodied the quintessential French woman.[73] For instance, although she was a besmirched divorcée, she abandoned one husband only to marry two more. These endeavors suggest that she never entirely forsook heterosexual love, nor did she completely renounce the middle-class institution that esteemed it. There were also important limitations to her libertinage. She may have seduced an underage stepson and carried on same-sex love affairs, but she identified neither as a sexual profligate nor as a liberated lesbian. Rather, she characterized her relationship with Bertrand as mutual and consensual, a necessary component of the awkward young man's coming of age, and she vocally derided same-sex female love as inferior to its heterosexual counterpart.

In her unwillingness to engage the heady politics of her age, moreover, Colette, like so many of her female contemporaries, embodied the *feminine* rather than enacted the *feminist.* She supported women's participation in the arts, but, as she told Walter Benjamin in his series "The Great Contradiction of

Our Time," she did not believe that women were temperamentally suited for public life. Politics, she explained, revealed a "taste for power" and a "brutality of the feminine character" that "masculinized women"[74] By depicting women who advocated for female political participation as "masculinized," Colette echoed the prejudices of her class. Her position on this issue, of course, reflected her privileged position in the polity. As a middle-class French woman with the financial freedom and social connections necessary to pursue her chosen career as well as her personal pleasures, she need not concern herself with the plight of other women for whom such options were not available. In this way, Colette's exceptionalism, indeed her very ability to see herself as Other, enabled her to uphold the values of the status quo, even as she herself undermined them. She also shared with many of her republican counterparts the belief that women were not devoid of power but that they simply exercised a particular form of it. Woman's authority, she maintained, derived not from the "throne room, but from the bedroom. It [sex] is," she maintained, "the only power that a woman ever wanted and with it she achieves what no man could."[75] In other words, while women might influence public affairs through their male representatives, they need not meddle in those matters themselves. It is through this perspective, importantly, that the abstract individual at the heart of French republican ideology perseveres. By declaring her support for such a notion, Colette reasserted her loyalty to a class that embraced gender complementarity as the bedrock of social stability, and she reaffirmed her allegiance to a nation whose republican ethos required it.

Comparing the boudoir to the throne room rather than to the boardroom or the National Assembly hall, Colette also unwittingly echoed the connection drawn between these two institutions in the Cleopatra myth. Like Cleopatra, Colette envisioned a politics in which a woman's sexual potency and political influence might work in tandem. Colette was not a leader of state, but by reiterating republican values she acknowledged how sex functioned as a powerful political tool. Whereas Cleopatra's privilege, rooted in her birthright as well as in a political system in which women could openly wield power, permitted her to exercise authority over men in both the public and private arenas, Colette's birthright as a middle-class French woman enabled her to promote a political system premised on the separation of those interlocking spheres.

Although rooted in the values of liberty, equality, and fraternity, in practice, French republicanism foreclosed opportunities for women's political participation, limiting their power to the private realm. In her disregard for feminism as well as in her dismissal of same-sex female love, Colette aligned herself with the status quo and demonstrated her devotion to the republican nation to which she belonged. Indeed, her scorn for so-called masculinized, unnatural women (suffragettes, bluestockings, even other writers), reverberated throughout her literary oeuvre as these figures contrasted sharply with her cast of ultrafeminine protagonists who were often crippled by their desire to love and to be loved by men.[76] Although they acted in profligate ways, many of Colette's characters fixated on domestic love. Like her they also remained silent on issues regarding women's political investment in the nation. Inasmuch as she ever talked politics herself, Colette parroted a contemporary insistence on the special status of French women. Woman exercised her greatest power in the boudoir; her citizenship, like her class status, thus derived from her ability to always know her place.

Colette's point of view, which she hinted at rather than systematically elucidated, contradicted her very public actions. Just as openly as she criticized the cult of Lesbos, she pursued same-sex love affairs. Although she seldom offered her opinion on state affairs, she reported on serious issues for the French press, even taking on the role as war correspondent from the battlefield. And, although she seemed to endorse the natural divisions between the sexes and the separate sphere ideology that they bolstered, neither she nor any of her heroines found happily-ever-after in domesticity. Through her words, Colette affirmed her French middle-class womanhood, reinstated herself in the *patrie,* and bolstered her privilege. But these words also, and perhaps more importantly, provided her a platform for exploring her own fantasy of exceptional womanhood. As a career-oriented, pleasure-seeking, self-involved celebrity who lived as she pleased and loved as she desired, Colette embraced that which made her different—she cast herself as Other and rendered the Other legible to the status quo. Through this process, she demonstrated that the woman who appeared *just like us* might not be anything like us at all. At the same time, she insinuated the Other's centrality to the self, suggesting that French women might all be just like her; and just like her, they too might have the power to author exceptional lives.

In contemporary reviews and scholarly treatments of her work, critics maintain that by vocalizing women's issues and concerns, Colette wrote in the voice of the feminine. During her lifetime and for several decades thereafter, readers praised the author's intuitive approach to writing, pointing to her focus on both the sensual female body and the natural world as evidence of her particularly "feminine sensibility."[77] In his 1910 review of *La Vagabonde,* for example, J. Ernest-Charles celebrated Colette's "truly feminine" personality. "A spontaneous, instinctive woman," Colette, he extolled, is also an "affected, precious, brutally realistic and delicious poet."[78] Scholars would later echo Ernest-Charles's assessment, asserting that Colette reflected a French singularity, a "common essence" of womanhood, that became a hallmark of French literature and a trademark of French national identity in the early twentieth century. By naturalizing and nationalizing gender, Colette's work, in content, in style, and in authorial voice, they suggested, revealed the intimate interconnectedness between constructions of femininity and productions of Frenchness.[79]

Colette wore her "Frenchness" as a badge of honor. Proud of her provincial roots, the woman who spoke throughout her life with a thick Burgundian accent seemed to embody a certain idea of France—an idea ensconced in the timeless pastoral, in the myth of an endlessly fecund, ethnically homogeneous *patrie.* And yet, what made Colette perhaps more authentically French was the fact of her *métissage* ancestry. Colette's maternal forebearers, to whom she referred as colonial "cocoa harvesters colored by island blood, with frizzy hair and purple fingernails," circumscribed her identity as much as her father's southern culture had.[80] In *La Maison de Claudine,* she explains that the family home displayed only one daguerreotype, an image of Colette's maternal grandfather, Henri Marie Landois. In the portrait, Colette discerned "the head and the shoulders of a "coloured man"—a quadroon, I believe—wearing a high white cravat, with pale, contemptuous eyes, and a long nose above the thick Negro lips that had inspired his nickname [the orange Gorilla]." Sido insisted that her father, though "ugly," was "well-built . . . in spite of his purple fingernails" and "awful mouth."[81] Sido's family may have originated in the peasant stock of the Champagne region, but it fled to Martinique to escape religious persecution in the seventeenth century after having converted to Protestantism. On an archipelago in the eastern Caribbean Sea, not on the rolling hills and amid the sprawling vineyards of eastern France, the heretic Landois clan prospered in the spice trade, amassed enough wealth to enslave Africans, and produced a first generation of mixed-race children.[82] Through Sido, the Landois line bequeathed, according to Colette, an eccentric earthiness, a stubborn disregard for convention, and a strong work ethic. But it also gave Colette her "frizzy hair," and it was responsible, as she divulged in a letter to Francis Jammes, for the "stain of black in my blood."[83]

Ambivalent about what she called the "stain of black" in her blood, Colette referred to her grandfather as the "orange gorilla," lamented her own, uncontrollable "frizzy hair," and played up her provincial roots to cover over any racial difference that might have othered her. At the same time, however, by acknowledging these ancestral ties and calling attention to them, she recognized them as part of her identity. She may have derogatorily racialized her grandfather as the "orange gorilla," but it was his image alone that decorated the Colette household, and it was his story, rather than the story of her paternal grandfather, for example, that she wrote about. Although she recognized her own racial ambiguity, Colette did not necessarily regard it as antithetical to her Frenchness. We can only speculate as to her opinion on this issue, but the fact that she supported the French colonial project in her fictive works, that she playfully nicknamed her second husband "Sidi" and supported Missy's adoption of the moniker "Yssim," for her stage name, and that she portrayed a revivified African princess in either a *Dream of Egypt* or a *Song of the Orient* suggests that she considered racial identity as mutable as gender identity.[84]

We might also speculate that Colette announced her racial ambiguity to further complicate her gender subversions. Through her textual, theatrical, and real-life appropriations of the racialized Other, Colette produced imperialist images in ways that made her appear to be an agent of Orientalism.[85] By exploiting the salient cultural narratives surrounding the French imperialist mission and revealing the ways in which ideologies of race and gender comingled in imperialist discourse, she seemed to insert herself into a national political conversation. Whether Colette engaged Orientalist themes and stereotypes to propagandize French imperialism is unclear; however, we see how she mobilized these tools to promote her personal agenda. The Moulin Rouge performance, for example, enabled Colette to monetize popular fascination with the exotic at the same time that its racialized elements afforded her a cover for challenging bourgeois heteronormativity. Whereas Bernhardt deemed it necessary to "stain" her white skin with body paint to represent Cleopatra more accurately, Colette mobilized the subversive possibilities of whiteness in her portrayal of the Egyptian mummy. The pantomime scandalized Parisian audiences not because it reflected back to them their own narrow-minded jingoism but because it provided a "living tableau of queerness," an "erotic cipher" that functioned as "a form of outing . . . consonant with putting on an act."[86] French audiences who associated the Orient with the erotic expected to see same-sex sexual encounters transpire in the foreign lands of North Africa. Yet these same spectators were discomforted by the fact that the players in the scene were not the fetishized, colonial Other but "quintessentially French" women from their own social class. It was the kiss between two white French women, the sexual awakening of a bourgeois female by an aristocratic woman, not the faraway setting of the pantomime that twisted the dream of Egypt, a potent French fantasy, into a tortured nightmare.

The performance was also threatening because a woman regarded as "quintessentially French" could so easily portray the racialized Other. In the figure of the white-skinned racially ambiguous Egyptian queen, Colette "played" with race and nationality, revealing both as arbitrary social constructions. She also demonstrated how the Other exists not only in opposition to the self but also within the self. In short, she showed French audiences that, in many ways, the Orientalized Other was *just like us.* This revelation had wide-reaching implications not only because it obfuscated cultural differences but also because it potentially expanded and contracted notions of Frenchness. Secure in her position as a middle-class French woman, Colette shuffled the categories of race, class, and gender to manufacture her own culturally illegibility. The genius of her fantasy of exceptional womanhood thus resided not in her appropriation of labels that others placed upon her, but in claiming the Other for herself.

Arthritic, hard of hearing, and increasingly immobile, Colette spent the last ten years of her life working and receiving visitors from the daybed in her last apartment, which overlooked the Palais-Royale. In the secluded work-room of this third-story perch she penned the *Evening Star,* wrote the dialogue for the film version of *Gigi,* reedited her collected works, and, at the age of seventy-nine, began to keep a diary.[87] Her hair permed and hennaed, her face enhanced with makeup, Colette received her rare guest as an aged but still vibrant woman of letters. Meeting the recluse in her apartment in March 1948, Simone de Beauvoir found herself captivated by the writer's "brilliant blue eyes." Nestled in her cramped hideaway, "between her collection of paper-weights and the gardens framed by her windows," Colette reigned "paralyzed and sovereign, like a formidable Mother-Goddess."[88]

Though physically removed from the public eye, Colette remained a public figure. On January 28, 1948, newspapers across the country celebrated the seventy-fifth birthday of "Our Colette." Five years later, another media out-pouring of articles, documentaries, and news pieces commemorated her life and work. Yet many of those celebrating her life struggled to understand the woman who lived and wrote it. In his January 24, 1953, article, "A Kind of Feminine Dandyism . . . ," André Billy failed to reconcile her morality with her sex, explaining that "Colette has her morality . . . an aristocratic morality. There is a dandyism of Colette . . . a kind of feminine dandyism." Her words "pass for contradictory, a supreme elegance, shrouded in mystery and silence," and in her prose we find "a refusal to say it all, a horror of gossip. Before her," he concludes, "no woman had given us such an example."[89] Like Bernhardt before her, Colette (as Billy characterized her) was a moral shape-shifter; a classless libertine for whom the "horror of gossip" was as delectable as the mystery it came shrouded in.

If Colette resembled the chameleon Bernhardt in her ability to blur bound-aries of class, she echoed both her theatrical predecessor and Cleopatra in her uncanny ability to embody both the masculine and the feminine in her person. Pierre Brisson argued that in "tone, authority, and clairvoyance," Colette was "masculine in her dealings with other women." In her prose, Colette may have privileged sensuality over sexuality but always in "front of love, or rather in front of feeling, she is both man and woman," the "masculine and feminine to-gether."[90] But if Colette was both man and woman together, a perfect union of the sexes within one person, how could she also be the quintessentially French woman? How could she, above all others, personify the "woman's writer"? It is possible that because she embodied a perplexing repository of seemingly end-less contradictions, because she revealed sex itself as an unresolvable paradox, that she ultimately exemplified French womanhood.[91] It is also possible that it is precisely because she combined the masculine and feminine in complete harmony that she signified the quintessentially French. After all, was it not the perfect harmony of the male and female, the perfect complementarity of the sexes, upon which the republic itself was built?

Although the press made much of her profligate sexuality and gender nonconformity, commentators presented her celebrity as an indisputable matter of fact. Colette wrote very little about her own stardom, but she acknowledged the power of celebrity in *La Maison de Claudine.* In the text, a teenaged Colette accumulates all sorts of promotional trinkets and commercial keepsakes associated with famous stage performers. The most prized items in her collection, she tells her readers, were the "empty matchboxes, of a new kind at the time, decorated with the photographs of actresses whose names I was quick to memorize and to repeat without blunder: Théo, Sybil Sanderson, Van Zandt. They belonged to an unknown, enviable race, invariably dowered by nature with huge eyes, very dark lashes, hair curled in a fringe on the forehead, one bare shoulder, and the other veiled in a wisp of tulle."[92] In the next sentence, she confides that as an enchanted thirteen-year-old, she whimsically mimicked these poses in her bedroom mirror, envisioning her adolescent self in the image of her idols.

It was not only in her role as a fan but also in her relationship to the media that Colette previewed what would become commonplace elements of twentieth-century celebrity culture. Like Bernhardt before her, Colette realized early on the important role the press played in shaping public opinion. Determined to manage her own publicity, she fed reporters stories about her professional endeavors. Whether announcing an opening night or advertising the launch of an ill-fated beauty business, Colette manipulated the press to advance her professional agenda. Additionally, she sent photos of herself to magazine editors with precise instructions for captions and placement; she gave interviews to most who requested them, and she even, as coverage of her divorce from Willy illustrated, allowed the media to make the darkest details of her private life public. The media thus provided Colette another opportunity to conflate personality with personhood and to package her celebrity persona for mass consumption. A persuasive cultural broker, like future celebrities, Colette embodied and defied the values of the dominant culture; she reflected the interests and challenged the assumptions of the status quo; she embodied national aspirations; and she fueled the collective imagination. Colette achieved all of this because even as her self-produced cultural illegibility made her interesting, newsworthy, and exceptional, her quintessential Frenchness ensured that her contemporaries saw in her a woman who, at the end of the day, was *just like us.*

Colette took her last breath at 7:30 p.m. on Tuesday, August 3, 1954. After days of fever, in and out of consciousness in the insufferable late-summer heat, she had passed her last hours with Maurice and a few trusted caretakers. Having actively curated her public identity for decades, Colette left others to be its steward in her death. Believing that death "should never be something public," the woman who avoided memorial services throughout her life left no instructions for her own.[93] Fortunately, the state would intervene. At 7:00 a.m. on August 7, the republic held the first ever state-sponsored funeral for a woman. Colette's coffin was draped in the tricolor and 2,500 guests were invited to pay their respects. The streets were flooded with an additional 6,000 mourners, many of them women from both France and abroad. A reporter for *Le Figaro* observed that the crowd came not only to respect a writer's life work but also to demonstrate their "love for a woman" whom they had all lost.[94] It would be another twenty-three years before a woman's death would attract such attention. This time it would not be for "Our Colette," the quintessentially French woman, but for "Our Josephine," the adopted African American expatriate, for whom the country would mourn.

4

Josephine Baker

"A WILD SPLENDOR"

*In the short pas de deux of the savages, which came as the finale of the
Revue Nègre, there was a wild splendor and magnificent animality.*

—ANDRÉ LEVINSON

In his opening-night review of *La Revue Nègre,* renowned dance critic André Levinson celebrated the Harlem troupe's breakout star Josephine Baker. Characterizing her frenetic dancing as a "wild splendor," he described how, on one magical night in 1925, a mesmerizing African American woman, the quintessence of "African Eros," held court at the Théâtre des Champs-Élysées in Paris.[1] Her "violently shuddering body" and her "springing movements" replicated the throes of passion. According to Levinson, Baker was not merely overcome by the music's impassioned pulsating; she was the "gushing stream of rhythm" who ignited it. "It was as though the jazz, catching on the wing the vibrations of this body," he declared, "was interpreting word by word its fantastic monologue. The music is born to dance, and what a dance!"[2] Rather than follow, Baker "led" the "spellbound drummer and the fascinated saxophonist." It was she who forcefully, through the "harsh rhythm of the blues," drove the players, the music, and the audience to the point of ecstatic release.

In his commentary on the "Danse Sauvage," the final number of the revue, Levinson presented Baker as the living embodiment of hypersexualized Black womanhood. In so doing, he tapped into the broader collective fantasies of the production's audience, in which unfettered access to the sexually available Black female body signaled French racial and cultural superiority. At the same time, however, Levinson also revealed how Baker's titillating performance threatened the very hierarchies of race and gender that authorized the French-man's privilege to look. "The gyrations of this cynical yet merry mountebank, the good-natured grin on her large mouth," he noticed, "suddenly give way to visions from which good humor is entirely absent."[3] Levinson pointed out that the "good-natured grin" of the "merry mountebank" (read: docile, sub-missive woman of color) was not merely a signal of acquiescence but itself a mask, a veil that paradoxically concealed and advanced the performer's power.

He elaborated the point, moving from stereotype to Freudian analysis. Describing "Miss Baker's poses, back arched, haunches protruding, arms en-twined and uplifted in a phallic symbol," he referenced her symbolic appropri-ation of the phallus and insinuated the Black woman's challenge to white mas-culinity. He tempered her threat, however, by explaining that the "compelling potency" of Baker's pose was not simply in her metaphoric claiming of the phallus but in her ability to represent the "finest examples of Negro sculpture." Objectifying Baker in this way, literally rendering her inanimate and stripping her of the vitality that he previously admired, Levinson transformed "a gro-tesque dancing girl" into "the black Venus that haunted Baudelaire."[4] By iden-tifying her with the Black Venus, Levinson reasserted the authority of French men (himself and Baudelaire) to act as cultural arbiters, and he positioned them as important brokers in the mediation between Black bodies, Black art forms, and French audiences. Drawing on stereotypes of the racial Other and elaborating the phantasmagoric fantasies of the fragile postwar French male psyche, moreover, Levinson made Baker's Black female body legible by describ-ing her performance in a language that European audiences could understand.

This would be neither the first nor the last time that commentators com-pared Josephine Baker to the Black Venus.[5] Following her opening-night performance in *La Revue Nègre,* Baker would live and perform in France for another fifty years. Undoubtedly, the public's initial fascination with the en-tertainer, its determination to see her as the embodiment of the exotic, re-inforced Eurocentric notions in which blackness signaled a curious, and for the French, colonial Other.[6] Despite fetishizing Baker as a hypersexualized novelty, however, the French would also come to revere her as a fashionable symbol of modern womanhood, a gifted artist, a generous humanitarian, and a true daughter of the *patrie.* Unlike Colette and Bernhardt, whose racial iden-tities were somewhat easily obscured, Baker could not hide her blackness; her racial otherness was always visible, always written on the surface of her body.

What makes her the more remarkable, then, is her inimitable ability to infiltrate the very culture that regarded her as Other.

As an African American émigré and as a Black woman, Baker was literally and metaphorically a transnational figure, a cultural import whose racial hybridity challenged preconceived notions of otherness. Scholars have argued that her look and her form of dance reflected an emergent "Black aesthetic"; they have scrutinized how Europeans fetishized her body as both a source of sexual fantasy and as an anxiety-producing marker of the modern; they have illustrated the numerous ways that she both symbolized and subverted white fantasies of exotic Black womanhood; and they have explained how she took center stage in the colonial metropolis of interwar Paris.[7] She did all of these things, and yet she could never fully escape the politics of race and gender that circumscribed her celebrity. Baker understood that in both America and France simply being a Black woman in the public eye was itself a political act. Within this charged context, she fashioned a fantasy of exceptional womanhood that subverted and exploited racial difference. In the process, she exposed how two of the world's most powerful democracies perpetrated perverse injustices rooted in racial disparity.

Examining Baker's biography and her celebrity memoirs, analyzing three of her signature performances, considering her emergence as a French beauty icon, and briefly exploring her personal passion project, creating a world village for racial harmony, this chapter demonstrates how Josephine Baker, a Black woman from St. Louis, became French. Baker's celebrity, as this chapter reveals, was premised on an elision of self and Other, on making French audiences forget her differences from them, so that even as they acknowledged her otherness, she appeared *just like us.* In her fantasy of exceptional womanhood, Baker enacted Orientalist tropes, playing upon colonial desires to possess the Black female body, to reveal race and sexuality as arbitrary constructs. Through her execution of this fantasy, she not only challenged the French to see Black female bodies in new ways, but she also implored them to reconsider the national body, to reassess who was French and who was Other.

INVENTING JOSEPHINE BAKER

Whereas Sarah Bernhardt and Colette *remained* daughters of France even as they became international icons, Josephine Baker *became* a daughter of France through her global celebrity. As was the case with Bernhardt and Colette, Baker's life story produced news items and memoirs, but it also provided the material for several "farewell tours," a "Fabulous Life of Josephine Baker Revue," and even a personal museum, before becoming the subject of numerous posthumous biographies.[8] Since her death in 1975, scholars, journalists, family members, and friends have told Baker's story, relying in part upon her words, in part upon their own recollections, and in part upon a voluminous if somewhat spotty historical archive to do so.[9] Each biographical work promised to reveal the real Josephine Baker; however, they often repeated or merely nuanced the often unsubstantiated truths that Baker told about herself. Her story thus unfolds piecemeal in the memoirs she supposedly recounted to Marcel Sauvage and André Rivollet, whose works reinforced her reputation as the exotic Black Venus and in the posthumous texts authored by her one-time husband Jo Bouillon and her unofficial "son" Jean-Claude Baker, who managed her reputation for posterity.[10] Filtered through the pens and the lens of white French male authors, Baker's life stories, like Colette's and Bernhardt's, emerged at the intersection of fact and fiction. Whereas Bernhardt relied on the press to enhance her cultural visibility and Colette used autofiction to construct a culturally illegible persona, Baker authorized male storytellers to narrate her life to maintain her enigmatic unknowability.

Although she exercised limited control over producing her story, there are many facts about her life upon which her biographers agree. Josephine Baker was born Frieda J. McDonald on June 3, 1906. The plump baby girl, whom her mother, Carrie, would nickname "Tumpy," a playful spin on the children's book character Humpty Dumpty, arrived at the St. Louis Female Hospital at eleven o'clock Sunday morning. Adopted by Richard and Elvira McDonald, a formerly enslaved couple of African and Native American ancestry, Carrie was the first literate member of her family. The McDonald elders hoped Carrie might enjoy a financially secure, respectable life; however, she preferred the vibrant nightlife to the humdrum of academics and the monotony of domesticity. It was not altogether surprising, then, when the free-spirited twenty-year-old announced her unplanned pregnancy. The identity of Baker's father, like that of Bernhardt's, remains unknown. Her birth certificate hints at a mysterious figure, *Edw,* which has led to speculation that he may have been a white man. Others have suggested that he was Carrie's favorite dance partner, vaudeville drummer Eddie Carson. Whether or not Josephine ever knew the real identity of her father, throughout her life she fashioned an array of potential candidates for the role. He was, by turns, and depending upon the audience, a Washington lawyer, a Spanish dancer, a Jewish tailor, or an olive-skinned man named Eddie Moreno.[11]

Unlike Colette, who enjoyed the placid ennui of comfortable country living as a child, Baker was hired out as a scullery maid at the age of seven to supplement the family's meager income. Leaving behind her younger siblings, Richard, Margaret, and Willy Mae, she earned her room and board performing physically strenuous household chores under the supervision of temperamental white employers. Released from service, Baker contributed to the family coffers by collecting coal and scavenging for food and other valuables. Although money was scarce, she managed to scrape enough together to take her siblings to the weekly ten-cent Sunday variety shows held at the Booker T. Washington Theatre. Owned, operated, and staffed entirely by Black men and women, the Washington played movies, presented musical comedies, and included a wide array of vaudeville acts. Inspired by this new world of commercial entertainment, the young entrepreneur began performing for pennies outside the theater.[12] It was in this capacity that she met the Joneses, a family of musicians with whom she traveled the Strawberry Road circuit as a hired stagehand. Enraptured by the glamorous nightlife of Black dance halls and exposed to the thrilling promiscuity of life on the road, she grew up quickly. Ready to take command of her own life, the precocious thirteen-year-old illegally married Willie Wells, a steelworker more than ten years her senior, in December 1919.

Not long thereafter, she accompanied the traveling Black troupe the Dixie Steppers on their dance revue across the American South. Both the marriage and the tour proved short-lived, however. The disappointed teenager found herself back in St. Louis, waitressing and washing dishes at the Old Chauffeur's Club restaurant, where she attracted the attention of Clara Smith, an acclaimed singer who would become her mentor, literacy teacher, surrogate mother, and occasional paramour.[13] She even served as her protégé's booking agent, securing her a position with the renowned Russell Company as a chorus girl. Josephine's prospects improved when the Theater Owners' Booking Association (TOBA), a predominantly white-owned agency that ran the Black Vaudeville circuit, hired the company to tour the United States. "BOB RUSSELL and His 25 Hottest Coons in Dixie" played at sold-out Black venues as often as four times a day. During this tour, Josephine traveled to New Orleans, the "birth-place of Creoles," "the French and the Blacks" for the first time. New Orleans acquainted the impressionable teenager with an ethnically diverse "high soci-ety" that dazzled her, but it was Philadelphia that introduced the fifteen-year-old to a twenty-three-year-old "pretty boy with fair skin" named Billy Baker.[14]

Still legally married to Wells, she wed Billy Baker in Camden, New Jersey, on September 17, 1921. Rather than settle quietly into domestic life, however, she honed her comedic craft at the Standard in Philadelphia before being cast in the second company of Eubie Blake and Noble Sissle's musical comedy *Shuf-fle Along,* the first all-Black hit on Broadway. As the offbeat chorus girl Happy Honeysuckle, her exaggerated facial expressions, awkward knee bending, and comical eye crossing entertained the predominantly white audiences but ir-ritated many of her female castmates, who ridiculed her for her darker skin and envied her popularity. This was neither Baker's first nor her last encoun-ter with colorism. For years neighbors had commented that she looked "too light" to fit into her family. Now she appeared "too dark" for her female col-leagues. Possibly in response to these coworkers, she spent a good deal of her discretionary income purchasing cosmetics from color specialist Mrs. Lucille, whose products notoriously matched (even altered) skin tone.[15] It is unclear whether she desired to appear lighter-skinned or if she regarded darker skin as a potential impediment to her career. Whether or not she could alter her skin color, however, she could lay claim to her identity by changing her name. Consequently, it was at this point in her career that she announced, "My name is not Tumpy anymore. My name is Josephine Baker."[16]

Commentators would remark on Baker's racial ambiguity, on her ability to be both "too dark" and "too light" for the next five decades. While perform-ing as part of all-Black troupes, of course, the issue was subsumed by broader racial prejudices operating in Jim Crow America. One example of this phe-nomenon involved Baker's success in Blake and Sissle's follow-up to *Shuffle Along, In Bamville.* Featuring 125 performers, three live horses, and opulent sets, the production traveled to Rochester, Pittsburgh, Detroit, and Chicago, where one reporter opined that it was not only "too beautiful for a colored show" but that there was "too much platitudinous refinement . . . too much 'art' and not enough Africa."[17] For some white Americans, Baker and her cast-mates, whose skill and talent easily rivaled that of their white counterparts, were not Black enough. Likely aware of this line of critique, Baker petitioned to perform solo in full blackface wearing clown shoes and a "picaninny" pinafore.[18] She might have made the request to pander to white nostalgia for the Old South, to capitalize on the success of minstrel shows, to mock an audience that pigeonholed Black performers, or to make a broader political point, but she never explained her reason behind this decision. By the time the show opened on Broadway as *The Chocolate Dandies,* Baker, in her picaninny pinafore—a clowning caricature that enabled, even encouraged white spectators to laugh at Black entertainers—emerged as the audience favorite. Over its sixty-week run, the show lost money; however, it earned Baker a salary on a par with her male costars and paid for her chic brownstone on Harlem's Seventh Avenue.[19] By indulging white America's racial prejudices, by playing with and at race itself, Baker ultimately launched her solo career. In this regard, it was she who would have the last laugh.

As "Josephine Baker" made her name in New York City, the white wife of an American diplomat named Caroline Dudley Reagan began planning an all-Black revue for Paris. Enticed by the promise of a two-hundred-dollar-per-week salary, Baker, along with twenty-five singers, dancers, and musicians, sailed for Paris in September 1925.[20] Whereas *In Bamville* only registered moderate success and lost money, "Une Revue Nègre avec Josephine Baker et Louis Douglas" and "Les 8 Charleston Babies" became an overnight sensation. Rather than join the production on its European tour, Baker abandoned the troupe to sign a lucrative contract with the Folies Bergère. She was hired to headline Paul Derval's *La Folie du jour,* a production that, unlike the all-Black *Le Revue Nègre,* featured a mixed-race cast including seventeen Tiller Girls and a variety of exiled Russian dancers. In addition to performing at the Folies, Baker moonlighted at Le Jardin des Acacias in the afternoon and at the L'Abbaye de Thélème cabaret at night, working eighteen-hour days. Her efforts enabled her to purchase a home on the Champs-Elysées and to send three hundred dollars a month to her family in St. Louis.[21]

Within a few years of her arrival in Paris, the American entertainer who barely spoke a word of French was the toast of the town. Not only had she signed a profitable contract with the Folies, but she also endorsed a variety of commercial products, including the popular aperitif Pernod and her own line of Bakerfix hair pomades.[22] By December 1926, fans could purchase their very own Josephine Baker doll at the Galeries Lafayette department store and visit her nightclub, Chez Joséphine. Open twenty-four hours a day and frequented by the who's who of Paris—including Colette, who left personal notes on the club's paper doilies for her "little brown daughter"—Chez Joséphine proved as big a triumph as the woman who owned it.[23] Shortly after launching her nightclub, she performed onstage in *Un Vent de folie,* she appeared in her first motion picture *La Sirène des tropiques,* and she embarked on a twenty-five-country tour. Accompanied by "Six Baker Boys" (a white band), an assortment of assistants, two dogs, 196 pairs of shoes, sixty-four kilos of face powder, and thirty thousand publicity photos, Baker was poised to conquer the world.

Along the way, she accumulated a stable of lovers (representing various races and nationalities) before casting her lot with a savvy, multilingual Sicilian named Giuseppe Abatino Pepito. Short in stature but brimming with panache, Pepito became Baker's manager and her next husband. It was under his tutelage that the "little savage" who, according to his sister Christina Scotto, "did not know how to behave at the table" and who "ate with her hands," transformed into a cosmopolitan woman. Pepito hired a countess to give Baker lessons in diction and comportment, he taught her about books and paintings, and, to the chagrin of imperiled Parisian motorists and pedestrians, he helped her get her first driver's license at the age of twenty-one.[24] "My 'husband' was a superb manager," Baker recounted later. "He taught me how to present my calling card to embassies; how to establish good relations with the press. 'It's important to get as much publicity as possible,' he explained. 'Remember, you're the black Venus who drives men mad.'"[25]

Throughout the 1930s, Baker continued to "drive men mad" as the "Black Venus." After returning from her world tour, she headlined at the legendary Casino de Paris. On September 26, 1930, *Paris qui remue* (*Bustling Paris*), in which she played both "La Petite Tonkinoise" and an ambiguous "African" alongside a trained cheetah named Chiquita, ran for thirteen months. Not only did the production intersect the colonial exposition, but it also introduced the world to what would become her signature song, "J'ai deux amours." Trading places with established Casino star Mistinguett, who derisively referred to her as "La Négresse," Baker performed in *La Joie de Paris* in 1932, headlined at the Folies in *En Super Follies* (1937), and enjoyed a second box-office hit with *Zouzou* (1934).[26] By the time that she sailed to Tunisia in 1936 to shoot her next motion picture, *Princess Tam-Tam,* whose Pygmalion plot focused on a French novelist's efforts to transform Baker's character Alwina into a high-society princess (much as Pepito reported to have done for her), the entertainer was financially flush enough to purchase a Louis XIII–style villa.[27] Complete with romantic turrets, storybook dormers, and illuminated outdoor statues of Diana, Venus, and Ceres, Baker's Beau Chêne estate was tucked away in the bucolic western outskirts of Paris in Le Vésinet. Here she entertained Parisian elites, recounted her life story to journalists and biographers, presided over the start of the 1933 Tour de France, and, until after the Second World War, nurtured her ever-expanding ensemble of monkeys, birds, ducks, geese, pigeons, pheasants, rabbits, and turkeys.[28]

French critics praised Baker's metamorphosis from comedic chorus girl to revue superstar. They celebrated the "beautiful savage [who] has learned to discipline her instincts" and acknowledged that having "left us a *négresse,* droll and primitive, she comes back [from her world tour] a great artist." In his 1931 *Voyages et aventures de Joséphine Baker,* Sauvage points out the many ways in which countries outside the Hexagon, particularly those in eastern and central Europe, ostracized Baker for both her blackness and her sexuality. In their efforts to undermine her popularity, he maintained, European press outlets often blackened Baker's body, emphasizing the darkness of her skin in their reportage. With a few notable exceptions, the French press, by contrast, had abandoned such practices and even began to lighten her skin tone, referring to it in equally problematic terms, such as "café au lait" or "butterscotch." For Sauvage, the media's lightening of Baker, as well as its focus on her newfound elegance and poise, reflected the country's growing acceptance of her as one of their own. It also, conversely, turned Baker into a symbol—an example of the ability of French culture to civilize the racial Other.[29] In the eyes of imperialists and conservatives determined to maintain Gallic superiority, it was through this conversion that Josephine Baker first became French.

For their part, American reviewers and audiences seemed less impressed by the entertainer's transformation. Employing the same language as some of her French colleagues, American journalist Janet Flanner lamented that her "caramel-colored body . . . has become thinned, trained, almost civilized." Rather than celebrate her metamorphosis, Flanner focused on how Baker's "lovely animal visage" possessed "now a sad look, not of captivity, but of dawning intelligence."[30] Other American commentators echoed Flanner's disappointment. On her mostly unsuccessful 1935 tour of the United States, which culminated in the financially disastrous Broadway revival of the *Ziegfeld Follies,* they accused her of refining her art until there was nothing left of it, claiming that she offered her presence instead of her talent. They disparaged Baker's dancing as "only ordinary, if agile," describing her as nothing more than a typical French cabaret performer.[31] Characterizing Baker as an ordinary French cabaret performer, these writers othered Baker in a new way. Now she was not only a hyphenated American, an African American, but also French, a designation that distanced her from her patrimonial birthright and contributed to her cultural illegibility.

Black audiences, in both America and France, could be equally unsympathetic to the new Josephine Baker who "insisted on speaking only French" and who acted "like a white woman, a French white woman at that." Publicly criticized by other African Americans for looking and acting both "too white" and "too French," Baker no longer belonged to the racial community into which she was born. Feeling this slight, Baker fled Harlem to "find again my France, and my freedom."[32] Yet, the Black community in France, a constituency that initially celebrated Baker, even claiming her as one of its own in the 1920s, had also cooled on her by the 1930s.[33] In the context of emergent authoritarian regimes across Europe and political uncertainty in France, Black activists in both the colonies and the metropole amplified their demands for equality. By refusing to speak at "The French Colonial Policies" conference and distancing herself from the Black intelligentsia and the Black workers of Paris, Baker, who for so many white Frenchmen and women embodied the colonial ideal, rejected any political association with colonial men and women living in the metropole. Her unwillingness to ally with this community led the Black Parisian press to characterize her as Other; as a "negrophobe" unsympathetic to the plight of her colonial brethren. For them, her transformation marked a renunciation of her Black roots and signaled a full-on embrace of white republican ideals from which they were summarily excluded.[34]

Baker separated from Pepito after the American debacle, and in November 1937 she married her fourth husband, Jean Lion, a bourgeois, Jewish Frenchman with political ambitions. She later claimed that she married Lion because "I wanted to exchange the artificial life of a star for that of a wife and mother. I mustn't let the real things in life pass me by."[35] Although she adored her new extended family, living under the same roof with them and experiencing the "real things in life" proved tedious. The painful loss of a miscarried child finally ended her domestic fantasy, and the pair separated in 1939. In the meantime, she carried on an affair with Jean Menier, continued to work, and, like the rest of her adopted nation, prepared for war.[36]

After France declared war on Germany in September 1939, Baker, adorned in her military issue helmet and overcoat, gave outdoor concerts for Allied troops in Tunis, Libya, Tripoli, Tobruk, and Alexandria. She continued to play the Casino, toured southern Europe, and hosted a Sunday-afternoon radio show. She sent autographed photos, records, and hand-knitted scarves to men at the front, secured exit visas for Lion's family and friends, and worked with an underground network that acquired Spanish Moroccan passports for Jews fleeing eastern Europe.[37] When in Paris, she ran a homeless shelter for refugees on the rue du Chevaleret, personally ministering to the infirm and the elderly.

When the Nazis occupied the North, purging Blacks and Jews from the theater, film, and radio, Baker moved south. She requisitioned a delipidated chateau (Les Mirandes, which she would later purchase and rename Les Milandes) in the Dordogne, three hundred miles away from the capital city. She relocated to her pastoral estate with her maid Paulette, a Polish valet, an aged Belgian refugee couple, and several Lion family members.[38] Yet Baker did not sit out the war in her bucolic hideaway. When she was recruited to work with Jacques Abtey, an officer in the Deuxième Bureau of the French military intelligence service, she eagerly undertook secret missions between Portugal and Morocco, proudly proclaiming that "France made me what I am. I am prepared to give her my life."[39] Under the pretext of preparing for a South American tour, she collected intelligence by day and played to sold-out audiences at night. Using her celebrity as a cover, she hid photos and diplomatic missives, coded in invisible ink and disguised as sheet music, in her underwear. In this way, Baker became an official operative in the French Resistance.[40]

Although hospitalized for much of 1941 and all of 1942, she continued her covert activities by engaging envoys in her sickroom. As she slowly recuperated, the German-controlled press fallaciously reported that she was dying from syphilis, while Nazi-sympathizer Maurice Chevalier claimed that he found Baker, who refused to see him, "dying and penniless' in the Casablanca hospital."[41] Rumors of Baker's ill-health spread like wildfire. The *Chicago Defender* reported that she had died, and even the venerable Langston Hughes penned an obituary for her, mourning her as "a victim of Hitler." Not everyone was convinced of Baker's demise, however. When Carrie heard the news, she responded bluntly, "Tumpy ain't dead." She was right; Tumpy was not dead. In fact, as Baker reassured the *Afro-American* newspaperman Ollie Stewart, she was "much too busy to die."[42]

Released from medical care at the end of 1942, Baker resumed her wartime activities. She pawned her jewelry to purchase veal, vegetables, and coal for those in need; she gave charity concerts; she performed at benefits for the Free French forces; and she never missed an opportunity to promote the agenda of her hero Charles de Gaulle.[43] As the conflict drew to a close and the liberation of Europe was underway, Baker performed for Allied troops, even appearing at Buchenwald. Hospitalized for yet another infection, Baker was decorated with the Medal of the Resistance with rosette in her infirmary gown on October 6, 1946.[44] Years later, on August 28, 1961, attired in her beloved, though by then threadbare, military uniform, Baker received the Croix de Guerre with palm and France's highest commendation, the Légion d'Honneur. In its recognition of her service to the state, the French government officially claimed Baker, who had long been "proud to be French because this is the only place in the world where I can realize my dream," as one of its own.[45]

The war behind her, Baker returned her attention to her career and pursued a new mission: promoting global racial equality. In 1947, with her then husband Jo Bouillon, she began converting Les Milandes and its surrounds into an international tourist attraction. Here Baker would play the "universal mother" to a motley crew of orphaned children whom she would call her "rainbow tribe." Baker populated her racial utopia with twelve adopted children: Akio, Janot, Jari, Luis, Jean-Claude, Moïse, Noël, Marianne, Brahim, Koffi, Mara, and Stellina, who collectively represented eight countries and seven religions.[46] Intended to embody her particular vision of universal brotherhood, the children were transformed into costumed performers, caricatures, and stereotypes who, despite their cultural differences, lived, played, and prayed together in front of a live, paying audience.

Curious spectators flocked to the mountain retreat eager to catch sight of the music hall diva "at home" with her international family. Les Milandes received more than ten thousand guests when it opened on September 4, 1949.[47] As both a tourist destination and a fairy-tale village, for the next nineteen years, Les Milandes welcomed guests with games, refreshments, and fanfare. Patrons were invited to view the working farm and encouraged to visit her sister Margaret's pastry shop and to patronize her brother Richard's Esso station.

After a comfortable night in one of the attraction's hotels, visitors could wander through the zoo, catch a Baker performance at the winter theater, stroll through a wax museum depicting scenes from her life, and admire the estate grounds complete with a statuary group depicting "La Baker in ancient saintly wraps, arms outstretched in benediction over kneeling figures of seven kiddies of various races."[48] At Les Milandes Baker parlayed her cultural illegibility into a new vision of Frenchness that put the republic's promise of universal rights into practice for the world to see. Finally, France would have a band of brothers (notably all racially ambiguous, multiethnic immigrants) upon which to realize its cherished values of liberty and equality.

In the three decades following World War II, Baker's racial justice mission extended far beyond Les Milandes. After touring the US South with Black journalist Jeff Smith and an *Ebony* magazine photographer, posing as a "simple black woman" named Miss Brown and recording her experiences for *France-Soir,* she became more visibly active in the American civil rights movement. She paid for the funeral of Willie McGee, a Black man wrongfully convicted and executed for rape in Mississippi. She passionately defended the Trenton Six, Black men accused of killing a New Jersey shopkeeper. She canceled engagements in Atlanta after three hotels refused to lodge her, she desegregated the Miami club scene as well as the Las Vegas strip, refusing to perform if Black people were denied admission, and she demanded that Black stagehands and musicians be employed in all of her shows. She led a busing boycott in San Francisco protesting the lack of Black drivers. She launched a notorious media war against famed gossip columnist Walter Winchell, who had refused (at least from her perspective) to support her when the New York City Stork Club snubbed her. She spoke at historically Black colleges, addressed the Chicago Women's Division of the American Jewish Congress, and lectured under the auspices of Ligue Internationale Contre le Racisme et l'Antisémitisme at the national museum in Copenhagen. In the 1960s she held a benefit at Carnegie Hall with all proceeds going to the NAACP, CORE, SNCC, SCLS, and her International Children's Camp, she participated in the International Festival of Negro Arts in Dakar, and she marched on Washington alongside Martin Luther King.[49] She was, consequently, the only woman to speak at that momentous event.

Along the way she attended Queen Elizabeth's coronation, talked politics with Eva and Juan Perón, raised money for the Castro brothers, lunched with

Eleanor Roosevelt, secured a lasting friendship with Grace Kelly, then princess of Monaco, and sent letters of support to Robert Kennedy and Charles de Gaulle. She peddled her revisionist history of World War II in which de Gaulle's Free French saved the day; she defended herself against charges of anti-Semitism, pointing out that she had married a Jew and that she "fought injustice at any cost"; and she reasserted her right to criticize racial injustice in the States by misleadingly reminding Americans that she was a citizen of France and that "in our country racial problems do not exist." Determined to demonstrate that color lines, like chorus lines, were made to be broken, Baker became the first person of color elected president of the French Actors Guild, she received a lifetime membership to the NAACP, and on May 20, 1951, Harlem celebrated Josephine Baker Day.[50]

Despite her myriad accomplishments, Baker struggled to fully realize her vision of racial conciliation. She divorced Bouillon in 1961, replacing him twelve years later with Bo Brady, a wealthy homosexual, whom she married "spiritually" in a small Catholic ceremony in Mexico. The ill-suited union lasted only a year. She continued to perform, mostly to retain Les Milandes, which was in financial peril, despite battling a variety of health issues.[51] After a failed attempt to borrow money from German banks, Baker took her plight to save Les Milandes to the media, holding a press conference asking "housewives everywhere" for donations. Moved by her plight, "It Girl" Brigitte Bardot made a plea of her behalf on French television, King Hassan II of Morocco gave her property outside of Marrakesh and donated $20,000 a year for the children's care, and Sylvain Floirat, the owner of radio station Europe 1, offered to pay off her debts and to purchase the property for 146 million francs. Baker refused to sell, and she managed to hold onto the estate for four more years. By 1968, however, her luck expired. Les Milandes was put up for auction. The chateau, farm, hotels, restaurants, amusement park, and forest sold for 125 million francs, one-fifth of its assessed value. Baker stayed on at the property until she was physically forced to leave. She then moved with her sixteen-member family into a two-bedroom apartment on the rue MacMahon in Paris. Her financial situation was so dire at this point that she had to put the apartment in her friend Marie's name to escape her creditors. Later that year Princess Grace of Monaco came to her rescue, securing for her, with the assistance of the Red Cross, a four-bedroom, two-bathroom villa in Roquerbrune where Baker and her children were permitted to live in perpetuity.[52]

Suffering from a brain hemorrhage, a comatose Josephine Baker died at 5:30 a.m. on Saturday, April 12, 1975, at the Salpêtrière Hospital in Paris. Unlike previous rumors of Baker's passing, this time, Tumpy was indeed dead. Paris grieved the loss of its adopted daughter, as thousands of mourners solemnly trailed the funeral procession across the city. Followed by a bearer carrying Baker's decoration and by twenty-four flags representing all branches of the French military, Baker's casket made its way to the funeral home where a harpist played her signature song, "J'ai deux amours." A second, more private funeral took place in Monaco on April 19. Here, her children, close friends, and scores of veterans came to pay their respects before Baker was laid to rest on October 2, 1975, fifty years to the day that she first danced in Paris.[53]

Future generations would come to "know" Josephine Baker through a series of biographical works including the celebrity memoirs that she "coauthored" with Marcel Sauvage. The third in a trilogy of memoires the pair produced, *Les Mémoires de Joséphine Baker recueillis et adaptés par Marcel Sauvage* (1949) provides a collage of memory snippets, press releases, and conversations both real and imagined. A commercial vehicle designed to promote her international celebrity, Baker's investment in the project itself is unclear. She flippantly reminded Sauvage, "You may be the writer of my life, but my life belongs to me," but she also claimed not to "know anything about my book. I never wrote nor read a line of it!"[54]

The memoir opens with a twenty-page preface in which Sauvage explains his initial encounters with Baker in 1926, whom he describes as "a wild little girl, playful and charming, illuminated by a laugh with thirty-two teeth bright and solid, oily hair hurriedly, plaited on the skull." Filling more than three hundred pages and comprised of ten chapters, the book focuses on her days in Paris, her triumphant world tours, and her professional successes. Along the way, readers encounter Baker's commentary on Colette, Mistinguett, and Édith Piaf, her recipes for food and skin care concoctions, her behind-the-scenes insights into various professional projects, and numerous press-review excerpts of her performances. Collecting information over "long intervals of time," Sauvage explains that the memoir traces Baker's transformation from an unknown "American girl" who "did not yet sing and dance in . . . a belt of bananas" into a "comedienne and a Frenchwoman, universally known," a diva who "sang Schubert's Ave Maria."[55] On so doing, he perhaps inadvertently situated her within an imperialist narrative of cultural uplift and conversion.

Baker's story, as Sauvage presented it, was not a cautionary tale about the irredeemability of the Other but a testimony to the efficacy of the civilizing mission. It was, in this regard, as much about France as it was about Baker.[56]

Devoting fewer than fifteen pages to her early life in America, the memoir meticulously chronicles the outsider's love affair with cosmopolitan Paris. In the modern city of high art and good taste, Baker is amused by her own old-fashioned clothing and delighted by a place where "the houses are small, but the women's heels are very high." The popularity of the *Revue Nègre*, in which "Europeans saw [modified and became possessed by] the Charleston dance [performed] by the Negroes," convinced Baker that she shared something in common with the spectators who paid to watch her perform. "I quickly understood Paris and I love it passionately," Sauvage's Baker exclaims. "Paris adopted me on the first evening. It made me feel overwhelmed . . . loved too. . . . Paris is dancing, and I love dancing." Impressed by the "pretty women, the pretty dresses," and the "eyes full of promises," Baker instantly came to "love Paris, its movement, its noise, its mysteries, all its mysteries."[57]

Although enchanted by the modern metropolis, Baker recognized that her place in it was circumscribed by her sometimes "very painful job" as "a curiosity." When Chez Joséphine catered to *toute Paris,* she claimed a place for herself in the city where she could feel, as the name suggests, at home. At the club, Sauvage's Baker explains, "I make jokes, I caress the skulls of the gentlemen, I pull the beards of gentlemen with beards." Whether making "the big ladies dance" or enrapturing "the midnight savages, who swallow you with their eyes," she turned passive spectators into enthusiastic participants, bringing French patrons into her world.[58] Steeped in European stereotypes of the female primitive, Baker's early performances reinforced French misconceptions of the exotic Black Other. By insinuating herself first into the nightlife and then into the heart of the city through the creation of Chez Joséphine, she illustrated the centrality of the Other in the metropole and provided, for those so inclined to see it that way, a new rationale for France's *mission civilisatrice.*[59]

Whereas Sauvage's memoir ends at the height of Baker's career, Jo Bouillon's posthumous account spans the entirety of her life. Combining snippets of material found in "desk drawers crammed with folders labeled in large, bold hand, 'For the book,'" with press clippings, excerpts from a three-hundred-page rough draft of an autobiography Baker began fifteen years earlier, and scores of interviews, Bouillon examines the "woman of a hundred faces" who lived "a collection of lives in one." Rather than focus on Baker's rise to fame and the ways in which she ingratiated herself with the French early in her career, Bouillon's account explores how Baker experienced fame, especially as it related to her race. For example, although both Sauvage and Bouillon's texts acknowledge her time at the Plantation, the latter version reveals that it was here that Baker first encountered colorism: "I was gradually learning that there was discrimination between blacks as well: the darkest versus the lightest, pale skin versus black. It made me what to turn and run. Wasn't there any place in the world where color didn't matter?"[60] This experience not only shaped how she saw herself vis-à-vis other Black performers but would later inform her efforts to manifest a postracial utopia.

Bouillon's Baker also undergoes a transformative experience when she arrives in France. She learns the foreign language by using press reviews as "textbooks," she naively wears a real snake named Kiki around her neck when she hears that "snakeskin" is fashionable, and she acknowledges how she attempted to differentiate her stage persona from her offstage identity. "Since I personified the savage on the stage" in *La Revue Nègre*, she explained, "I tried to be as civilized as possible in daily life." But for the woman whose money "ran through my fingers like water" and who "needed to be constantly in motion, driving my roadster, flying my plane, running through the fields with my dogs," reconciling public expectations with personal desire did not come easily. "I was drawn, painted, sketched, caricatured, photographed, filmed. My voice was even recorded. . . . Let them call me heartless and temperamental if they like," she exclaimed. "I had decided to do as I pleased. When I was summoned to a social function to be shown off like a circus animal in fancy dress, I would glue myself to the buffet table . . . then quietly slip away."[61]

Attentive to Baker's many contradictions, Bouillon highlights the period in her career and life in which "two Josephines" coexisted. On the one hand, there was "the Josephine of the Casino who rode horseback in the Bois de Boulogne, drove a roadster, took flying lessons . . . [who] posed at Monsieur Poiret's in fancy clothes and [who] inaugurated the *Josephine Show*." On the other there was "the Josephine of Le Vésinet who fed her ducks and rabbits, caressed her cats, exercised her dogs and napped with Chiquita. The Josephine of the Casino appeared at countless functions and gave endless autographs . . . [while] the Josephine of Le Vésinet wore Peter Pan collars." Bouillon's Baker straddled public and private life, and although she adapted easily to French society, he could not resist the urge to see her as an "African goddess . . . or Egyptian queen."[62]

Aware of her own in-betweenness, Bouillon's Baker gravitated toward others who seemed to share her predicament. She disclosed a particular affinity for Colette, claiming that "I would have called her the white Negress had I dared, because of her kinky hair and natural grace. Of all the women I knew, she was the only one who seemed completely open, deeply attuned to animals and growing things, a potential soul mate. She offered to send me a copy of her book about backstage life at the Folies." Baker also felt a similar kinship with the Lion family, especially Jean's mother, whom she labeled a "warm, charming woman." "Was it because Jean was Jewish," she wondered, "that there seemed to be no family opposition to his marrying a Negro? 'Mixing blood produces fine children,' the Lions insisted."[63] That Baker felt an intimate connection with the Lion family and with Colette, figures distinguished in Bouillon's text by their racial otherness, suggests her awareness of how one's racial ambiguity marked them as Other. Despite their racial differences, however, the woman with "kinky hair," the family willing to "mix blood," and eventually Baker herself were welcomed into the family of France. In their figures, Frenchness did not require racial homogeneity inasmuch as it necessitated devotion to the republic and its values.

It was the "Josephine of the Casino," moreover, who sacrificed herself to the republic by participating in the resistance during the Second World War. Baker "drove herself mercilessly during day: writing letters to boys at front, preparing packages for them, engaging in service work, giving and attending parties to raise money." Overwhelmed with invitations to attend diplomatic functions, diligently engaged in subversive resistance activities, tending the dislocated while rubbing shoulders with dignitaries, Baker was changed by the war that brought her "face to face with herself." Until now, "her life as an entertainer had been perpetual performance. She was now immersed heart and soul in the human adventure, and it gave her days new meaning."[64]

As life slowly returned to normal in war-torn France, Baker married Bouillon and began building her "World Village" devoted to racial harmony. Admittedly the part of Baker's life in which he featured most prominently, the Les Milandes years occupy the largest part of Bouillon's text. Like his partner, Bouillon romanticized the crumbling chateau, envisioning in the "real France" of the medieval Dordogne a future society in which it would be "possible for children of different races to grow up together as brothers." According to Bouillon, from the moment Baker purchased her pastoral parcel until she lost it in 1968, every job she took, every speech she made, every controversy she roused, was aimed at achieving her dream of racial equality and funding her harmonious community. "Photographed in local dress, her arms filled w/ flowers; perched on her huge Diesel-Map tractor; in her spacious aviary surrounded by cockatoos and monkeys; on her outdoor stage; shaking hands; kissing children; washing dishes," Baker put her vision of domestic racial harmony on display for the world to see.[65]

Whether challenging Jim Crow, pledging her allegiance to de Gaulle, or commanding the Roxy in a "cloak made of sixty-six feet of satin trimmed in fifty-five pounds of pink fox and jeweled headdress" so as to be one of "only two women in the world could carry that thing off: Josephine and Cleopatra," Bouillon's Baker used her celebrity to promote her political agenda. Although the financial failure of Les Milandes crushed her, it did not dissuade her from pursuing her broader goal. "Surely the day will come when color means nothing more than skin tone," she explained not long after the court verdict, "when religion is seen uniquely as a way to speak one's soul; when birth places have the weight of a throw of the dice and all men are born free; when understanding breeds love and brotherhood." For the woman who had "come to France to forget my blackness," the erasure of racial difference was a dream deferred, not a dream forgotten.[66]

If Sauvage's memoir highlighted Baker's career to demonstrate her transformation from Other to French, Bouillon's revealed how Baker mobilized her celebrity status as a daughter of France to achieve her broader political aims. Masquerading as Baker's true-life story, these white-male-authored texts deliver only half-truths, and they are limited by their commercial purpose as celebrity memoirs. Despite these drawbacks, however, they offer some insight into how the French saw the many faces of Josephine Baker. Anything but straightforward, Baker's life story was always mediated by others, embellished by herself, and framed by ambiguities of race and nationality. At turns Baker was considered American, African American, or French. She was always Black, but she was criticized by some as too light-skinned and by others as too dark. Although technically neither Oriental nor colonial, she represented both in a limited French imaginary that constructed otherness through racialized imperial categories. At all levels, Baker scrambled the cultural registers through which the French understood race and national identity. That France would eventually claim Baker as one of its own suggests how a fantasy of exceptional womanhood rooted in racial difference and enacted through celebrity might broaden the definition of Frenchness itself. To see Baker as French required that the republic make good on its promise of universal rights and maybe even see the abstract individual as an embodied woman of color.

CLEOPATRA'S RUSE: THE BLACK FEMALE BODY AS IMPERIAL FETISH

In 1920s Paris, however, it was Baker's ability to evoke the timeless non-Western Other that initially enchanted French audiences. Whether cast as an African princess or as a colonial Creole, Baker's Black female body stoked imperialist fantasies of sexual and territorial conquest.[67] Although she was American and in no way connected to the French Empire, on the stage and in the broader French imaginary, she came to symbolize the colonial Other, whether that Other was North African, Caribbean, or Indochinese. In this way Baker, like Cleopatra, signified a repository of racial otherness, a synthetic conglomeration of cultural misappropriations and temporal dislocations that Europeans ascribed to nonwhite bodies to stabilize their own identity. Audiences read Baker as a composite figure, as a woman who belonged nowhere and everywhere, to no time and to all time. Whereas such typecasting might have impeded some entertainers, Baker flipped the imperialist script, using her celebrity to carve out a place for the racialized Other in the heart of the Hexagon. In this regard, Baker's "Danse Sauvage" in *La Revue Nègre* (1925), her "Banana Dance" in *La Folie du jour* (1926), and her ballad "J'ai deux amours," as performed in *Paris qui remue* (1930) became important vehicles through which she expressed her own fantasy of exceptional womanhood. In this fantasy, the racially ambiguous woman transformed how Black bodies might be seen by white audiences.

On *La Revue Nègre*'s opening night, it was "Josephine whose appearance filled the stage," Théâtre des Champs-Élysées director André Daven raved. Offering audiences "a glimpse of another world," she "was eroticism personified."[68] Paris correspondent for the *New Yorker* magazine Janet Flanner elaborated the scene: "She made her entry entirely nude except for a pink flamingo feather between her limbs." Balanced "upside down and doing the split on the shoulder of a black giant," her male partner Joe Alex, Baker appeared as a hypersexualized nymph, whose "magnificent dark body" proposed a "new model" of beauty as it seduced "the white masculine public in the capital of hedonism."[69] "Precisely at the moment when black is being worn again," Flanner mused, "Josephine Baker's Colored review has arrived at the Champs-Élysées Theater and the result has been unanimous. Paris has never drawn a color line. It likes blondes, brunettes, or Bakers, more now than ever."[70] Although naïve in its assertion that Paris had "never drawn a color line," Flanner's initial portrait of Baker rendered blackness a function of "fashion." Pointing out how she appealed to French fetishes as well as to French aesthetics, however, she also positioned Baker within broader Orientalist discourses in which nonwhite female bodies were designed for white male pleasure.

Baker's gyrating signified all of the erotic otherness that a performance entitled the "Danse Sauvage" would imply. However, she was not a colonial export but an American who encapsulated the modern jazz age. Transposing Old South caricatures onto contrived African jungle canvasses and mixing tom-tom drumbeats with booming percussion, brass, and horns, La Revue Nègre invited spectators into "another world." This new world, signified by musical forms that blended past and present, was not so different from the old one when filtered through the French gaze. While some spectators were disappointed to see light-skinned "American mulattos" rather than "Black Africans" onstage, others commented on the ways in which the performance mixed the primitive with the modern. Still others situated the revue within a longer history of familiar African American art forms that included the cakewalk, ragtime, and the performances of Scott Joplin and John Philip Sousa.[71] Whether French audiences imagined Black performers pejoratively as Louisiana slaves or equally problematically as West African witch doctors, they saw in their ecstatic movements a total lack of constraint, a freedom of the body, and a sexual abandon that was simultaneously threatening and exhilarating. In this way, Baker's performance reinforced deeply embedded French imperial fantasies regarding the racialized Other even as it generated new ones in which that Other was distinctly American and modern.[72]

As jazz music radiated across the city, another form of popular entertainment was reaching its apogee in Paris: the Grande Revue. The centerpiece of the interwar music hall, the Grand Revue featured opulent sets, intricately choreographed musical numbers, which were often accompanied by full orchestras and chorus lines, lavish costumes, and, of course, sensational star performers, including the *gommeuse* turned songstress Mistinguett and the comedic showman Maurice Chevalier.[73] Unlike the Folies-Bergère or the Casino de Paris, music halls that enjoyed tremendous financial success in the 1920s, some theaters struggled to make the transition from small-scale concert hall to large performance venue. This was the case for the Théâtre des Champs-Élysées, an exquisitely designed art deco auditorium that had frequently hosted Diaghilev's wildly popular Ballet Russes before the war but that had fallen on hard times after 1917. Desperate to reestablish itself, in the autumn of 1925 the Théâtre des Champs-Élysées gambled on *La Revue Nègre*. Before Baker ever stepped on stage at the Champs-Élysées, two Frenchmen doggedly concerned themselves with her introduction to Paris. Moulin Rouge producer Jacques Charles was hired to modify the "Danse Sauvage," tasked with making the number "more African" by including jungle rhythms (beating drums, tom-toms) and by stripping the performers' costumes back so that they appeared almost entirely nude. He eliminated the revue's chorus line and precision dancing, which he believed audiences would find "too pretentious and inappropriate" for Black performers who, stereotypes held, danced by instinct.[74] The spectacle transpired in a jungle setting and featured a choreography in which Baker's character morphs from a cosmopolitan American into an animal-like object of prey. These elements, designed to portray a wild Africa untouched and untampered by the civilizing hand of Western culture, reinforced French imperial fantasies of blackness.[75]

As Charles created the theatrical tableau that would introduce Baker and *La Revue Nègre* to French audiences, painter Paul Colin, an artist from Nancy, generated publicity materials for the revue. Colin's posters, which drew on and, in many ways, reproduced racist American stereotypes of Black people, exaggerated performers' features, highlighted their dark skin, enlarged their eyes, and emphasized their smiling faces with deeply reddened lips (figure 11). Portraying Baker "as a symbol of torrid, exotic black sexuality," Colin differentiated her from her male counterparts by lightening her skin tone, limiting and illuminating her clothing, and by suggestively tilting her hip.[76] As exaggerated caricatures, Colin's image of Baker and her castmates reiterated racialized Vaudeville tropes that simultaneously sexualized and infantilized Black performers.

Colin's initial impression of Baker set the tone for his future poster portrayals of her. At their first meeting, he encountered the entertainer "dressed

FIG. II. Poster by Paul Colin, *Josephine Baker and La Revue Nègre,*
Théâtre des Champs-Élysées, Paris, 1925.

in rags," describing her as "part boxing kangaroo, part rubber woman, part
female Tarzan." Once in motion, "she contorted her limbs and body, crossed
her eyes, shimmied, puffed out her cheeks, and crossed the stage on all fours,
her kinetic rear end becoming the mobile center of her outlandish maneu-
vers. Then, naked but for green feathers about her hips, her skull lacquered
black, she provoked anger and enthusiasm," he waxed. "Her quivering belly
and thighs looked like a call to lubricity, like a magical return to the mores of
the first ages."[77] Baker's "kinetic rear" and "quivering belly" mesmerized Colin,
whose prints in turn used these attributes to commodify and to hypersexual-
ize Baker's Black body. Lightening her skin and positioning her in seductive
rather than comedic poses, moreover, Colin's posters highlighted Baker's otherness from her castmates and from white French viewers. Portraying her as

less Black than her colleagues and as less white than her audience, these images highlighted her racial ambiguity and cultural hybridity—they marked her as exceptional.

Equally captivated by the performer's physical "lubricity" and blinded by their own fetishistic preoccupation with the Black female body, French audiences would, like Colin and Charles, receive Baker with a mixture of fear and fascination.[78] The prefect of Paris might threaten to shut down *La Revue Nègre,* claiming that "the color black alone does not dress one," but French theatergoers would shower Baker with applause, gifts, and love letters.[79] Baker and Douglas's somatic dance number entranced audiences, bringing them to a point of euphoric "intoxication." In the crowd on opening night, *L'Humanité* reporter Marcel Fourrier noted that, "carried away by instinct," Douglas and Baker "do not think." Rather, "the soul of dance is in them: the mystical contagion emanates from imperious rhythms which control their nerves. In truth, they are no longer in Paris, on the Champs-Élysées in front of an audience of snobs and civilized fools"; they are transported outside of place and time by the rhythmic sensations that enliven their bodies.[80] Commenting retrospectively on Baker's debut, the Black expat and Paris institution in her own right, Bricktop, recalled, "French people, who loved all that [was] chic, went out of their minds. Josephine was gorgeous ... naked or with clothes."[81]

Reception of the "Danse Sauvage" thus illustrates the contradictory ways in which the Black female body excited and unsettled French spectators. Baker's sensual manipulation of her partially nude body reinforced colonialist fantasies of the sexually available Black woman. For *Candide* correspondent Pierre de Régnier, Baker's performance jumbled categories of race and gender so much that she became a living embodiment of music itself. In his much-cited review of Baker's performance, he asked, "Is this a man? Is this a woman? Her lips are painted black, her skin is the color of a banana, her hair, already short, is stuck to her head as if made of caviar, her voice is high-pitched, she shakes continually, and her body slithers like a snake. . . . The sounds of the orchestra seem to come from her." He ponders her further asking, "Is she horrible? Is she ravishing? Is she black? Is she white? . . . Nobody knows for sure. There is no time to know. She returns as she left, quick as a one-step dance, she is not a woman, she is not a dancer, she is something extravagant and passing, just like the music."[82] Baker herself later reflected on her performance, "The first time I had to appear in front of the Paris audience . . . I had to execute a dance rather . . . savage. I came onstage and . . . a frenzy took possession of me . . . seeing nothing, not even hearing the orchestra, I danced!"[83] Mortal, goddess, Black, white, male, female, an illusion "extravagant and passing," Baker crafted her unique fantasy of exceptional womanhood not by merely epitomizing the phantasm of the exotic Other but by troubling the very assumptions that underwrote it.

Charles acknowledged this point when he assumed that French audiences would demand that revue performers appear "more African." To meet this perceived imperative, performers applied black body paint to their dark skin, and Daven's publicity for the revue promised "twenty-five Negros, in typical scenes and in their crude state." Efforts to reproduce a white, French image of African blackness onstage suggest that audiences not only desired to see a particular fantasy of the Other reflected back at them but that they also depended upon these racialized fantasies to bolster their own sense of Frenchness.[84] The jungle setting, the feathers, the drums, the semi-nude dancers (although topless dancers and ostrich feathers were a common feature in interwar Parisian music halls), even the title of the finale "Danse Sauvage," were all evoked to conjure a collective image of the untamed Other. Across the revue's ten-week run, Colin's posters increasingly darkened Baker's skin and emphasized her protruding hips and buttocks. These depictions, suggestive of both indigenous African dance forms and reminiscent of the Hottentot Venus, whose oversized sex organs transfixed European spectators in the nineteenth century, situated Baker firmly within French colonial fantasies of Black womanhood. Never mind that Baker was a light-skinned, professionally trained American artist who had not yet stepped foot on African soil; in the "Danse Sauvage" she, like Black women more broadly, embodied European fantasies of the sexually available Other.[85]

At the same time that she personified the premodern colonial Other, she also signaled a break with the past, a dislocation from the moorings of Old Europe. Pepito would later tell Baker that she was "just what people needed after the restrictions of war. They craved something wild, natural, extravagant— you . . . You represented freedom."[86] But, if Baker represented freedom to her French audiences, her own was curtailed by her inability to root herself in either time or place. On the one hand, her ability to cross national boundaries and to move seamlessly across cultural borders liberated her from the constraints of Jim Crow America and enabled her to pursue a profession that made her an international celebrity. On the other hand, because she belonged to both and to neither America nor France, to the vibrant Black communities or to the established white ones therein, like many Black performers of the age, she was perpetually trapped between worlds.[87]

Precisely because Baker appeared to belong nowhere and everywhere she represented the Other writ large to white audiences. Baker's Folies-Bergère début as the indeterminate "native girl" Fatou in *La Folie du jour* (1926), emphasizes this point (figure 12). In the production, Baker quite literally reproduced the European male fantasy of colonial conquest as her character Fatou materializes, as Colette's mummy had done for Missy's Egyptologist, in the dreams of slumbering white imperialists.[88] Costumed in a risqué belt of rubber bananas and surrounded by tom-tom drumming "natives," themselves adorned only in loincloths, Baker enacts the femme Orientale. Having come to life through the European imagination, she is first *seen* exclusively through an imperial lens that fetishizes and objectifies the Black female body. Although she emerges from the white male imagination, Baker's Fatou appropriates the act of looking herself. She enters the stage surrounded by strategically positioned mirrors that reflect, refract, fragment, and multiply her image. The audience, encountering many Bakers at one time, is confused about which image is the real Baker and which is merely her reflection.[89] Through this entrance, Baker dismantles the homogeneous European gaze, reducing it to a contrived visual effect. Itself a myth constructed to confirm and legitimize imperial systems of authority, the powerful "gaze" is exposed in this kaleidoscopic moment as a haphazard compilation of disconnected and disempowered individual looks. Through her fragmented figuration, Baker's Fatou reveals the fragility of the imperialist gaze, and she challenges its authority to construct and perpetuate stereotypes of the Other.

Through this chimera of interpolating mirrors Baker also exposes the single truth behind her staged illusion: the European's fantasy of otherness is neither real nor natural. It is simply a phantasmagoric perversion, a flimsy fiction possible only in the imperialist's dream. As Fatou, an anonymous colonial collage, and through her signature "Banana Dance," Baker exposes how power structures rooted in manufactured categories of racial difference were merely figments of the imperialist's imagination. An indeterminate racial and cultural hybrid, adorned in little more than a belt of rubber bananas, which was itself a nod to modern musical comedy and a marker of the non-Western

FIG. 12. Photograph by Walery of Josephine Baker dancing in her girdle of bananas, Paris, 1926.

exotic, Baker's Fatou embodied and subverted stereotypes of the Black Other. Through parody and masquerade, she enacted a form of cultural appropriation that upended social conventions and that suggested how race, sexuality, and gender functioned as transposable masks that individuals simply put on.[90]

Baker's most enduring visual celebrity signature, the banana skirt and the dance that accompanied it, further differentiated her from white music-hall performers and embedded her more firmly within a tradition of Black expressive forms. On the stage, Black female performers "negotiated the currencies that their bodies commanded on the world markets," Jayne Brown argues. "Their artistic efforts were multi-signifying practices of dissemblance." Objects of the white gaze, Black performers achieve autonomy first by looking at the self through the eyes of non-Black Others. In so doing, they engage in a "double operation" in which playing to expectation devolves into a satire that challenges arbitrary racial differences.[91] At a moment when Europeans regarded Black art as an elixir for the degenerative effects of war, hybrid performers like Baker, symbolized, for better and for worse, the ways in which the colonial Other was produced in and belonged to the metropole.[92]

As an amalgamation of interchangeable colonial types, Baker became a repository of French perceptions of otherness; however, as a foreigner, a modern American, who transplanted herself into the center of France and into the hearts of French audiences, she complicated a superficial narrative in which the Other was always primitive, or non-Western. When she embarked on her first world tour after *La Folie du jour* wrapped, she announced that she was leaving France to be reborn. "The Charleston, the bananas, finished," she explained, "to be worthy of Paris, I have to become an artist."[93] Baker's transformative journey abroad further negates any sense that she is in any way unmodern, unworldly, or, indeed, unworthy of the European audiences she entertains. Following her successful twenty-five-country tour, she returned to France a cosmopolitan superstar, an international celebrity, and a woman of the world.

This was the same tour, interestingly, that Sauvage celebrated as having made Baker more French. Focusing on the racial discrimination she faced in eastern and central Europe and explaining how she had to modify her performances so as to be less sexually stimulating, Sauvage suggests that Baker not only refined her style but that she also more strongly identified with a France that accepted her. Parisians would first encounter this new Baker at the Casino de Paris in the lavish Grand Revue *Paris qui remue*.[94] For *Paris qui remue*, Casino proprietors Henri Varna and Oscar Dufreene created an over-the-top extravaganza that featured a glamorously costumed Baker performing several elaborate dance numbers, some of them, especially those involving her feline costar Chiquita, reminiscent of the "Danse Sauvage." Yet in this production, Baker would not only dance, but she would also sing—in French. Vincent Scotto composed "J'ai deux amours," a ballad tailored to Baker's vocal strengths in which she extols her "two loves," her native country and Paris.

The song, which highlights Baker's in-between status, positioning her as both an insider and an outsider, would become her celebrity anthem.

In the first verse, Paris comes to Baker, as Fatou came to life, through a dream, a fantasy of the unknown. But this time, the fantasy is her own:

They say beyond the seas,	*On dit qu'au-delà des mers,*
There beneath the pale sky,	*Là-bas sous le ciel clair,*
There exists a city, an enchanted escape.	*Il existe une cité au séjour enchanté.*
And under the big black trees,	*Et sous les grands arbres noirs,*
each night, Towards it go all my hopes.	*Chaque soir, Vers elle s'en va tout mon espoir.*

Located beneath a "pale (or clear) sky" and nestled tellingly "under big *black* trees [my emphasis]," Baker's "enchanted escape beyond the seas" anticipates a promised land, where her dreams come true. Focusing not on the moment when that dream is realized but rather on the transition between worlds, "J'ai deux amours" complicates Baker's relationship to both of her loves, new and old.[95] The next verse reveals the singer's inner turmoil, her sense of dislocation, and her desire to belong:

I have two loves,	*J'ai deux amours,*
My country and Paris,	*Mon pays et Paris,*
Always by these two,	*Par eux toujours,*
My heart is delighted.	*Mon cœur est ravi.*

The lyrics here beg the question, is it better to be torn between two loves, never fully possessing one or the other, or to be fully in love with one? Whereas "Manhattan is beautiful / *Manhattan est belle,*" the tune continues and is repeated until the end, "What bewitches me, is Paris / *Ce qui m'ensorcelle, c'est Paris* / it's only Paris / *c'est Paris tout entier.*" Paris bewitches the forlorn singer, it becomes clear in the refrain, because she has not yet seen it.

To see it one day,	*Le voir un jour,*
that's my dearest wish,	*c'est mon rêve joli,*
I have two loves,	*J'ai deux amours,*
my country and Paris.	*Mon pays et Paris.*

The underlying premise of "J'ai deux amours," that Baker is torn between two worlds, rests upon a false equivalency that compares that which is known (Manhattan) to that which is imagined (Paris). In this way, Baker's relationship to self and Other replicates rather than refutes imperialist fantasies—both Baker and the imperialist romanticize the unknown. At the same time, however, the dream itself, as Baker and her audience both know, is based entirely on an untruth. Baker not only *knows* Paris, but, by this point in her career, she is a centerpiece of the city's cultural and commercial life. Was Baker a woman without a country or a woman with two countries? Was she the fantasy or was Paris? Where is the center and where is the periphery? Who is "us" and who is Other? "J'ai deux amours" asks all of these questions. Envisioned by its composer as a ballad expressing an African woman's anguish when she is forced to choose between her French colonizer and her homeland, the song, which so eloquently captured Baker's cultural hybridity, was routinely interpreted as exemplifying her position between two nationalities.[96] In many ways, "J'ai deux amours" exposed home itself as a fantasy, an imaginative manifestation, as fragile as the dreamers who contrived it.

For many the appeal of Baker's cultural hybridity was that it provided them a clean slate upon which to project their own desires and anxieties. In the context of 1920s "negrophilia" and the desire for all things new and modern, Baker's early performances ignited the sexual appetites of white men and echoed white women's demands for personal freedom. In the shadow of the Great War and amid the rise of regimes for whom political ideology intersected racist worldviews, she prophesized the decline of civilization and embodied fears of racial degeneracy. And, as France came to recognize that the value of its empire resided not only in its ability to bolster the country's reputation as an international power but also in its capacity to resuscitate an ailing republic, she encapsulated the promises and perils of the *mission civilisatrice*.[97] Her ability to signal all of this simultaneously underwrote her meteoric rise to celebrity and explained, to some extent, why she was ultimately accepted as a daughter of France. In these early performances, Baker oscillated erratically between the past and the present and, caught between two worlds, she struggled to claim her place in a rapidly changing republic. In all of these ways, the Black African American Baker resembled her white French audiences. If French imperialists sought world domination by capturing territory and asserting political authority and economic dominance over peoples living far away, then Baker conquered France from within, acquiring all of these things by penetrating the French imagination. Despite efforts to typecast her as such, she was never a colonial possession; however, by so expertly playing the role of the colonial Other, she manipulated the perverted logics of imperialism to build her own empire in France.

REVERBERATIONS

Whereas Colette's fantasy of exceptional womanhood stemmed from her privileged position among the status quo and Bernhardt's unfolded through subversive acts of dissemblance that marked her singularity, Baker's version intertwined sameness and difference in even more intricate ways. Black and foreign, Baker could never be *just like us* in the French mind; and, reductively stereotyped as the colonial Other, neither could she be completely singularized. Nevertheless, French men and women adopted Baker as one of their own, paradoxically celebrating and erasing her otherness. Rooted in racial, temporal, and geographic ambiguity and enacted through the illusion of cultural hybridity, Baker's fantasy of exceptional womanhood endlessly shuffled the categories of self and Other. As an international celebrity, a globalized woman of the world as well as a particularized Black woman, Baker upended fixed notions of identity. Baker would rely on the same tactics that permitted her to construct her universal appeal onstage to ingratiate herself with the French and, ultimately, to promote her vision of a world devoid of racial difference.

As commentators at the time and since have noted, Baker arrived in Paris at a particularly fortuitous moment.[98] In the aftermath of the Great War, she provided a beacon of light for a new, energized future in which men might be reinvigorated and women might be empowered. Men had returned from the front physically depleted, psychologically damaged, and emotionally withdrawn. While some actively resumed their prewar professions and activities, for many returning to prewar normalcy was not possible. Their jobs had been filled by noncombatants, women, and colonials during the war, while their position as head of house had eroded during their prolonged absences. Indeed, when they returned from the front, many Frenchmen found themselves at the center of a foreign world. Faced with women in the workforce, new social norms, a perceived dilution of their sexual potency, and general uncertainty about the future, they sought ways to reestablish order and to reclaim their place in French public life.[99]

At the same time that men attempted to do this, French women continued carving out new roles for themselves. The wartime economy and the demand for women to replace men serving at the front in the workforce enabled many women to earn their own wages, to live independently, and to see themselves as active participants in the nation-state. Working-class women left low-wage domestic service (especially after the unemployment benefit declined and the cost of living skyrocketed in 1916) for higher-paying jobs in the munitions, steel, and iron industries or to work in the service sector as public-transit operators, hairdressers, and sales clerks. Once women entered the university, the tertiary sector, and the factory, they desired to maintain their hard-won independence.[100]

As they gained entry in the workforce, women became publicly visible economic agents. Consequently, these changes in women's lives prompted a reassessment of French beauty standards. The curvy voluptuousness that characterized the female silhouette of the Belle Époque, Bernhardt's sinewy "S" and Colette's toned musculature, gave way to a shapeless, slender, androgynous physique. New fashions dictated a flattening of form and accompanied a masculinized aesthetic characterized by cropped hair and unisex clothing. Angular, geometric patterns, such as Elsa Schiaparelli's cubist- and, later, surrealist-inspired creations, and straight-line cuts featuring masculine accents, like Coco Chanel's unisex jersey knits, collars, and ties, and trousers for women, accentuated the modern woman's boyish frame. Whereas proponents of the new fashions maintained that they offered the freedom of movement necessary to emancipate women from both the physical constraints imposed by the old fashions and the social conventions that governed them, critics read them as a means for erasing the visual markers of sexual difference that underwrote the entire social order. Vulgar and unfeminine, they claimed, the new fashions unsexed women and indicated a rejection of maternity.[101]

In many ways, Baker's look modeled this new beauty aesthetic. Her slim, dancer's body exuded youthful vigor while her corporeal contortions mimicked the disjointed angularity popularized in modernist art forms and fashions. Moreover, by transforming her body into both a suitable mannequin for the new French fashions (Paul Poiret, renowned for his corset-less tube dresses, outfitted her throughout 1925–26) as well as into a "cubists' *art Nègre* in naked, human form," Baker's fashioned body elided racialized cultural differences.[102] If jazz was the hallmark of modernity, then the jazz dancer, an object in perpetual motion that reflected the speed as well as the rhythm of modern daily life, was, by definition, completely *à la mode.*[103]

Another way that Baker signified the modern was her adoption of the "bob" hairstyle. Although it is unclear who originated the popular look—some credited Victor Margueritte's fictional *garçonne,* some Coco Chanel, others the Parisian coiffeur Antoine Cierplikowski with its invention—women, who had started wearing shorter hair during the war, eagerly embraced the trend after it.[104] Critics argued that the style threatened the social order because it visually marked woman's loss of femininity. The cropped cut unsettled traditionalists because it confused categories of gender, making women look like men, and it obscured class differences by making it impossible to distinguish working-class women from their middle-class counterparts. Yet it also invited controversy because, fashionably worn by both white and Black women, it undermined racial distinctions. Indeed, whereas the hairstyle would have previously announced Baker's racial otherness, in the 1920s it created common ground between her and her white female audience.

As short hairstyles evolved throughout the decade, women of every class and race sought out new ways to manage them. It was in this context that Baker not only provided a model for how to wear the cropped style but that she also manufactured and successfully sold hair care products. French consumers clamored for Bakerfix pomade, which promised to retain curl, to tame wayward locks of hair by slicking them down, and (implicitly) to help the user achieve the fashionable Baker "look." Advertisements for the product appeared in women's magazines like *Vogue* and *Votre Beauté* but also in mainstream dailies like *Le Figaro* and *Le Journal.* In contrast to publicity materials generated to promote her stage performances and films, Bakerfix advertisements rarely revealed any part of Baker's body below the shoulder. Focusing on her hair (where the product would be applied) and on her face (thereby associating her image with her product), Bakerfix adverts highlighted not the dancer's raw sexuality but her fashionable beauty. In an interesting twist, Baker used hair, a feature most often evoked to highlight racial differences, especially between Black and white women, to forge a common ground among them. The popu-

FIG. 13. *Femme de France*, 1926.

larity of Bakerfix thus demonstrated how a shared gender could not only cover over but actually trump racial difference, how it could make us look just like the Other and make the Other look *just like us.*

In their zeal for her hypersexualized stage performances, French men objectified Baker as an erotic symbol of Black exoticism. In their adoption of her look and their use of her beauty products, French women envisioned her as an aspirational model of modern womanhood. In both instances, Baker's allure resided in a fantasy of exceptional womanhood rooted in the cultural illegibility of her Black female body. Men fetishized her body because it promised sex and rejuvenation; women because it insinuated freedom, modernity, and autonomy.[105] Baker capitalized on these sentiments by presenting her body as a commodity. She understood the value of her brand and worked hard to shape it across the entirety of her career. By constantly reinventing herself, appearing as the hypersexual jazz dancer one minute, the savvy fashion maven or the fun-loving girl next door the next, and altering her image as frequently as she changed costumes, she determined how audiences would see her and, by extension, how they would see Black female bodies more generally. As suggested by the full-page article "Josephine Baker: Étoile Noire" (figure 13), which, through Baker's image, visually encapsulated the femme Orientale's transformation into the ultramodern femme de France, the Black body was no longer merely a repository of otherness; it was now also a mirror of the self.

Interestingly, because so much of the scholarship regarding Baker's reception has presumed a homogeneous "French audience," scholars have overlooked a crucial difference in the ways that French women and French men *saw* her. To resolve the beauty contradictions that Baker posed, these constituencies entertained two very different fantasies of Black womanhood. Through the semi-nude feathered form shown in figure 13, French men resurrected colonial fantasies of the Black exotic to keep Baker in her place as an object and Other. French women, who envisioned Baker adorned in the latest sartorial trends, by contrast, dislodged her from those narratives and upheld her as both a fashion icon and as a symbol of modern womanhood.[106] The former response highlighted Baker's difference; the latter emphasized her sameness. Both interpretations were central to Baker's popularity. As these competing perspectives suggest, however, the star's broader cultural impact was situated in both the legacy of French colonialism and in the context of postwar desires for liberation.

As Sauvage and Pepito so astutely pointed out, the Great War had upended French social norms, and, in so doing, it created the conditions necessary for Baker's cultural invasion. The male fantasy of the sexually available Black woman acquired new meaning in a postwar world in which French male virility and national prestige had been powerfully tested. In this context, the color of Baker's skin, the frenetic motion of her dancing, and the literal staging of blackness in the constructed environment of the Grand Revue excited male viewers eager to reassert their vitality and to rejuvenate a depleted nation. At the same time, they repulsed spectators who read in Baker's body all the signs of Western degeneracy, overcivilization, and decline. The French woman's fantasy of modern womanhood was also rooted in the war experience. Baker reinforced and challenged interwar beauty standards. On the one hand, her fit, youthful body, and cropped hair exemplified a universal, modernist beauty aesthetic; on the other, her Black body signified, as her detractors were all too willing to point out, the "ugly" Other through which whiteness itself was normalized as the standard of beauty.[107]

Yet if the war experience gave the French new eyes, it was Baker who taught those eyes how to see. Portraying the primitive sex object as well as personifying the American modern on stage and screen, Baker indulged colonial fantasies by impersonating racial stereotypes. By playing these roles, however, she also exposed the fictions that underwrote them.[108] Through her self-fashioning, Baker shaped how white spectators would see blackness, otherness, womanhood, and the modern. To "see" Baker as beautiful, the French had to concede that Black, female, and American/non-European, all categories antithetical to the criteria of French identity, were no longer simply Other but also, in some way, *just like us.* For the French coming to terms with the devastating impact of the Great War, Baker's cultural illegibility, her capacity to combine, conceal, and conjoin differences of class, race, and gender, muddied an already murky republican politics premised on a universalist vision that itself attempted to obscure particularities. Baker could be all things to all people precisely because she was particular and universal, embodied and abstract, Other and self. Her chameleon-like ability to appear to play each of these roles simultaneously was the key to her popularity and the essence of her celebrity. But it was also the very thing that could challenge ingrained prejudices and broaden the identity categories through which one might envision how to become French.

If Baker redirected the French gaze, holding up a mirror to her white audience after the Great War to reflect upon its values, then her efforts to create a racial utopia in the heart of France after the Second World War asked the rest of the world to engage in the same self-appraisal. Building a multiracial, multinational family at her home Les Milandes, Baker endeavored to turn the republic's abstract universalism into a reality. Through her multiethnic family, a band of brothers (her first inclination was to adopt only boys) who would live in peace under the direction of a universal mother (Baker herself), she proposed a new optics of race. In principle, her effort echoed the lofty ideals of 1789, in which democratically elected men (brothers working together under the banner of *fraternité*) would ensure the natural and civil rights of all French citizens. Like the revolutionaries, however, Baker too encountered many unanticipated problems when she attempted to put her vision into practice. Although Baker's appeal resided in her ability to merge identity categories, she could not think of a way to create her utopia without relying on those same categories to do so. Indeed, to construct this world village she plucked children from various countries and assigned them names and religions based on their skin color and birthplace. In so doing, she relied on the same stereotyping and tokenism as those who used race and place to justify the arbitrary hierarchies of imperial power.[109]

Baker brought this world, a somewhat bizarre mixture of show business glamour, social justice activism, and domestic harmony, to life at Les Milandes. For most of her life, Baker had longed for motherhood; however, she was unable to have children. Adoption provided her the means to fulfill her maternal desire and to enact her social experiment. She organized Les Milandes in the same way that she choreographed her music-hall performances: with precision. Here, each occupant had a role to play, and each trained and costumed child was tasked with representing his or her nation of origin, religion (often assigned by Baker), and race in front of a live, paying audience. Adorned in their regional dress, taught their native languages and customs, and temporarily returned to their homelands to reinscribe them with a "richer sense of their own blood inheritance," Baker's motley entourage followed "mother's" script. As her son Jarry would later acknowledge, the family was show business, a labor not a love affair.[110]

Indeed, the children were intended to function not only as siblings bound together by a "universal" mother's love but also as political symbols, "human metaphors who could provide visual contrast to make bigger claims about humanity and roots of racism."[111] Baker's manufactured, Technicolor world of racial harmony, as well as the children's fable she authored promoting it, "La Tribu Arc-en-Ciel" (The Rainbow Tribe), advanced the notion that race could unite rather than divide humanity. In making this claim, she once again positioned herself between two worlds: on the one hand, she rejected the prejudices of Jim Crow America; on the other, she reinforced the central fiction of French republicanism in which the valence of universalism eroded difference altogether. Yet, like many of her French contemporaries, she emphasized rather than diminished the racial differences of her adopted children, suggesting that she could not fully envision a world in which race did not matter. In Baker's idealized world, as in republican France, color lines encumbered color-blindness. In this way, as in so many others, Baker proved to her French compatriots that she was *just like them.*

On November 30, 2021, Josephine Baker became the first Black woman, the third Black person, and the sixth woman ever to be entombed in France's hallowed Panthéon.[112] "Inducting Baker into the Panthéon would be a powerful symbol of national unity, of emancipation and of France's universalism," writer Laurent Kupferman, who petitioned for her induction, argued.[113] Although supportive of the idea, Baker's children refused to have her remains removed from the familial burial site in Monaco, where she lay alongside her husband Pepito's buried heart, one of her deceased children, and her friend Princess Grace. Rather than exhume her body, they permitted the government to fill a coffin with soil from the United States, France, and Monaco. It would be Baker's spirit, signified by the soil of the places she called home, if not her body, that entered the nation's venerated necropolis (figure 14).

President Emmanuel Macron presided over Baker's induction ceremony. Five months earlier, Macron defeated Marine Le Pen's xenophobic, anti-immigrant, "France First" National Front party in a particularly contentious presidential election. Tensions around French identity were thus front and center in Macron's mind as he celebrated the "courage and audacity" of "an American who found refuge in Paris and captured what it is to be French." Upholding Baker as a symbol of unity who signified "the beauty of collective destiny," the president portrayed her as an exemplar of immigrant success.[114] Baker's full integration into French society was possible, he proposed, because she did not "define herself as Black before defining herself as American or French." Baker sought to be "a free and dignified citizen," he continued. "She did not defend a certain skin color. She had a certain idea of humankind and fought for the freedom of everyone. Her cause was universalism, the unity of

FIG. 14. French president Emmanuel Macron, standing in front of the cenotaph containing soil from various places where Josephine Baker lived, presides over her induction ceremony into the Panthéon in Paris, November 30, 2021.

humanity, the equality of everyone ahead of the identity of each single person." For Macron, as for many of the ceremony's spectators, Baker was French and "France was Josephine," precisely because she personified and promoted the promises of universal equality upon which the republic built its own identity.[115] In other words, the abstract individual at the heart of French republicanism, who had for so long been configured exclusively as male, white, and native-born, could, in the guise of Josephine Baker, now also be female, Black, and foreign.

Baker's cenotaph symbolized an inclusive France, a republic whose pledge of *liberté, égalité,* and *fraternité* applied to all. However, as persistent debates around immigration policy, the strength of anti-Muslim sentiment, and particular discomfort with North African populations residing in the Hexagon make clear, a vast gulf remained between the promise of universalism and its realization. Writing for the *Nation,* Gary Younge, a Black British national who had resided in France as a student, reiterated that it was Baker's exceptionalism, especially her status as a Black American artist, that made her integration possible in the first place. Black expat artists in Paris "inhabited a liminal racial and political space in which their racial difference was embraced because the French found themselves neither familiar with nor implicated in the conditions that made their exile necessary," he explains. "Theirs was an honorary, if contingent, racial status. They were free, for example, to write about racial atrocities in America—but not to comment on colonial atrocities committed by France, either at home or abroad."[116] Baker provides an excellent case in point. Although she spoke at the March on Washington, openly criticized Jim Crow, and attempted to create her own racial utopia in response to the repressive racial politics she experienced in America, she never spoke out against de Gaulle's repression of protesters in 1968, never publicly commented on the republic's debacle in Algeria, and never criticized its treatment of immigrants. Her vision of France reverberated in the republic's view of itself; both were cloaked in the fantasy of universalism that enabled each to believe and ultimately to perpetuate the timeless myth of a color-blind France.

Manufactured through the French colonist lens as well as through her performances, Baker's racial ambiguity played on multiple registers simultaneously. By putting on the costume of the colonial Other, she reinforced French stereotypes in which people of color blended seamlessly into a hodgepodge of racial otherness that differentiated them from their white counterparts. But appropriating this generic Other was not an indicator of consent for Baker; it was a strategy through which she made herself legible and that enabled her to upend seemingly fixed notions of race. By playing the femme Orientale in its various guises, she exposed the arbitrariness of race-based identity categories and reflected back to French audiences the Black/white world that they proclaimed not to see. A truly color-blind France, a France that could see Baker as African, Caribbean, Indochinese etc., should also see her as French, as white, as *just like us.* In Baker's fantasy of exceptional womanhood, it was sameness, not difference, that made one French. In light of the recent honors bestowed upon her, it would appear that the French continue to embrace Baker as one of their own. The extent to which they have embraced the fantasy she embodied, however, remains an open question.

Conclusion

What did it mean, ultimately, to "play Cleopatra" in Third Republic France? For Sarah Bernhardt, Colette, and Josephine Baker, it meant tapping into a transhistorical fantasy of exceptional womanhood rooted in cultural illegibility. Perhaps the first famous figure to enact this fantasy, Cleopatra enlivened a supple model of exceptional womanhood that reverberated across time and that echoed in the performances of the women in this book. Playing on her own racial hybridity and gender fluidity (especially in her capacity as head of state), Cleopatra's fantasy confounded Rome and provided future women a script for subverting republican values and institutions. Incapable of reconciling her influence within the republic with her status as a foreign, African woman, her Roman adversaries and their historians relegated Cleopatra to the margins, focusing on her exceptionalism, her difference, to neutralize her political power. In so doing, however, they also inadvertently acknowledged the cultural potency of the female Other and cemented the Egyptian queen's exalted place in history. By differentiating the female Other from the status quo, male actors, as we have seen, stoked rather than diminished the fantasy of exceptional womanhood, contributing to its mythology and imbuing the "exceptional" woman with a formidable cultural authority.

Echoing the fantasy of exceptional womanhood originated by Cleopatra, Bernhardt, Colette, and Baker extended the authority of the female Other into modern France and offered it a new vehicle of expression, celebrity. For each of these women, the work of this fantasy was manifold and multifaceted. Bernhardt mobilized the fantasy of exceptional womanhood to blur fact and fiction, to defy classification, and to author a culturally relevant model of female celebrity. Colette evoked it to create her own illegibility, to uphold and to subvert norms of gender and sexuality, and to illustrate the fragility of the French family. Baker, for her part, relied upon it to transport the nonwhite female body from the periphery to the center of imperial politics, to challenge fixed notions of time and place, and to envision her dream of racial harmony. In a variety of ways, the fantasy of exceptional womanhood provided these women with a framework for reimagining the female self. It enabled them to become shape-shifters, chameleon-like figures who won public adulation by revealing that the distance between us and Other was never that very far.

At the same time that the fantasy of exceptional womanhood provided Bernhardt, Colette, and Baker a vehicle for pursuing their own agendas, it also united them in a much broader critique of republican identity politics. As fantasy echoes of Cleopatra, these performers evoked and overturned a persistent narrative of the eternal feminine. They reinforced and challenged the ideology of complementarity circumscribed by sex difference to reveal womanhood as a dynamic site of becoming. A choreographed performance rather than an inert state of being, womanhood could not be limited to a collection of anatomical parts, nor could it be reduced to a series of ascribed sex characteristics. Embodying the Other, Bernhardt, Colette, and Baker exposed the inherent fictions of pervasive stereotypes, manipulating them in ways that undermined seemingly fixed identity categories. By incessantly juxtaposing race with Frenchness, these women questioned the degree to which one could be distinguished from the other. In their persons as well as in their personas, they have complicated notions of whiteness and blackness. They managed to do this so elegantly by appearing as both the "Other" and as a woman who was inherently and authentically *just like us.*

It was in their capacities as celebrities, ultimately, as intimate strangers who exploited the contradiction of being not like us (exceptional) and *just like us,* that they challenged the abstract individual at the heart of the republic's own sacred mythology. In their figures, they particularized the abstract individual and revealed Frenchness as an ethnically heterogeneous, sexed construct. They undermined an exclusionary political ethos premised on the commensurability of the sexes and unsettled seemingly fixed biologically situated categories to nuance the story that the nation told about itself. Through their myriad performances, moreover, they glamorized exceptionalism and sanitized subversion in ways that made the fantasy of French republican belonging accessible to all people, regardless of their class, race, age, sexual orientation, or even, in the case of Josephine Baker, their nationality. Through their efforts they may not have single-handedly liberated women or fully realized the promises of a multiracial France, but they did envision a more inclusive nation, one that made room for women and people of color, and in which the promise *of liberté, égalité,* and *fraternité* might reverberate in figures who looked just like them.

As celebrities, Bernhardt, Colette, and Baker transmitted their own fantasies of exceptional womanhood and upheld a mirror to a republic whose values they deemed worthy but incomplete. As recent scholars have explained, by transforming individuals into spectacles, stereotypes, and personalities who are both singular and ubiquitous, celebrity, almost by default, confers upon otherwise ordinary individuals political and cultural capital.[1] As political actors and as cultural brokers, celebrities navigate the possible and provide aspirational models for the seemingly impossible. Precisely because they were public figures, the actions of the women featured in this book were politicized, even if they pretended, as in the case of Colette, to be themselves apolitical. Their elevated status, furthermore, empowered them to participate in state affairs and to claim their place within the nation. During three catastrophic events that punctuated the Third Republic—the Commune, the Great War, and the Second World War—these women, who could neither vote nor serve at the front, ministered to the displaced and the injured, engaged statesmen and military leaders, and acted as state agents. Whether they aligned themselves with Dreyfus or de Gaulle, supported the plight of workers or indulged the desires of libertines, Bernhardt, Colette, and Baker assumed roles of active citizenship foreclosed to most of their female contemporaries.

The female celebrity's political agency, of course, was inextricably linked to her cultural relevance. Constructed through signifiers of race, class, gender, and nationality, celebrities are more than embodied personalities; they are also themselves mythic figures who, through their ephemeral ubiquity, their uncanny ability to appear *just like us,* impact the daily lives of ordinary people.[2] Celebrities are, as Rachel Brownstein reminds us, "made up of fictions . . . images as well as actual persons" who although "remarkable for their doubleness" nevertheless manage to "seem more or less real than the rest of us."[3] As evidenced by their fabricated memoirs and press releases, Bernhardt, Colette, and Baker, who were never willing to let the truth get in the way of a good story, enchanted audiences not only through their stage performances but also through their *staged* performances. In prose as well as in practice, these celebrities were beguiling storytellers, dream weavers who magically brought fantasy into communion with reality. Constantly playing a double game that tested the limits of time and space and that blurred distinctions between the real and the fictive, they suggested alternatives for women who, through their identification with and reverence for them, might imagine new life stories for themselves.

The paradox of being both unique and *just like us* underwrote Bernhardt, Colette, and Baker's commercial success at the same time that it cemented their roles as social influencers. Entrepreneurs as well as entertainers, these women actively engaged in the process of their own commodification. Ordinary women clamored for their beauty products, books, and dolls while fans made pilgrimages to their theaters and domiciles, displayed their portraits and posters, and collected their autographs. By bringing the celebrity, via her branded product, into their homes, consumers could claim not only to possess a part of them but to participate in the fantasy that they signified. One need not sleep in a coffin, amass a menagerie of animals, or harbor a complicated relationship to one's mother to identify with her idol; she could access them vicariously through media and through the commodities associated with her. The modern fan, like the Egyptomaniacs of the early twentieth century, could pillage her tombs, reinvent her stories, and even, if it suited her, enact the same fantasies of exceptional womanhood.

In the theaters, café-concerts, and music halls of Paris, as well as in their memoirs and in the cultivation of their public personas, Bernhardt, Colette, and Baker achieved these feats by crafting enduring models of modern female celebrity. Within a burgeoning mass consumer society, they employed the stage and the media to reveal personhood itself as an act, a social construction. Role-playing enabled these women to pursue lucrative careers, to live and to love on their own terms, and to claim for themselves a place in the history of France. Awarded the country's highest commendation, the Legion of Honor, buried in its most sacred spaces (Père Lachaise for Bernhardt and Colette, the Panthéon for Baker), remembered in its history books, frequently featured in its twentieth- and twenty-first century news reportage, resurrected in biographies, works of fiction, and cinematic biopics, and commemorated on postage stamps and street names, these mesmerizing figures have woven their personal narratives into a broader national story. In the process, they have become familiar to new generations of fans, scholars, and ordinary people, who know their names if not their stories, and who unquestioningly consider them French. Throughout their long careers and even after death, these entertainers never left the public eye. In their longevity, they achieved a legendary status. As icons, they have transcended time, they have entered into myth, and they have each spawned fantasies and echoes of their own.

In this regard, these women share much in common not only with the exceptional women who preceded them but also with another select group of individuals in the republic, the immortels. Since its founding by Cardinal Richelieu in 1635, the prestigious Académie Française has charged certain intellectuals with safeguarding the integrity of the French language. For centuries, these men (remarkably few women have been inducted into this hallowed society) have acted as gatekeepers, as standard-bearers not only of the French language but also, in many ways, of the national culture. By determining the language, the very words that animate ideas, through which individuals come to know themselves and to understand Frenchness, they, too, reinforce and reflect the republic's most sacred values. They compose the lexicon through which the French communicate with one another, but they also provide the raw material, the vocabulary, necessary for authoring the national story.

Despite their important role in arbitrating the French language, however, the Académie Française immortels are not the only individuals responsible for articulating Frenchness. What if we expand the notion of the "immortel?" What happens if "immortel" not only references a handful of intellectuals but also includes celebrities like Bernhardt, Colette, and Baker who provided generations of French men and women with entirely new lexicons for self-expression? In manufacturing their cultural illegibility, these women challenged stereotypes, ideas rooted in language, divesting some words of their original meanings altogether to carve out a space for new identities. Indeed, one of the difficulties of writing about these women is that they move physically and discursively across several registers at the same time, they shuffle the categories of identity, and their words, whether in the media or in their memoirs, can never be taken at face value. Precisely because these women defy the limits of language, words alone do not adequately express the important cultural work that their fantasies of exceptional womanhood performed. To understand their contributions then, we need a new language. We need to think beyond stereotypes and categories, to problematize what we mean by words like "race," "class," "gender," "sexuality," and "Frenchness." In so doing, we better ascertain how these women became part of the conversation about the French patrimony, and we more fully understand the thorny contests, past and present, over what it means to be French.

As celebrity immortels, if not as immortels in the strict sense of the term, Bernhardt, Colette, and Baker, like Cleopatra, enjoy a perpetual afterlife. They live on in the popular imagination not only through the cultural artifacts that animated their existence but also via the dozens of female celebrities who echo them. We glimpse them, for example, in contemporary figures whose politics and personal lives, like those of the women in this book, often compete with their work onscreen, in text, and onstage for public attention. Of course, Cleopatra herself has not been lost in the cacophony of echoes generated by her cultural progeny. Over the past century she has materialized in biopics, academic papers, news items, and on the cinematic screen. Perhaps the most compelling of these iterations—Elizabeth Taylor's portrayal of her in the epic 1963 biopic or Beyoncé's incarnation of the charismatic "Foxxy Cleopatra" in the 2002 feature film *Austin Powers in Goldmember*—attest to our continued fascination with a queen whose fantasy of exceptional womanhood has stood the test of time. Like their predecessors, this new generation of celebrities is also composed of unreliable narrators, dynamic women who do the unexpected, who write in the interrogative, and who live in the transitive. Like them, they engage in subversive acts that mark them simultaneously as unruly and exceptional, extraordinary and *just like us.* And like them, they also hold up a mirror to their own societies and cultures, asking us to expand our lexicons, to think more critically about how difference shapes who we are. Only time will tell if they, like Cleopatra, Bernhardt, Colette, and Baker, will achieve immortality.

Notes

1. Datta, *Heroes and Legends* 11, 47.

2. Scott, *Fantasy of Feminist History* 48.

3. Male preoccupation with defining womanhood in the late nineteenth century emerged in a variety of texts. Markedly more sympathetic to the plight of women than most, Georges Montrogueil's *La Parisienne peinte par ells-même* (1897) and Octave Uzanne's *Parsiennes de ce temps* (1894), for example, offered encyclopedic inventories of female types. See also Menon, *Evil by Design;* and Mitchell, *Venus Noire.*

4. Menon, *Evil by Design* 3.

5. Scott, *Fantasy of Feminist History* 43, 45–46.

6. A psychically infused work of the imagination, fantasy, Scott asserts, "extracts coherence from confusion, reduces multiplicity to singularity, and . . . enables individuals and groups to give themselves histories" (Scott, *Fantasy of Feminist History* 51).

7. By making the incoherent intelligible, fantasy articulates silences, and it signals continuities often otherwise obscured.

8. Hughes-Hallett, *Cleopatra* 50–51; Bridenthal, Stuard, and Wiesner-Hanks, *Becoming Visible.*

9. A. Clark, *Desire* 27.

10. Roberts, "True Womanhood Revisited."

11. L. Clark, "Bringing Feminine Qualities in the Public Sphere" 129, 146.

12. Grout, *The Force of Beauty* 72; Berlanstein, *Daughters of Eve* 9.

13. Berlanstein, *Daughters of Eve;* Roberts, *Disruptive Acts;* J.-J. Rousseau, "Letter to Alembert on the Theater."

14. Scott, *Fantasy of Feminist History* 48, 49, 52, 53.

15. In the late nineteenth-century imperial age, France, Britain, Germany, and Italy, among other nations, restricted populations within their borders, marginalized groups based on race, religion, sexuality, and class, and, guided or misguided by their own myths of *civilisation* or *Kultur,* they colonized parts of the non-Western world.

16. Humbert in Humbert, Pantazzi, and Ziegler, *Egyptomania* 21–22, 26.

17. Meskell, "Consuming Bodies" 63.

18. Humbert, *Egyptomania* 24.

19. Meskell, "Consuming Bodies" 66; Hughes-Hallett, *Cleopatra* 203–4.

20. Carroll, *The Politics of Imperial Memory* 213–14.

21. Maier, "Is Cleopatra Black?" 68. In *Disruptive Acts,* Roberts examines the impact women deemed "not quite" had on the Third Republic.

22. Scott, *Fantasy of Feminist History* 11.

23. Conor, *The Spectacular Modern Woman* 3; Roberts, "Acting Up."

24. Berlanstein, "Historicizing and Gendering Celebrity Culture" 65–91.

25. Selections above published previously in Grout, "Celebrity Matters," *Aeon,* July 16, 2019.

26. Ferris, "The Sociology of Celebrity."

27. Braudy, "The Dream of Acceptability" 185.

28. Rojek, *Celebrity* 9; Weber, *Women and Literary Celebrity.*

29. Lilti, *The Invention of Celebrity* 7, 11.

30. Douglas and McDonnell, *Celebrity* 3, 4–5, 9; Rojek, *Celebrity* 10.

31. Berenson and Giloi, *Constructing Charisma* 1, 17; Kuhn, *The Media in France* 18–20; Rojek, *Celebrity* 1.

32. Rojek, *Celebrity* 103.

33. Douglas and McDonnell, *Celebrity* 78–80. In 1839 Louis Daguerre exhibited the photographic process, and over the next decade daguerreotype galleries emerged in Paris and London. By 1849, Gaspard-Félix Tournachon, or Nadar, used this technology to create a template for staging celebrity (Rojek, *Celebrity* 125).

34. Berenson and Giloi, *Constructing Charisma* 2; Datta, *Heroes and Legends* 20–29.

35. Berenson and Giloi, *Constructing Charisma* 2; Douglas and McDonnell, *Celebrity* 75; Garval, *Cléo de Mérode* 5.

36. Douglas and McDonnell, *Celebrity* 18; Garval, *Cléo de Mérode* 4; Rojek, *Celebrity* 120.

37. Douglas and McDonnell, *Celebrity* 88.

38. Redmond and Holmes, *Stardom and Celebrity,* 257; Holmes and Redmond, "A Journal in Celebrity Studies" 4, 7.

39. Richard Dyer argues that celebrities enable "access to political matters of class, gender, race, and sexuality that underline the dominant ideology of that society at the time" (Dyer cited in Redmond and Holmes, *Stardom and Celebrity* 258).

40. In his canonical text, Dyer identified the star's uncanny ability to be special and ordinary simultaneously as the central contradiction of celebrity. Dyer, *Stars* 43.

41. Berlanstein, "Historicizing and Gendering Celebrity Culture" 67–68.

42. Gaffney and Holmes, *Stardom in Postwar France* 1.

43. Poet André Rivollet coauthored Baker's other autobiography from the early period in her career, *Une Vie de toutes les couleurs,* with André Rivollet, 1927 and 1935. Sauvage's 1949 memoir was a culmination of twenty years of interviews and was based on two earlier editions.

44. Popkin, *History, Historians, and Autobiography.* Scholars working in media studies and in the relatively nascent fields of celebrity and persona studies have more recently turned their attention to these sources (see Bennett, "Approaching Celebrity Studies"; Lee, "Reading Celebrity Autobiographies"; and Marshall, Moore, and Barbour, "Persona as Method").

45. Popkin, *History, Historians, and Autobiography* 11, 26, 34; Eakin, *Fictions in Autobiography* 3.

46. Banet-Weiser, "Am I Pretty or Ugly?" 83–101.

47. Lee, "Reading Celebrity Autobiographies" 87–89.

48. Eakin, *Fictions in Autobiography* 3; Popkin, *History, Historians, and Autobiography* 22, 13, 27; Smith and Watson, *Reading Autobiography* 10, 12–13; Marshall, Moore, and Barbour, "Persona as Method."

49. Lengthy excerpts from this section have appeared in print before in Grout, "Authorizing Fictions"; Grout, "Celebrity Matters"; and Grout, "European Celebrity in Historical Perspective."

50. Lacour, "Cléopâtre"; Menon, *Evil by Design* 261, 325n110.

51. Certeau, *The Writing of History* 303.

1. CLEOPATRA: A "MOST WOMANLY WOMAN"

1. Hughes-Hallett, *Cleopatra* 203–8; Humbert, Pantazzi, and Ziegler, *Egyptomania* 22; Meskell, "Consuming Bodies" 63–64.

2. "As a woman, as an Oriental," Lucy Hughes-Hallett explains, Cleopatra "offers strangeness and the inscrutable vacancy of imagined space" (Hughes-Hallett, *Cleopatra* 203).

3. Said, *Orientalism* 2.

4. More than a mere "airy European fantasy about the Orient," moreover, Orientalism has, Said argues, "created a body of theory and practice in which, for many generations, there has been a considerable material investment" (Said, *Orientalism* 3, 4, 6).

5. Lewis, *Gendering Orientalism* 16.

6. Lewis, *Gendering Orientalism* 20.

7. The Ptolemaic dynasty's legitimacy rested on its association with Alexander the Great. Egyptians considered Cleopatra VII as a Macedonian—Greek, not Egyptian (Schiff, *Cleopatra: A Life* 21).

8. Roller, *Cleopatra: A Biography* 2, 3, 15; see also Jones, *Cleopatra: A Sourcebook.*

9. Hughes-Hallett, *Cleopatra* 72; Roller, *Cleopatra: A Biography* 1, 3, 45, 46, 72; Schiff, *Cleopatra: A Life* 4–8.

10. Schiff, *Cleopatra: A Life* 25–26.

11. Roller, *Cleopatra: A Biography* 82, 92, 95, 105–10.

12. Roller, *Cleopatra: A Biography* 2, 5, 69.

13. Hughes-Hallett, *Cleopatra* 14; Roller, *Cleopatra: A Biography* 70.

14. Roller, *Cleopatra: A Biography* 5, 70, 82.

15. Hughes-Hallett, *Cleopatra* 14, 90.

16. Roller, *Cleopatra: A Biography* 114, 115, 117. Consequently, Cleopatra also met Antony for the first time on her vessel *Isis*. The crown of cobras was also worn by Cleopatra's predecessor Arsinoe II, with whom she frequently aligned herself to evoke Egyptian identity.

17. Hughes-Hallett, *Cleopatra* 74, 77.

18. Roller, *Cleopatra: A Biography* 100, 154.

19. For more on Cleopatra as myth, see Mann, *Joseph in Egypt;* and Pucci, "Every Man's Cleopatra."

20. Hughes-Hallett, *Cleopatra* 38–39, 45, 57, 59. "The Cleopatra of the Octavian story unmanned Antony by a dual strategy," Lucy Hughes-Hallett explains. "Not only did she refuse to

play a properly feminine role, thereby denying him the right to act the man; she also seduced him, drawing him into the realm of the sensual and sexual pleasure which was perceived as being essentially gynocratic."

21. Cited in Jones, *Cleopatra: A Sourcebook* 33–34.

22. Jones, *Cleopatra: A Sourcebook* 33–34, 105.

23. Roller, *Cleopatra: A Biography* 131.

24. Ziegler, "Cleopatra or the Seductions of the East" 554.

25. Horace, "Cleopatra Ode"; Roller, *Cleopatra: A Biography* 130, 132.

26. The exact date for this text is unknown. It is likely from the early second century.

27. Jones, *Cleopatra: A Sourcebook* 105; Roller, *Cleopatra: A Biography,*131.

28. Boccaccio, *De Claris mulieribus/On Famous Women* 192–98.

29. Hughes-Hallett, *Cleopatra* 2.

30. Hughes-Hallett, *Cleopatra* 113–14; Jones, *Cleopatra: A Sourcebook* 207.

31. The play first appeared in print in the 1623 Folio.

32. The version of the play cited and referenced throughout this section is William Shakespeare, *Antony and Cleopatra,* ed. Mowat and Werstine, Folger Shakespeare Library.

33. Hughes-Hallett, *Cleopatra* 1, 150–51, 156. In his *Notes on Antony and Cleopatra* (1819), Samuel Taylor Coleridge cast Cleopatra as both a criminal and a femme fatale.

34. Shakespeare, *Antony and Cleopatra* 1.1.2–6; 1.5.32–34.

35. Recent controversy over the Netflix film featuring a Black Cleopatra demonstrates the centrality of the queen's racial ambiguity to her identity (see Bethonie Butler, "Was Cleopatra Black?," *Washington Post,* May 12, 2023; "Egyptians and Others Are Upset a Black Actress Stars in Netflix's 'Queen Cleopatra,'" National Public Radio, May 11, 2023; and Gwen Nally and Mary Hamil Gilbert, "Fear of a Black Cleopatra," *New York Times,* May 10, 2023).

36. MacDonald, "Sex, Race, and Empire" 63, 65, 69.

37. MacDonald, "Sex, Race, and Empire" 70.

38. Shakespeare, *Antony and Cleopatra* 2.5.22–27.

39. Pucci, "Every Man's Cleopatra" 196.

40. Jones, *Cleopatra: A Sourcebook* xiv–xv.

41. Hughes-Hallett, *Cleopatra* 1, 170.

42. The two versions of the story authored by women during the period, Sarah Fielding's, *The Lives of Cleopatra and Octavia* (1757) and Charlotte Brontë's *Villette* (1853), offer a more sympathetic rendering of the queen (Jones, *Cleopatra: A Sourcebook* 247).

43. Osmond, "'Her Infinite Variety.'" For a wider discussion linking *Antony and Cleopatra* to the British Empire, see Little, *Shakespeare Jungle Fever;* and McCombe, "Cleopatra and Her Problems." Similar themes appeared in nineteenth-century French productions of the play; more on those below.

44. Royster, *Becoming Cleopatra* 48. Royster explains that while the historical sources Shakespeare drew upon most likely portrayed Cleopatra as Macedonian and white, he figured "her as black-skinned, the product of a monstrously strong sun."

45. Little, *Shakespeare Jungle Fever* 163. Little contends, "Whether racialized as white or black[,] Cleopatra, from the days of Augustan propaganda through today, sports a body of hybrid-

ity. Whether white or black[,] Cleopatra finds herself the object of racial passing" (Little, *Shakespeare Jungle Fever* 24).

46. Little, *Shakespeare Jungle Fever* 167; Royster, *Becoming Cleopatra* 20.

47. Little, *Shakespeare Jungle Fever* 103–4.

48. Hughes-Hallett, *Cleopatra* 143, 208.

49. Royster, *Becoming Cleopatra* 34.

50. Between 1859 and 1866 François-Victor Hugo published his fifteen-volume translation of Shakespeare's complete works. Considered the most accurate translation of the original texts, Hugo's translations circulated widely under the Third Republic. Other examples of fictional works beyond France include Alexander Pushkin's *Egyptian Nights* (1825), a novel in which Cleopatra prostitutes herself, and George Bernard Shaw's *Caesar and Cleopatra* (1898), a play that strips the queen of her sexual power altogether by infantilizing her. Egyptian themes were a mainstay of English literature and visual arts across the nineteenth century. Keats, Shelley, and Byron were all captivated by the distant country, and historical novels about her appeared with some frequency after the annex of Egypt as a British protectorate in 1882. J. M. W. Turner, John Martin, David Roberts, and Benjamin Haydon painted Egyptian capriccios (works based on studies of artifacts, archives, and the *Description de l'Égypte*), and Carl Haag and John Frederick Lewis painted scenes of Egyptian daily life. Perhaps the most popular artist to focus on Egypt was the Dutch-born Lawrence Alma-Tadema, who settled in England. Alma-Tadema devoted twenty-six works to the country and completed a series of Cleopatra portraits from 1859 to 1883 (M. M. D. Smith, "HRH Cleopatra" 151, 154–55, 157).

51. Dykstra, "The French Occupation of Egypt, 1798–1801."

52. Jones, *Cleopatra: A Sourcebook* 255. For example, after discovery of the Rosetta Stone in the 1820s, Jean-Françoise Champollion led another excursion into Egypt to collect more hieroglyphic inscriptions (Miles, "Cleopatra in Egypt" 7).

53. Carroll, *The Politics of Imperial Memory* 16.

54. M. M. D. Smith, "HRH Cleopatra" 151.

55. Humbert, Pantazzi, and Ziegler, *Egyptomania* 21; Wyke and Montserrat, "Glamour Girls."

56. Flaubert, *Flaubert in Egypt* 35.

57. Lojo Tizón, "Le Mythe de Cléopâtre."

58. Perhaps some better-known examples include Gérôme's *The Dance of the Almeh* (1863); Moreau's *Salomé* (1876); and Eugène Delacroix's, *The Massacre at Chios* (1824).

59. Royster, *Becoming Cleopatra* 60.

60. Hughes-Hallett, *Cleopatra* 208.

61. Kent, "Nude Bodies."

62. Pina Polo, "The Great Seducer" 178. The painting was originally commissioned by the French courtesan La Païva, who returned it, unsatisfied. Gérôme exhibited the painting in 1871 at the Royal Academy of Arts.

63. Meskell, "Consuming Bodies" 66.

64. Datta, *Heroes and Legends*; Lowe, *Critical Terrains* 76, 93.

65. Hughes-Hallett, *Cleopatra* 201, 204.

66. Burlesque shows featuring Cleopatra proliferated in England: James Draper's *Antony &*

Cleopatra: A Classical, Historical, Musical, Mock-Tragical Burlesque and Cowley Burnand's *Antony and Cleopatra, or, His-tory and Her-story in a Modern Nilo-metre* provide two examples (Wyke and Montserrat, "Glamour Girls" 174).

67. Hughes-Hallett, *Cleopatra* 262; Humbert, Pantazzi, and Ziegler, *Egyptomania* 508.

68. Bellow, "Fashioning Cléopâtre" 7–8.

69. Salomé, the biblical vixen who demanded the head of John the Baptist, was one of the most prominent figures on European stages at the fin de siècle. The Old Testament embodiment of the Eastern femme fatale, like Cleopatra, she provided a shorthand for masculine anxiety at the turn of the twentieth century. This had much to do with Oscar Wilde's play devoted to her, a part he wrote for Sarah Bernhardt. A rich and robust scholarship, one far too vast and beyond the scope of this project to engage here, examines the ways in which Salomé represented and subverted fin-de-siècle anxieties through her performance of the exotic Other (Cucullu, "Wilde and Wilder Salomés"; Dierkes-Thrun, *Salomé's Modernity;* Freedman, "Transformations of a Jewish Princess"; Gilman, "Salomé, Syphilis, Sarah Bernhardt").

70. Osmond, "'Her Infinite Variety'" 56.

71. Koda and Bolton, "Paul Poiret (1879–1944)."

72. Bellow, "Fashioning Cléopâtre" 8, 15, 34.

73. Maclatchie, "Foreign Fantasies" 3.

74. Humbert, Pantazzi, and Ziegler, *Egyptomania* 509.

75. Elliot, "Art Deco Worlds in a Tomb" 124; Humbert, Pantazzi, and Ziegler, *Egyptomania* 509.

76. Maier, "Is Cleopatra Black?" 1.

77. De Grazia, "Mass Culture and Sovereignty" 53–87, 57, 63.

78. Osmond, "'Her Infinite Variety'" 55, 56.

79. Wyke and Montserrat, "Glamour Girls" 178, 180–81.

80. Despite introducing two-color Technicolor, the 1928 silent MGM short featuring Dorothy Revier has been largely overshadowed by Colbert and Taylor's box office smashes.

81. Wyke and Montserrat, "Glamour Girls" 181–82.

82. Maier, "Is Cleopatra Black?" 3, 8, 13, 15.

83. Hall and Neale, *Epics, Spectacles, and Blockbusters* 166.

84. E. Lacey Rice, "Cleopatra (1963)." Turner Classic Movies archive.

85. On masquerade and the femme fatale, see Osmond, "'Her Infinite Variety'" 59.

86. Wyke and Montserrat, "Glamour Girls" 173.

87. Hughes-Hallett, *Cleopatra* 279; Royster. *Becoming Cleopatra* 97, 114.

88. Jones, *Cleopatra: A Sourcebook* xiv–xv.

89. Hughes-Hallett, *Cleopatra* 1.

2. SARAH BERNHARDT: "INCREDIBLE MIRAGE!"

1. Adler, "The Unlacing of Cleopatra" 462.

2. Hamer, *Signs of Cleopatra;* Hughes-Hallett, *Cleopatra;* Roberts, *Disruptive Acts.*

3. Berlanstein, *Daughters of Eve* 20. Berlanstein counts no fewer than 360 café-concerts.

4. Berlanstein, *Daughters of Eve;* Glenn, *Female Spectacle* 6–7.

5. Berlanstein, *Daughters of Eve* 18; Roberts, *Disruptive Acts* 12.

6. "Masculin et féminin"; Rostand, *Sarah Bernhardt,* 94. Rostand identifies two Sarahs: "Il y avait deux êtres en Sarah: un être extraordinairement viril et un être extrêmement féminin, et elle était en somme le couple réuni."

7. This is the full name entered on her baptismal certificate.

8. After her baptism in 1857, Bernhardt chose to go by "Sarah" rather than "Rosine." Some scholars speculate that she did so "to retain a prominent sign of her Jewishness" (Bergman-Carton, "Negotiating the Categories" 59).

9. Gold and Fizdale, *The Divine Sarah;* Gottlieb, *Sarah.*

10. Duckett, "The Actress-Manager and the Movies."

11. Gottlieb, *Sarah* 75, 80, 110, 112–15, 120, 168, 171.

12. Roberts, *Disruptive Acts* 167.

13. Roberts, *Disruptive Acts* 212.

14. Bernhardt, *My Double Life,* trans. Tietze Larson, 1999. I have consulted both the French- and English-language versions of this text. I cite the English version because the translations accurately and fluidly convey the meanings within the original.

15. Bernhardt, *My Double Life* 49, 56–59, 69.

16. Bernhardt, *My Double Life* 176.

17. Bernhardt, *My Double Life* 183–84.

18. Bernhardt, *My Double Life* 109–17, 117–25, 129–33; 157. Bernhardt's efforts during the war were reported as well in the contemporary press (*The Week's News,* June 14, 1879: 757).

19. Bernhardt, *My Double Life* 256.

20. Bernhardt, *My Double Life* 181.

21. Gottlieb, *Sarah* 156.

22. Bernhardt, *My Double Life* 221.

23. Bernhardt, *My Double Life* 89.

24. Bernhardt, *My Double Life* 199. Bernhardt's debut in Victor Hugo's much-anticipated revival of "Ruy Blas," in February 1872, marked the return of the playwright from exile but also elevated Bernhardt's status (Gold and Fizdale, *The Divine Sarah* 92–94).

25. Bernhardt, *My Double Life* 217–18; Gold and Fizdale, *The Divine Sarah* 146–47. Becoming a prestigious sociétaire made Bernhardt a lifetime partner at the Comédie and guaranteed her a pension in retirement.

26. Bernhardt, *My Double Life* 158, 163.

27. Bernhardt, *My Double Life* 195.

28. Bernhardt, *My Double Life* 195–96.

29. Bernhardt, *My Double Life* 226.

30. Mesch, "A Belle Epoque Media Storm" 117.

31. Mesch, "A Belle Epoque Media Storm" 116–17; Berlanstein, *Daughters of Eve* 238.

32. She also contradicts this claim outright: "I had fancied, and up to this performance of *Zaïre* I had always heard and read in the papers that my voice was pretty, but weak; that my gestures were gracious, but vague; that my supple movements lacked authority, and that my glance lost in heavenward contemplation could not tame the wild beasts (the audience). I thought then of all that" (Bernhardt, *My Double Life* 182).

33. Bernhardt, *My Double Life* 174–75.

34. Roberts, *Disruptive Acts* 203, 204, 207.

35. Although Colombier was convicted for publishing obscene material, for which she was imprisoned for three months and fined three thousand francs, the book was an instant bestseller. Bernhardt also sued Colombier for libel and defamation, which likely increased sales and kept the scandal in the media.

36. Colombier, *The Memoirs of Sarah Barnum* 33, 36, 39, 67, 91, 94.

37. Colombier, *The Memoirs of Sarah Barnum* 37, 73.

38. Colombier, *The Memoirs of Sarah Barnum* 3, 7, 29, 153, 144.

39. Cited in Gottlieb, *Sarah* 153.

40. Bergman-Carton, "Negotiating the Categories" 55; Roberts, *Disruptive Acts* 207.

41. Duckett, "The Actress-Manager and the Movies" 45–47.

42. In Greek and Roman mythology, the Lernaean Hydra was a serpentine water monster believed to provide entrance into the underworld. Characterized by poisonous breath, a deadly scent, and regenerative heads (one which was immortal), the hydra is ultimately killed by Hercules and transformed into the constellation Cancer.

43. Roberts, *Disruptive Acts* 170.

44. Lesueur, "Prêtresse de la Beauté" 1.

45. Émile Moreau is accredited with coauthoring the play with Sardou. Bernhardt won critical acclaim six years earlier in Sardou's popular *Théodora*.

46. Sardou, *Cleopatra* 17.

47. Sardou, *Cleopatra* 18, 26.

48. Although I could not find evidence in promotional materials or reviews confirming the identity of the performers who played the "Nubian slaves," it is unlikely that they were portrayed by performers of African descent. Black performers were rare on the Paris stage generally, but even more so in the theater, which still drew actors primarily from the prestigious conservatoire. Rafael Padilla, "Chocolat," who would become one of the most notable Black performers in Third Republic France, had only recently infiltrated the French circus and vaudeville circuit in 1888.

49. Maier, "Is Cleopatra Black?" 12.

50. *Nation,* November 20, 1890.

51. *St. James Gazette,* October 9, 1860: 15. Published between 1880 and 1905, the conservative *St. James Gazette* and its first editor, Frederick Greenwood, endorsed Britain's occupation of Egypt in 1882.

52. *St. James Gazette,* October 16, 1860: 5.

53. Sardou, *Cleopatra* 36.

54. Sardou, *Cleopatra* 36, 37.

55. "Sarah Bernhardt in 'Cleopatra'" 2.

56. Bauer, "Cléopâtre."

57. Sardou, *Cleopatra* 41.

58. Sardou, *Cleopatra* 52, 53.

59. Sardou, *Cleopatra* 82, 92, 98.

60. *Le Figaro,* October 24, 1890.

61. Sardou, *Cleopatra* 113.

62. Sardou, *Cleopatra* 131, 133.

63. Sardou, *Cleopatra* 155, 158, 165.

64. *Nation,* November 20, 1890.

65. Menon, *Evil by Design* 261.

66. Gottlieb, *Sarah* 180; McPherson, "Sarah Bernhardt: Portrait of the Actress" 415.

67. Ockman, "Was She Magnificent?" 35–36.

68. *Black and White,* June 4, 1892.

69. Augustin-Thierry, "The Theater."

70. Augustin-Thierry, "The Theater," 316.

71. *Black and White,* June 4, 1892.

72. Bauer, "Sarah Bernhardt."

73. *Le Figaro,* October 24, 1890.

74. Séverine, "Sarah" 1.

75. *Le Figaro,* October 24, 1890.

76. Quoted in Roberts, *Disruptive Acts* 219.

77. Hughes-Hallett, *Cleopatra* 113.

78. Scott, *Fantasy of Feminist History* 48.

79. *Le Figaro,* October 24, 1890.

80. Claretie, *Histoire de la littérature française* 602.

81. James, "The Comédie-Française."

82. Braudy, *The Frenzy of Renown;* Berenson and Giloi, *Constructing Charisma* 6–7; Evans and Hesmondhalgh, *Understanding Media* 4; Redmond and Holmes, *Stardom and Celebrity* 98.

83. McPherson, "Sarah Bernhardt: Portrait of the Actress" 410. Rachel M. Brownstein identifies "doubling" as a central characteristic of stardom: "Stars are remarkable for doubleness above all; perhaps they represent doubleness. They seem to be both singular and reminiscent, simultaneously false and true. As such they reflect, reveal, and focus a problem that has preoccupied Western culture for at least two hundred years: the shape and depth of individual character, the outlines of the integral, coherent self, the relation between the substance of a self—sometimes called character—and appearances, self-presentations, temporary social roles" (Brownstein, *Tragic Muse* ix).

84. Glenn, *Female Spectacle* 11, 12.

85. Glenn, *Female Spectacle* 27–29, 34–35.

86. Artists Jules Chéret, Alphonse Mucha, and Georges Clairin and photographers Nadar and Napoleon Sarony, perhaps the most well-known among them.

87. McPherson, "Sarah Bernhardt: Portrait of the Actress" 409–10, 425, 426.

88. Glenn, *Female Spectacle* 29; Roberts, *Disruptive Acts* 198.

89. Bernhardt, *The Art of the Theater* 99, 141, 166, 201, 203.

90. Bernhardt, *The Art of the Theater* 201, 101.

91. Marcus, "Sarah Bernhardt's Exteriority Effects" 298–301, 308–10, 310–12.

92. Brunotte, "All Jews Are Womanly" 207.

93. Bergman-Carton explains that although Jews played prominent roles in French commerce, industry, politics, and intellectual life, the Jewish population hovered around only 75,000 in the Third Republic (Bergman-Carton, "Negotiating the Categories" 57).

94. Bergman-Carton, "Negotiating the Categories" 57; Garb, "Modernity, Identity, Textuality" 20, 22, 23.

95. Brunotte, Ludewig, and Stähler, *Orientalism, Gender and the Jews* 5; Ludewig, "Between Orientalization and Self-Orientalization" 221, 223; Garb, "Modernity, Identity, Textuality" 26; Ellenzweig, "Sarah Bernhardt at the Jewish Museum" 29.

96. Brunotte, Ludewig, and Stähler, *Orientalism, Gender and the Jews* 11, 15; Bergman-Carton, "Negotiating the Categories" 57.

97. Bergman-Carton, "Negotiating the Categories" 58, 60.

98. Ockman, "Was She Magnificent?" 121, 124, 139.

99. Bergman-Carton, "Negotiating the Categories" 58.

100. Garb, "Modernity, Identity, Textuality" 27; Lathers, "Posing the 'Belle Juive'" 27.

101. Brunotte, "All Jews Are Womanly" 201; Pellegrini, "Sarah Bernhardt, Live" 43; Roberts, *Disruptive Acts* 115.

102. London *Times*, March 28, 1923.

103. Gottlieb, *Sarah* 208–10.

104. Roberts, *Disruptive Acts* 226.

105. Fair, "Bernhardt" 6.

106. Rostand, *Sarah Bernhardt* 111–12.

107. Gottlieb, *Sarah* 204.

108. de Flers, "À Sarah Bernhardt."

109. Berlanstein, *Daughters of Eve* 31.

110. Berlanstein, *Daughters of Eve* 171, 177, 209, 219.

111. McPherson, "Sarah Bernhardt" 412, 415, 434.

3. COLETTE: "AUDACIOUS SHAMELESSNESS"

1. Pascal, *L'Éclair de Montpellier*, January 7, 1907.

2. Colette made her professional debut at the Théâtre des Mathurins on February 6, 1906, playing the lead in *L'Amour, le desir, la chimère*, a pantomime by Francis de Croisset and Jean Nougués (Thurman, *Secrets of the Flesh* 166).

3. Thurman, *Secrets of the Flesh* 198, 203–6, 360.

4. Thurman, *Secrets of the Flesh* 24, 28.

5. Thurman, *Secrets of the Flesh* 42, 45.

6. Thurman, *Secrets of the Flesh* 59, 68, 71, 106. In addition to selling Claudine collars, lotion, ice cream, hats, cigarettes, perfume, candies, photo paper, and rice powder, Willy and Colette adapted the novels for the stage, and a costumed Colette and Polaire (the Algerian-born actress who portrayed Claudine onstage) paraded around Paris.

7. *Lettres de la vagabonde*, ed. Pichois and Forbin, 94.

8. In the five years following the war, she authored *Mitsou* (1919), *Chéri* (1920), *La Maison de Claudine* (1922), *l'Autre femme* (1922), and *Le Blé herbe* (1923).

9. Walker, *Outrage and Insight*; Bonal and Maget, *Colette Journaliste*.

10. Thurman, *Secrets of the Flesh* 350, 371.

11. In a journal from April 1943, friend Renée Hamon writes, "Colette is a born anti-Semite, especially toward Jewish women" (Bibliothèque Nationale: Dossier Renée Hammond, 210).

12. Thurman, *Secrets of the Flesh* 415.

13. Grout, *The Force of Beauty* 110–11.

14. Thurman, *Secrets of the Flesh* 437.

15. Thurman, *Secrets of the Flesh* 436–37, 443.

16. Flieger, *Colette and the Fantom Subject* 4–5.

17. Colette, *Break of Day* 33; Flieger, *Colette and the Fantom Subject* 6, 7, 10–11, 183. I have read these texts in both their original French publication format and in English translation. Rather than translate the selections, I have relied upon Una Vicenzo Troubridge and Enid McLeod's *"My Mother's House" and "Sido"* (New York: Farrar, Straus and Giroux, 1953); and Judith Thurman's *Break of Day* (New York: Farrar, Straus and Giroux, 2001), very reliable translations, for my own text.

18. In the 1937 English translation of the text the title was *The Mother of Claudine;* only later was "Claudine" replaced with "My," making the new title *My Mother's House.*

19. Colette, *"My Mother's House" and "Sido,"* trans. Troubridge and McLeod, 1953.

20. Colette, *My Mother's House* 5–10, 24–25.

21. Colette, *Sido* 147, 148, 158.

22. Colette, *My Mother's House* 48.

23. Colette, *My Mother's House* 30.

24. Cited in Thurman, *Secrets of the Flesh* 366.

25. Colette, *Break of Day* 4.

26. Colette, *Break of Day* 24.

27. Colette, *Break of Day* 77.

28. Colette, *Break of Day* 17, 43, 77.

29. Colette, *Break of Day* 17, 110.

30. Flieger, *Colette and the Fantom Subject* 206–8.

31. Tilburg, *Colette's Republic* 101, 148; Tilburg, "Earning Her Bread." See also Colette, *La Vagabonde* (1910) and *L'Envers du Music Hall* (1913).

32. She premiered as a scantily clad woodland nymph in *L'Amour, le desir, la chimère,* a risqué pantomime penned by Francis de Croisset and set to music by Jean Nougués.

33. As she pursued her stage career, she contributed regularly to *Le Matin;* authored a collection of autobiographical essays, *Les Vrilles de la vigne;* resurrected an unfinished novel, *L'Ingénue libertine;* and penned what many considered her first great masterpiece, *La Vagabonde.*

34. Phelps, *Belles saisons* 167, 175. In February 1922, Colette played Léa in the one-hundredth stage performance of *Chéri*—a role she would reprise numerous times over the next four years—and in 1927 she headlined once more as Renée Néré.

35. Fonds Rondel 11405 (January 5, 1907), "Théâtres de Paris." Despite Missy's initial refusal of payment, the pair earned the astronomical sum of 1,500 francs a day for the performance.

36. Cited in Thurman, *Secrets of the Flesh* 170.

37. Fonds Rondel 11405.

38. Cited in Thurman, *Secrets of the Flesh* 169. From this point forward, I rely primarily on archival sources as well as on Judith Thurman's vivid recounting of the event to tell the opening-night story.

39. Delilia, *Le Figaro* 1.

40. Delilia, *Le Figaro* 1.

41. Thurman, *Secrets of the Flesh* 171.

42. Rochefort, "Une Soirée historique."

43. Franc-Nohain, *Fantasio.*

44. "La Croisade au Moulin-Rouge"; "Une Scandale au Moulin-Rouge"; Thurman, *Secrets of the Flesh* 172.

45. Delilia, *Le Figaro.*

46. Glenn, *Female Spectacle* 33, 35.

47. Erber, "In the Flesh" 188.

48. "Théâtres et Concerts, avant-premières au Moulin Rouge."

49. Calmette, "Le Scandale du Moulin-Rouge."

50. Mortier, "La Croisade au Moulin-Rouge."

51. Thurman, *Secrets of the Flesh* 171.

52. Cited in Thurman, *Secrets of the Flesh* 172.

53. Thurman, *Secrets of the Flesh* 172.

54. Thurman, *Secrets of the Flesh* 173–74.

55. Berenson, "The Politics of Divorce" 33, 39; McBride, "Public Authority and Private Lives."

56. McBride, "Public Authority and Private Lives" 749, 763.

57. Berenson, "The Politics of Divorce," 48. Missy's divorce was finalized in 1903.

58. The 1792 law rendered marriage a contract dissolvable by the mutual consent. The 1884 law made no such provision.

59. McBride, "Public Authority and Private Lives" 749.

60. Berenson, "The Politics of Divorce" 52–53. Berenson illustrates that *Le Matin* headlines included "Divorce: Confession générale d'une époque" (February 9, 1908); "Les douleurs du divorce" (February 12); and "La Crise du mariage et du divorce est portée devant le Senat" (February 22).

61. Scholars have identified the period from 1870 to 1914 as a "golden age" for the French press. At this time, not only did the number or dailies increase dramatically (from 37 dailies for every 1,000 people in 1870 to 244 daily papers per 1,000 in 1914), but growing literacy rates increased the demand for information of all sorts (Kuhn, *The Media in France* 17).

62. Berenson and Giloi, *Constructing Charisma* 17; Evans and Hesmondhalgh, *Understanding Media* 2; Gaffney and Holmes, *Stardom in Postwar France* 8; Redmond and Holmes, *Stardom and Celebrity* 309–10.

63. Discourses around female homosexuality emerged in art, literature, sexological studies, exposés, guidebooks, and medical essays. Dr. Julien Chevalier's *Aberrations de l'instinct sexuel au point de vue ethnographique, historique et sociale* (Paris: Storck, 1905), Léo Taxil's [pseud. Gabriel Jogand-Pagès], *La corruption fin-de-siècle* (Paris, 1891), and Ali Coffignon's, *La corruption á* [sic] *Paris* (Paris, 1888), portrayed female homosexuality as a form of deviance that penetrated not only heterosexual brothels but also respectable middle-class homes (Erber, "In the Flesh" 181–82).

64. Thurman, *Secrets of the Flesh* 153.

65. Cited in Thurman, *Secrets of the Flesh* 136.

66. Erber, "In the Flesh" 184–85; Kerley, *Uncovering Paris.*

67. Ross, *Public City/Public Sex.*

68. Erber, "In the Flesh" 185.

69. Erber, "In the Flesh" 187–88.

70. Calmette, "Le Scandale du Moulin-Rouge."

71. Indeed, Colette had engaged in similarly scandalous performances with other women, including Christine Kerf, throughout her career, without inspiring such a reaction. My gratitude to the anonymous reader for LSU Press who reminded me of this fact.

72. "Le Baiser au Théâtre."

73. Antonioli, "Colette Française" 120, 117.

74. Cited in Thurman, *Secrets of the Flesh* 417–18.

75. Cited in Antonioli, "Colette Française" 113.

76. Antonioli, "Colette Française" 124–25, 118.

77. Antonioli, "Colette Française" 117.

78. Ernest-Charles, *L'Excelsior.*

79. Antonioli, "Colette Française" 115, 122–23, 126.

80. Cited in Thurman, *Secrets of the Flesh* 6–7.

81. Colette, *My Mother's House* 60.

82. Francis and Gontier, *Creating Colette.*

83. Cited in Thurman, *Secrets of the Flesh* 6–7.

84. Goellner, "Algeria in France" 485.

85. Goellner, "Algeria in France" 484; Lewis, *Gendering Orientalism,* 3, 21. Lewis argues that "women did play a part in the textual production that constituted Orientalism and, moreover, that gender, as a differentiating term, was integral to the structure of that discourse and individuals' experience of it" (18).

86. Goellner, "Algeria in France" 484; Apter, "Acting Out Orientalism" 106.

87. Thurman, *Secrets of the Flesh* 468.

88. Cited in Thurman, *Secrets of the Flesh* 484.

89. Billy, "Une Sorte de dandysme féminin."

90. Brisson, "Troisième anniversaire de sa mort."

91. Scott, *Only Paradoxes to Offer.*

92. Colette, *My Mother's House* 101, 109.

93. Thurman, *Secrets of the Flesh* 498.

94. *Le Figaro,* August 9, 1954.

4. JOSEPHINE BAKER: "A WILD SPLENDOR"

1. Levinson, *La Danse d'aujourd'hui* 277; Mackrell, *Flappers* 372.

2. Levinson, *La Danse d'aujourd'hui* 276.

3. Levinson, *La Danse d'aujourd'hui* 276–77.

4. Levinson, *La Danse d'aujourd'hui* 277.

5. For lengthier discussions of the Venus Noire/Black Venus in the French context, see Mitchell, *Venus Noire;* and Sharpley-Whiting, *Black Venus.*

6. The association between the hegemonic categories of "African" and "primitive" frequently appeared in reviews of African American dancers, including those of Baker and *La Revue Nègre*

(Lemke, *Primitivist Modernism,* 1998). On how Europeans "othered" non-Europeans, see Lewis, *Gendering Orientalism;* and Said, *Orientalism.*

7. Boittin, *Colonial Metropolis;* Dalton and Gates, "Josephine Baker and Paul Colin"; Ezra, "Silents Are Golden"; T. J. Gordon, "Synesthetic Rhythms"; Henderson, "Colonial, Postcolonial, and Diasporic Readings of Josephine Baker"; Ruiz, "Black States of Desire"; Sharpley-Whiting. *Black Venus;* Sowinska, "Dialectics of the Banana Skirt"; Stovall, "Gender, Race, and Miscegenation"; Stovall, "The New Woman and the New Empire."

8. In addition to works published with Marcel Sauvage, Baker coauthored *Une Vie de toutes les couleurs* (1935) with poet André Rivollet, and she was aided in publicizing her story by Pepito, who distributed a collection of news clippings entitled *Josephine Baker vue par la presse française* (1931).

9. Baker and Bouillon, *Josephine;* Baker and Chase, *Josephine Baker: The Hungry Heart.*

10. Boittin, *Colonial Metropolis* 14–15.

11. Baker and Chase, *Josephine Baker: The Hungry Heart* 17; Mackrell, *Flappers* 177. She changed her surname frequently, adopting McDonald, Martin, and Wells before settling on Baker.

12. Baker and Chase, *Josephine Baker: The Hungry Heart* 23–26.

13. Baker and Bouillon, *Josephine* 21, 24.

14. Baker and Chase, *Josephine Baker: The Hungry Heart* 43–44.

15. Baker and Chase, *Josephine Baker: The Hungry Heart* 46, 56, 58, 60. Baker used the drugstore skin lighteners Ko-Verra and Bleacho as well as Mary Congolene hair straighteners throughout her career.

16. Baker and Chase, *Josephine Baker: The Hungry Heart* 55.

17. Baker and Chase, *Josephine Baker: The Hungry Heart* 72.

18. Brown, *Babylon Girls* 206.

19. Baker and Chase, *Josephine Baker: The Hungry Heart* 72, 75, 80.

20. Baker and Bouillon, *Josephine* 36, 42–44.

21. Baker and Chase, *Josephine Baker: The Hungry Heart* 117, 137–39; Baker and Bouillon, *Josephine* 33.

22. Boittin, *Colonial Metropolis* 17.

23. Mackrell, *Flappers* 392–93.

24. Baker and Chase, *Josephine Baker: The Hungry Heart* 141–42, 143, 144, 146, 151, 154–55, 171.

25. Baker and Bouillon, *Josephine* 78.

26. Baker and Chase, *Josephine Baker: The Hungry Heart* 168–70, 176–77, 186, 212; Baker and Bouillon, *Josephine,* 93–94, 96.

27. Baker and Chase, *Josephine Baker: The Hungry Heart* 186–87.

28. Baker and Chase, *Josephine Baker: The Hungry Heart* 185; Baker and Bouillon, *Josephine* 82, 98.

29. Boittin, *Colonial Metropolis* 8–9; Sauvage, *Voyages et aventures.*

30. Cited in Baker and Chase, *Josephine Baker: The Hungry Heart* 171.

31. Section compiled from an amalgamation of reviews collected and cited in Baker and Chase, *Josephine Baker: The Hungry Heart* 202–3.

32. Cited in Baker and Chase, *Josephine Baker: The Hungry Heart* 189, 190–91.

33. Regester, "The Construction of an Image" 39–40.

34. Boittin, *Colonial Metropolis* 14, 31–32.

35. Baker and Bouillon, *Josephine* 112.

36. Baker and Chase, *Josephine Baker: The Hungry Heart* 227; Baker and Bouillon, *Josephine* 115.

37. Baker and Chase, *Josephine Baker: The Hungry Heart* 224, 227, 231, 242–43, 253, 257.

38. Baker and Chase, *Josephine Baker: The Hungry Heart* 228–29, 234.

39. Baker and Bouillon, *Josephine* 116.

40. Baker and Chase, *Josephine Baker: The Hungry Heart* 226, 232–24; Baker and Bouillon, *Josephine* 141.

41. Baker and Bouillon, *Josephine* 128.

42. Baker and Chase, *Josephine Baker: The Hungry Heart* 244–45, 247–49, 274.

43. Baker and Chase, *Josephine Baker: The Hungry Heart* 264, 266, 267; Baker and Bouillon, *Josephine* 131.

44. Baker and Bouillon, *Josephine* 146.

45. Baker and Chase, *Josephine Baker: The Hungry Heart* 35.

46. Baker and Chase, *Josephine Baker: The Hungry Heart* 276, 278, 284, 442.

47. Baker and Bouillon, *Josephine* 166.

48. Baker and Chase, *Josephine Baker: The Hungry Heart* 343.

49. Baker and Chase, *Josephine Baker: The Hungry Heart* 281, 294, 297, 300–303, 306, 312, 319, 325, 370, 374, 386. She did not publicly comment on the Algerian War or the Paris uprisings of May 1968.

50. Baker and Chase, *Josephine Baker: The Hungry Heart* 293, 296, 297, 302, 312, 320, 321,323, 392, 436, 460; Baker and Bouillon, *Josephine* 226, 176.

51. Bouillon reports that in 1952 Baker was twenty-seven million francs in debt; that amount rose to more than eighty-three million by 1957. She was hospitalized for exhaustion several times, she underwent six abdominal surgeries during her adulthood, and she suffered three heart attacks. The financial burden of her racial utopia forced her to keep working and likely contributed to her body's decline (Baker and Bouillon, *Josephine* 211).

52. Baker and Chase, *Josephine Baker: The Hungry Heart* 240, 380–81, 385, 396, 398, 400, 412–13.

53. Baker and Chase, *Josephine Baker: The Hungry Heart* 477, 486–88, 492.

54. Cited in Baker and Chase, *Josephine Baker: The Hungry Heart* 172, 149.

55. Baker and Sauvage, *Les Mémoires de Joséphine Baker* 7–8, 9–10.

56. Boittin, *Colonial Metropolis* 5–7.

57. Baker and Sauvage, *Les Mémoires de Joséphine Baker* 32–45, 49, 51–52, 53, 54, 55.

58. Baker and Sauvage, *Les Mémoires de Joséphine Baker* 55–60, 70, 191–92.

59. Brown, *Babylon Girls* 242, 254, 256.

60. Baker and Bouillon, *Josephine* xii, ix, x, 38.

61. Baker and Bouillon, *Josephine* 50, 53, 55–57, 66, 90.

62. Baker and Bouillon, *Josephine* 87, 92.

63. Baker and Bouillon, *Josephine* 71, 110.

64. Baker and Bouillon, *Josephine* 117, 125, 143.

65. Baker and Bouillon, *Josephine* 145, 160, 162, 169.

66. Baker and Bouillon, *Josephine* 169, 262–63, 230.

67. Guterl, *Josephine Baker and the Rainbow Tribe* 34–41.

68. Cited in Sharpley-Whiting, *Black Venus* 43. *La Revue Nègre* sold out the theater's two thousand seats when it opened on October 2, 1925.

69. Flanner, *Paris Was Yesterday* xx–xxi; Rose, *Jazz Cleopatra* 274n5. This version of Flanner's review appeared not in 1925 but decades later, in 1972, in the author's own memoir. Indeed, in Flanner's original assessment, Black was not "beautiful" (a popular refrain that reflected the racial politics of 1970s America) but, rather, "fashionable." Rose makes this point beautifully in her comparison of these two iterations of Flanner's review.

70. Cited in Rose, *Jazz Cleopatra* 30–31.

71. French enthusiasm for prewar ragtime and the cakewalk fueled its postwar zeal for jazz. Scholars quibble as to when jazz officially "arrived" in France; however, they agree that it was popularized by African American soldiers stationed there during the Great War. Black GIs not only listened to jazz, but several Black regiments, including the Harlem Hellfighters and the Seventy Black Devils, gave concerts. At the war's end, Black troupes performed to packed crowds at the Tuileries Gardens, the Apollo Theater in Montmartre, and the Théâtre des Champs-Élysées, where Baker later débuted. Dalton and Gates, "Josephine Baker and Paul Colin" 906–7; Jackson, *Making Jazz French*.

72. Guterl, *Josephine Baker and the Rainbow Tribe* 2.

73. Grout, "Authorizing Fictions."

74. Rose, *Jazz Cleopatra* 5–6.

75. Charles justified his decisions, explaining that "these French people, with their fantasies of black girls," demand "*des nichons* [tits]" (cited in Baker and Chase, *Josephine Baker: The Hungry Heart* 111).

76. Stovall, *Paris Noir* 53. Colin collected his materials on Baker in a series called *Le Tumulte*.

77. Colin, *La Croûte* 81.

78. Alby, "Quelques instants avec Joséphine Baker"; Fourrier, "Au Théâtre des Champs-Élysées 4; Patin, "Les Premières" 4; Raymond-Millet, "Joséphine Baker étoile noire" 29.

79. Baker and Chase, *Josephine Baker: The Hungry Heart* 115, 119, 121.

80. Fourrier, "Au Théâtre des Champs-Élysées" 4.

81. Cited in Baker and Chase, *Josephine Baker: The Hungry Heart* 119.

82. Pierre de Régnier, *Candide*.

83. Cited in Baker and Chase, *Josephine Baker: The Hungry Heart* 6.

84. Cited in Mackrell, *Flappers* 371.

85. Brown, *Babylon Girls* 179; Mitchell, *Venus Noire*.

86. Baker and Bouillon, *Josephine* 82.

87. Brown, *Babylon Girls* 15, 242.

88. Mackrell, *Flappers* 383.

89. Baker and Chase, *Josephine Baker: The Hungry Heart* 136.

90. Ruiz, "Black States of Desire" 133, 135; Sowinska, "Dialectics of the Banana Skirt." Bananas proved an effective marketing tool in Baker's commodification: fans could purchase a "Custard Josephine Baker," or dolls dressed in banana skirts; they found stickers publicizing *ZouZou* on bananas; and Baker offered banana-based recipes for homemade skin moisturizers.

91. Brown, *Babylon Girls* 6.

92. Boittin, *Colonial Metropolis* xvii; Brown, *Babylon Girls* 17, 244, 254, 256.

93. Cited in Mackrell, *Flappers* 397.

94. *Paris qui emue* ran at the Casino for thirteen months. "J'ai deux amours" far outlived the production, selling 300,000 records and becoming Baker's signature song.

95. Guterl considers "J'ai deux amours" a "tribute to diaspora and dislocation" (Guterl, *Josephine Baker and the Rainbow Tribe* 32).

96. Armianu, "Josephine Baker: Artist and Dissident" 46.

97. Boittin, *Colonial Metropolis* 11.

98. Boittin, *Colonial Metropolis* 2.

99. Roberts, *Civilization without Sexes*.

100. Roberts, *Civilization without Sexes*; Thébaud, "The Great War" 21–75. Women's wartime activities influenced some of their postwar civil liberties. Women could join labor unions without a husband's consent (1920), and they were permitted to take the male version of the baccalauréat exam (1924) (Sohn, "Between the Wars in France and England" 5:114). However, French women remained disenfranchised and enjoyed limited reproductive rights (further curtailed by anti-abortion and anticontraceptive legislation passed in the early 1920s), and spouses remained legally subject to paternal authority until 1938.

101. Grout, *The Force of Beauty*; Roberts, "Samson and Delilah Revisited."

102. Dalton and Gates, "Josephine Baker and Paul Colin" 933.

103. T. J. Gordon, "Synesthetic Rhythms." "Jazz ambiguously linked categories of race and gender," Liz Conor contends, "portraying the primitive and modern woman in the same social and significatory space" (Conor, *The Spectacular Modern Woman* 191).

104. Roberts, "Samson and Delilah Revisited."

105. "During *les années folles*, when the French tried to supersede the moral concepts of their father's generation," Lemke argues, "this display of Black female sexuality on stage was a conduit through which many spectators tried to subvert received social and religious attitudes toward sexuality, curiously enough, by symbolically embracing the Black other" (Lemke, *Primitivist Modernism* 101).

106. Mitchell, *Venus Noire*.

107. Raymond-Millet, "Joséphine Baker étoile noire" 29.

108. Lemke, *Primitivist Modernism* 103, 114.

109. Guterl, *Josephine Baker and the Rainbow Tribe* 9.

110. Guterl, *Josephine Baker and the Rainbow Tribe* 4, 86, 175, 127.

111. Guterl, *Josephine Baker and the Rainbow Tribe* 80, 95.

112. "Josephine Baker Becomes First Black Woman"; "Joséphine Baker, Chanteuse, Danseuse"; "Josephine Baker to Become First Black Woman to Enter France's Panthéon."

113. "France Petitions to Have Josephine Baker." On December 16, 2013, Régis Debray pushed for this same honor in an op-ed piece for *Le Monde*.

114. "Josephine Baker Becomes First Black Woman."

115. "Josephine Baker Becomes First Black Woman."

116. Younge, "Giving Josephine Baker a Hero's Grave."

CONCLUSION: IMMORTELS

1. Brownstein, *Tragic Muse* ix–x.
2. Redmond and Holmes, *Stardom and Celebrity* 1–2.
3. Brownstein, *Tragic Muse* ix.

Bibliography

PRIMARY SOURCES

Archives

Bibliothèque Arsenal—FOL Z Pièce 299
Bibliothèque Marguerite Durand: Fonds BER
Bibliothèque Marguerite Durand: Fonds SB
Bibliothèque Marguerite Durand: Fonds Col
Bibliothèque Nationale: Dossier Renée Hammond
Bibliothèque Opéra: Dossiers D'Artistes—Joséphine Baker
Bibliothèque Opéra: Dossier D'Artiste—Sarah Bernhardt
Bibliothèque Richelieu: 8-RO-15602
Bibliothèque Richelieu: Baker RO-15816 (1926–1928)
Bibliothèque Richelieu: FOL-W-1832
Bibliothèque Richelieu: Sardou (Victorien)—21 Lettres, cartes, et télégrammes à Sarah
    BERNHARDT—MN 506
Fonds Rondel RF 47,774—Cleopatra/Sardou
Fonds Rondel 11405

Periodicals

Black and White. June 4, 1892.
Candide. November 12, 1925.
Ciné. October 15, 1927.
Comœdia. October 9, 1930.
L'Écho de Paris. August 2, 1890; October 20, 1890; January 18, 1894.
L'Éclair de Montpellier. January 7, 1907.

L'Excelsior. December 19, 1910.

Fantasio. November 1, 1906.

Femme de France. December 19, 1926.

Le Figaro. October 21, 1890; October 24, 1890; January 4, 1907; October 7, 1925; August 9, 1954.

Guardian. August 22, 2021.

L'Humanité. October 18, 1925.

L'Intransigeant. January 5, 1907

Le Journal. January 3, 1907.

La Laterne/journal politique quotidien. January 6, 1907.

Le Matin. January 27, 1911.

Le Matin/dernier télégrammes de la nuit. January 4, 1907.

Le Monde. August 22, 2021.

Midinette. June 19, 1936.

Le Parisien Dimanche. August 22, 2021.

Le Petit Journal Illustrée.

St. James Gazette. October 9, 1890; October 16, 1890.

Nation. July 31, 1879; November 20, 1890; November 29, 2021.

New York Times. November 30, 2021.

Week's News. June 14, 1879.

Books and Articles

Alby, Marianne. "Quelques instants avec Joséphine Baker." *Ciné,* October 15, 1927: 15–16.

"Le Baiser au Théâtre." *Paris-Théâtre,* January 18, 1907.

Baker, Josephine, and Jo Bouillon. *Josephine.* Trans. Mariana Fitzpatrick. New York: Harper and Row, 1976.

Baker, Josephine, and Marcel Sauvage. *Les Mémoires de Joséphine Baker recueillis et adaptés par Marcel Sauvage.* Paris: Éditions Corrêa, 1949.

Bauer, Henry. "Cléopâtre." *Revue Illustrée,* December 15, 1896.

———. "Sarah Bernhardt." *L'Écho de Paris,* January 18, 1894.

Bernhardt, Sarah. *The Art of the Theater.* 1924. Trans. H. J. Stenning. New York: Books for Libraries Press, 1969.

———. *My Double Life: The Memoirs of Sarah Bernhardt.* 1907. Trans. Victoria Tietze Larson. New York: State University of New York Press, 1999.

Billy, André. "Une Sorte de dandysme féminin . . ." January 24, 1953. Bibliothèque Arsenal, FOL z, Pièce 299.

Binet-Valmer, *Sarah Bernhardt.* Paris: Flammarion, 1936.

Boccaccio, Giovanni. *De claris mulieribus/On Famous Women.* Trans. and ed. Guido A. Guarino. New York: Italica, 2011.

Bonal Gérard, and Frédéric Maget, eds. *Colette journaliste: Chroniques et reportages 1893–1955*. Paris: Éditions Seuil, 2010.

Bourgeois, Armand. *Conférence sur Sarah Bernhardt*. Paris: Bibliothèque d'Art de la Critique, 1898.

Brisson, Pierre. "Troisième Anniversaire de sa Mort: Colette et L'Amour." *Le Figaro Littéraire*, August 10, 1957: 1.

Calmette, Gaston. "Le Scandale du Moulin-Rouge." *Le Figaro,* January 4, 1907.

Claretie, Léo. *Le Dix-neuvième siècle*. Vol. 4 of *Histoire de la littérature française (900–1900)*. Paris: Société D'Éditions Littéraires et Artistiques, 1909.

Cochrane, Lauren. "Why Colette Is Queen of the Influencers." *Guardian,* January 9, 2019.

Colette, Sidonie-Gabrielle. *Belles saison: A Colette Scrapbook*. Comp. Robert Phelps. Trans. Matthew Ward. New York: Farrar, Straus and Giroux, 1983.

———. *Break of Day*. Trans. Enid McLeod. New York: Farrar, Straus and Giroux, 2001.

———. *The Collected Stories of Colette*. Ed. Robert Phelps. Trans. Matthew Ward, Antonia White, and Anne-Marie Calimocho. New York: Farrar, Straus and Giroux, 1983.

———. *Letters from Colette*. Selected and trans. Robert Phelps. New York: Farrar, Straus and Giroux, 1980.

———. *Lettres à Hélène Picard*. Ed. Claude Pichois. Paris: Flammarion, 1988.

———. *Lettres de la vagabonde*. Ed. Claude Pichois and R. Forbin. Paris: Flammarion, 1961.

———. *La Maison de Claudine*. 1922. http://www.gutenberg.net/1/3/7/0/13703/.

———. *Mes apprentissages*. Trans. Helen Beauclerk. New York: Farrar, Straus and Giroux, 1957.

———. *"My Mother's House" and "Sido."* Trans. Una Vicenzo Troubridge and Enid McLeod. New York: Farrar, Straus, and Giroux, 1953.

———. *Œuvres*. Vol. 1. Bibliothèque de la Pléiade. Preface by Claude Pichois. Paris: Gallimard, 1984.

Colette, Robert Phelps, Herma Briffault, and Derek Coltman. *Earthly Paradise: An Autobiography*. New York: Farrar, Straus and Giroux, 1966.

Colin, Paul. *La Croûte (Souvenirs)*. Paris, 1957.

Colombier, Marie. *The Memoirs of Sarah Barnum*. New York: S. W. Green's Son, 1884.

"La Crise du marriage et du divorce est portée devant le Senat." *Le Matin,* February 22, 1908.

"La Croisade au Moulin-Rouge." *Gil Blas,* January 4, 1907.

De Flers, Robert. "À Sarah Bernhardt." *Le Théâtre et Comœdia Illustré*—Numéro Spécial Sarah Bernhardt—Juin 1926.

Delilia, Alfred. *Le Figaro,* January 4, 1907: 1.

"Divorce: Confession Générale d'une époque." *Le Matin,* February 9, 1908.

"Les douleurs du divorce." *Le Matin,* February 12, 1908.

Ernest-Charles, J. *L'Excelsoir,* December 19, 1910.

Fair, Fanny. "Bernhardt." *New York Telegram,* December 1905: 6.

Flaubert, Gustave. *Flaubert in Egypt: A Sensibility on Tour.* Trans. and ed. Francis Steegmuller London: Penguin, 1972.

Fourrier, Marcel. "Au Théâtre des Champs-Élysées: *La Revue Nègre.*" *L'Humanité,* October 1925: 4.

"France Petitions to Have Josephine Baker Honoured with Voltaire, Rousseau at the Pantheon." *France 24,* May 30, 2021.

Franc-Nohain. *Fantasio,* November 1, 1906.

Gautier, Théophile. "Une Nuit de Cléopâtre." *La Presse,* November 29–December 6, 1838.

Gilbert, Augustin-Thierry. "The Theater: Men, People, and Things." *Illustrated Review* 10.18 (November 1, 1890): 314–16.

Hahn, Reynaldo. *La Grande Sarah souvenirs.* Paris: Hachette, 1930.

Horace, "Cleopatra Ode." World History Commons. http://worldhistorycommons. org/horace-cleopatra-ode.

James, Henry. "The Comédie-Française in London. *Nation,* July 30, 1879: 72–73.

"Josephine Baker Becomes First Black Woman Inducted into France's Tomb of Heroes." *New York Times,* November 30, 2021.

"Joséphine Baker, chanteuse, danseuse et figure de la Résistance, va entrer au Panthéon." *Le Monde,* August 22, 2021.

"Josephine Baker to Become First Black Woman to Enter France's Panthéon." *Guardian,* August 22, 2021.

Jules-Rosette, Bennetta. "Josephine Baker in Art and Life." *New York Times,* June 3, 2007.

Lacour, Léopold. "Cléopâtre." *Le Figaro,* October 21, 1890.

Lesueur, Daniel. "Prêtresse de la beauté." *La Fronde,* 28 January 1898.

Levinson, André. *La Danse d'aujourd'hui: Études, notes, portraits.* Paris: Éditions Duchartre et Van Buggenhoudt, 1929.

Mann, Thomas. *Joseph in Egypt.* New York: Knopf, 1938.

"Masculine et féminin." *Le Grélot,* May 2, 1897.

Un Monsieur de l'Orchestre. "La Soirée théatrale: Cléopâtre." *Le Figaro,* October 24, 1890.

Montorgueil, Georges. *La Parisienne peinte par elle-même.* Paris: Librairie L. Conquet, 1897.

Mortier, Pierre. "La Croisade au Moulin-Rouge." *Gil Blas,* January 4, 1907.

Pascal, Félicien. *L'Éclair de Montpellier,* January 7, 1907.

Patin, Jacques. "Les Premiéres." *Le Figaro,* October 7, 1925.

Raymond-Millet, J-K. "Joséphine Baker étoile noire." *Femme de France,* December 19, 1926: 29.

Régnier, Pierre de. *Candide,* November 12, 1925.

Rochefort, Henri. "Une Soirée historique." *L'Intransigeant* January 5, 1907.

Rostand, Maurice. *Sarah Bernhardt.* Paris: Calmann-Lévy, 1950.

Rousseau, Jean-Jacques. "Letter to Alembert on the Theater." *Letter to d'Alembert and Writings for the Theater.* Ed. and trans. Allan Bloom, Charles Butterworth, and Christopher Kelly. Hanover, NH: University Press of New England, 2004.

Ryner, Han. *Le Massacre des Amazones: Études critiques sur deux cents bas-bleus contemporains.* Paris: Chamuel, 1899.

"Sarah Bernhardt in 'Cleopatra,' A Splendid Stage Production." *Wanganui Herald,* December 15, 1890.

Sardou, Victorien. *Cleopatra: A Play in Five Acts.* Trans. Frank J. Morlock. Cabin John, MD: Wildside, 2010.

Sauvage, Marcel. *Les Mémoires de Joséphine Baker.* Paris: Éditions KRA, 1927.

———. *Voyages et aventures de Joséphine Baker.* Paris: Éditions Marcel Sheur, 1931.

"Une Scandale au Moulin-Rouge: La Marquise de Morny et Mme Colette Willy ont été sifflées et injuriées par le public." *Le Petit Journal,* January 4, 1907.

Séverine. "Sarah," *L'Écho de Paris,* December 11, 1896: 1.

Shakespeare, William. *Antony and Cleopatra.* Ed. Barbara A. Mowat and Paul Werstine. Folger Shakespeare Library. https://shakespeare.folger.edu/.

"Théâtres et Concerts, Avant-premières au Moulin Rouge." *Le Journal,* January 2, 1907.

Uzanne, Octave. *Parisiennes de ce Temps.* Paris: Mercure de France, 1894.

Villiéras, Henry. "Comment on Devient Étoile Joséphine Baker." *Midinette,* June 19, 1936: 28–29.

Younge, Gary. "Giving Josephine Baker a Hero's Grave Won't Bury the Truth . . . about France's Republican Racism." *Nation,* November 29, 2021.

SECONDARY SOURCES

Acocella, Joan, and Lynn Garafola, eds. *André Levinson on Dance: Writings from Paris in the Twenties.* Hanover, NH: Wesleyan University Press, 1991.

Adler, Doris. "The Unlacing of Cleopatra." *Theater Journal* 34.4 (December 1982): 450–66.

Antonioli, Kathleen. "Colette Française (et Fille de Zouave), Colette and French Singularity." *French Politics, Culture, and Society* 38.1 (Spring 2020): 113–28.

Apter, Emily. "Acting Out Orientalism: Sapphic Theatricality in Turn-of-the-Century Paris." *L'Esprit Créateur* 34.2 (Summer 1994): 102–16.

———. "Cabinet Secret: Fetishism, Prostitution, and the Fin-de-Siècle Interior." *Assemblage,* no. 9 (June 1989): 6–19.

Armianu, Irina. "Josephine Baker: Artist and Dissident." *International Journal of Francophone Studies* 20.1 and 2 (2017): 39–55.

Arnold, Rebecca. *Fashion, Desire, and Anxiety: Image and Morality in the Twentieth Century*. New Brunswick, NJ: Rutgers University Press, 2001.

Baker, Jean-Claude, and Chris Chase. *Josephine Baker: The Hungry Heart*. New York: Cooper Square, 2001.

Banet-Weiser, Sarah. "Am I Pretty or Ugly? Girls and the Market for Self-Esteem." *Girlhood Studies* 7.1 (Summer 2014): 83–101.

Bellow, Juliet. "Fashioning Cléopâtre: Sonia Delauney's New Woman." *Art Journal* (Summer 2009): 7–23.

Bennett, James. "Approaching Celebrity Studies," *Celebrity Studies* 6.3 (2015): 269–71.

Berenson, Edward. "The Politics of Divorce in France of the Belle Epoque: The Case of Joseph and Henriette Caillaux." *American Historical Review* 93.1 (February 1988): 31–55.

Berenson, Edward, and Eva Giloi. *Constructing Charisma: Celebrity, Frame, and Power in Nineteenth-Century Europe*. New York: Routledge, 2010.

Bergman-Carton, Janis. "Negotiating the Categories: Sarah Bernhardt and the Possibilities of Jewishness." *Art Journal* 55.2 (Summer 1996): 55–64.

Berlanstein, Lenard. *Daughters of Eve: A Cultural History of French Theater Women from the Old Regime to the Fin de Siècle*. Cambridge, MA: Harvard University Press, 2004.

———. "Historicizing and Gendering Celebrity Culture: Famous Women in Nineteenth-Century France." *Journal of Women's History* 16.4 (Winter 2004): 65–91.

Bernheimer, Charles. *Figures of Ill Repute: Representing Prostitution in Nineteenth-Century France*. Durham, NC: Duke University Press, 1997.

Berry, Sarah. *Screen Style: Fashion and Femininity in 1930s Hollywood*. Minneapolis: University of Minnesota Press, 2009.

Boittin, Jennifer Anne. *Colonial Metropolis: The Urban Grounds of Anti-Imperialism and Feminism in Interwar Paris*. France Overseas: Studies in Empire and Decolonization series. Ed. Philip Boucher et al. Lincoln: University of Nebraska Press, 2010.

Borelli, Melissa Blanco. "Performing Josephine Baker." *Dance Chronicle* 31.3 (2008): 466–70.

Braudy, Leon. "The Dream of Acceptability." *Stardom and Celebrity: A Reader*. Ed. Sean Redmond and Su Holmes. London: Sage, 2007. 185.

———. *The Frenzy of Renown: Fame and Its History*. New York: Oxford University Press, 1986.

Bridenthal, Renate, Susan Stuard, and Merry Wiesner-Hanks, eds. *Becoming Visible: Women in European History*. New York: Houghton Mifflin, 1998.

Brooks, Daphne. *Bodies in Dissent: Spectacular Performances of Race and Freedom, 1850–1910*. Durham, NC: Duke University Press, 2006.

Brown, Jayna. *Babylon Girls: Black Women Performers and the Shaping of the Modern*. Durham, NC: Duke University Press, 2008.

Brownstein, Rachel M. *Tragic Muse: Rachel of the Comédie-Française.* New York: Knopf, 1993.

Brunotte, Ulrike. "All Jews Are Womanly, but No Women Are Jews." *Orientalism, Gender and the Jews: Literary and Artistic Transformations of European National Discourses.* Ed. Brunotte, Anna-Dorothea Ludewig, and Axel Stähler. Berlin: De Gruyter OldenBourg, 2015. 195–220.

Brunotte, Ulrike, Anna-Dorothea Ludewig, Axel Stähler, eds. *Orientalism, Gender and the Jews: Literary and Artistic Transformations of European National Discourses.* Berlin: De Gruyter OldenBourg, 2015.

Butler, Judith. *Gender Trouble: Feminism and the Subversion of Identity.* New York: Routledge, 2008.

———. "Performative Acts and Gender Constitution: An Essay in Phenomenology and Feminist Theory." *Performing Feminisms: Feminist Critical Theory and the Theatre.* Ed. Sue Ellen Case. Baltimore, MD: Johns Hopkins University Press, 1990.

Canning, Kathleen. *Gender History in Practice: Historical Perspectives on Bodies, Class, and Citizenship.* Ithaca, NY: Cornell University Press, 2006.

Carroll, Christina B. *The Politics of Imperial Memory in France, 1850–1900.* New York: Cornell University Press, 2021.

Certeau, Michel de. *The Writing of History.* Trans. Tom Conley. New York: Columbia University Press, 1988.

Chadwick, Whitney, and Tirza True Latimer, eds. *The Modern Woman Revisited: Paris between the Wars.* New Brunswick, NJ: Rutgers University Press, 2003.

Cheng, Anne Anlin. "Josephine Baker: Psychoanalysis and The Colonial Fetish." *Psychoanalytic Quarterly* 75.1 (2006): 95–129.

———. *Ornamentalism.* Oxford: Oxford University Press, 2019.

———. "Wounded Beauty: An Exploratory Essay on Race, Feminism, and the Aesthetic Question." *Tulsa Studies in Women's Literature* 19.2 (Autumn 2000): 191–217.

Clark, Anna. *Desire: A History of European Sexuality.* New York: Routledge, 2008.

Clark, Linda. "Bringing Feminine Qualities in the Public Sphere: The Third Republic's Appointment of Female Inspectors." *Gender and the Politics of Social Reform in France, 1870–1914.* Ed. Elinor Ann Acampo. Baltimore, MD: Johns Hopkins University Press, 1995.

Conor, Liz. *The Spectacular Modern Woman: Feminine Visibility in the 1920s.* Bloomington: Indiana University Press, 2004.

Crane, Mary Thomas. "Roman World, Egyptian Earth: Cognitive Difference and Empire in Shakespeare's *Antony and Cleopatra.*" *Comparative Drama* 43.1 (Spring 2009): 1–17.

Cucullu, Lois. "Wilde and Wilder Salomés: Modernizing the Nubile Princess from Sarah Bernhardt to Norma Desmond." *Modernism/modernity* 18.3 (September 2011): 495–524.

Dalton, Karen C., and Henry Louis Gates Jr., "Josephine Baker and Paul Colin: African Dance Seen through Parisian Eyes." *Critical Inquiry* 24.4 (Summer 1998): 903–34.

Datta, Venita. *Heroes and Legends of Fin-de-Siècle France: Gender, Politics, and National Identity.* Cambridge: Cambridge University Press, 2011.

De Cordova, Richard. *Picture Personalities: The Emergence of the Star System in America.* Champaign: University of Illinois Press, 1990.

De Grazia, Victoria. *Irresistible Empire: America's Advance through Twentieth-Century Europe.* Cambridge, MA: Belknap Press of Harvard University Press, 2009.

———. "Mass Culture and Sovereignty: The American Challenge to European Cinemas, 1920–1960." *Journal of Modern History* 61.1 (1989): 53–87.

Dierkes-Thrun, Petra. *Salomé's Modernity: Oscar Wilde and the Aesthetics of Transgression.* Ann Arbor: University of Michigan Press, 2011.

Douglas, Susan J., and Andrea McDonnell. *Celebrity: A History of Fame.* New York: New York University Press, 2019.

Duckett, Victoria. "The Actress-Manager and the Movies: Resolving the Double Life of Sarah Bernhardt." *Nineteenth-Century Theatre and Film* 45.1 (2018): 27–55.

Duncan, Sophie. *Shakespeare's Women and the Fin de Siècle.* Oxford: Oxford University Press, 2017.

Dyer, Richard. *Stars.* London: British Film Institute, 1998. First published 1979.

Dykstra, D. "The French Occupation of Egypt, 1798–1801." *The Cambridge History of Egypt.* Ed. M. W. Daly. Vol. 2. Cambridge: University of Cambridge Press, 1998. 113–38.

Eade Guenoun, Katherine. "Between Synagogue and Society: Jewish Women in Nineteenth-Century France." PhD diss., University of Wisconsin–Madison, 2015.

Eakin, Paul John. *Fictions in Autobiography: Studies in the Art of Self-Invention.* Princeton, NJ: Princeton University Press, 1985.

Ege Samantha. "Restaging Respectability: The Subversive Performances of Josephine Baker and Nora Holt in Jazz-Age Paris." *Angelaki* 27.3–4 (2022): 112–24.

Ellenzweig, Allen. "Sarah Bernhardt at the Jewish Museum." *Studies in Gender and Sexuality* 8.1 (2007): 27–36.

Elliot, Bridget. "Art Deco Worlds in a Tomb: Reanimating Egypt in Modern(ist) Visual Culture." *South Central Review* 25.1 (Spring 2008): 114–35.

Erber, Nancy. "In the Flesh: Scandalous Women's Performances in Fin-de-Siècle Paris." *Proceedings of the Western Society for French History* 36 (2008): 181–93.

Evans, Jessica, and David Hesmondhalgh, eds. *Understanding Media: Inside Celebrity.* Maidenhead, Berkshire, UK: Open University Press, 2005.

Ezra, Elizabeth. "Silents Are Golden: Staging Community in *Zouzou.*" *FCS* 7 (1996): 149–61.

Ferris, Kerry O. "The Sociology of Celebrity." *Sociology Compass* 1.1 (2007): 371–84.

Fila-Bakabadio, Sarah. "Media and the Politics of "Re-presentation" of the Black Female Body." *Black French Women and the Struggle for Equality, 1848–2016.* Ed. Félix Germain and Silyane Larcher. Lincoln: University of Nebraska Press, 2018. 169–83.

Flanner, Janet. *Paris Was Yesterday: 1925–1939.* New York: Viking, 1972.

Flieger, Jerry Aline. *Colette and the Fantom Subject of Autobiography.* Ithaca, NY: Cornell University Press, 1992.

Francis, Claude, and Fernande Gontier. *Creating Colette: From Ingenue to Libertine 1873–1913.* Hanover, NH: Steerforth, 1998.

Francis, Terri Simone. *Josephine Baker's Cinematic Prism.* Bloomington: Indiana University Press, 2021.

Freedman, Jonathan. "Transformations of a Jewish Princess: Salomé and the Remaking of the Jewish Female Body from Sarah Bernhardt to Betty Boop." *Philological Quarterly* 92.1 (Winter 2013): 89–114.

Gaffney, John, and Diana Holmes, eds., *Stardom in Postwar France.* New York: Berghahn, 2007.

Garb, Tamar, "Modernity, Identity, Textuality." *The Jew in the Text: Modernity and the Construction of Identity.* Ed. Linda Nochlin and Tamar Garb. London: Thames and Hudson, 1995. 20–30.

Garval, Michael D. *Cléo de Mérode and the Rise of Modern Celebrity Culture.* Farnham, UK: Ashgate, 2012.

Germain, Félix, and Silyane Larcher, eds. *Black French Women and the Struggle for Equality, 1848–2016.* Lincoln: University of Nebraska Press, 2018.

Gever, Martha. *Entertaining Lesbians: Celebrity, Sexuality, and Self-Invention.* London: Routledge, 2003.

Giles, David. *Illusions of Immortality: A Psychology of Fame and Celebrity.* New York: Palgrave Macmillan, 2000.

Gillett, Rachel Anne. *At Home in Our Sounds: Music, Race, and Cultural Politics in Interwar Paris.* New York: Oxford University Press, 2021.

Gilman, Sander. "Salomé, Syphilis, Sarah Bernhardt and the Modern Jewess." *The Jew in the Text: Modernity and the Construction of Identity.* Ed. Linda Nochlin and Tamar Garb. London: Thames and Hudson, 1995. 97–120.

Glenn, Susan A. *Female Spectacle: The Theatrical Roots of Modern Feminism.* Cambridge, MA.: Harvard University Press, 2000.

Goellner, Sage. "Algeria in France: Colette's 'Le manteau de spahi." *French Review* 85.3 (February 2012): 483–88.

Gold, Arthur, and Robert Fizdale. *The Divine Sarah: A Life of Sarah Bernhardt.* New York: Knopf, 1991.

Gordon, Rae Beth. "Natural Rhythm: La Parisienne Dances with Darwin: 1875–1910." *Modernism/modernity* 10.4 (November 2003): 617–56.

———. *Why the French Love Jerry Lewis: From Cabaret to Early Cinema.* Stanford, CA: Stanford University Press, 2001.

Gordon, Terri J. "Synesthetic Rhythms: African American Music and Dance through Parisian Eyes." *Scholar and Feminist Online* 6.1–6.2 (Fall 2007/Spring 2008).

Gottlieb, Robert. *Sarah: The Life of Sarah Bernhardt.* New Haven, CT: Yale University Press, 2010.

Grout, Holly. "Authorizing Fictions: Narrating a Self in Mistinguett's Celebrity Memoir." *French Historical Studies* 42.2 (April 2019): 295–322.

———. "Celebrity Matters." *Aeon,* July 16, 2019.

———. "European Celebrity in Historical Perspective." *Making Modern Social Science: The Global Imagination in East Central and Southeastern Europe after Versailles.* Spec. issue of *Journal of Contemporary European History* 28.2 (May 2019): 273–82.

———. *The Force of Beauty: Transforming French Ideas of Femininity in the Third Republic.* Baton Rouge: Louisiana State University Press, 2015.

Guterl, Matthew Pratt. *Josephine Baker and the Rainbow Tribe.* Cambridge, MA: Belknap Press of Harvard University Press, 2014.

Hall, Sheldon, and Stephen Neale. *Epics, Spectacles, and Blockbusters: A Hollywood History.* Detroit, MI: Wayne State University Press, 2010.

Hamer, Mary. *Signs of Cleopatra: Reading an Icon Historically.* Exeter, UK: University of Exeter Press, 2008.

Haney, Lynn. *Naked at the Feast: A Biography of Josephine Baker.* 1995. London: Robson Books, 2002.

Hindson, Catherine. *London's West End Actresses and the Origins of Celebrity Charity, 1880–1920.* Iowa City: University of Iowa Press, 2016.

Harris, Gerry. "Regarding History: Some Narratives Concerning the Café-Concert, Le Music Hall, and the Feminist Academic." *TDR* 40.4 (1996): 70–84.

Harris, Jonathan Gil. "'Narcissus in Thy Face': Roman Desire and the Difference It Fakes in *Antony and Cleopatra.*" *Shakespeare Quarterly* 45.4 (Winter 1994): 408–25.

Hawkins, Ann R., and Maura Ives, eds. *Women Writers and the Artifacts of Celebrity in the Long Nineteenth Century.* London: Routledge, 2012.

Henderson, Mae Gwendolyn. "Colonial, Postcolonial, and Diasporic Readings of Josephine Baker as Dancer and Performance Artist." *Scholar and Feminist Online* 6.1–6.2 (Fall 2007/Spring 2008).

Holmes, Diana. *Colette.* London: Macmillan, 1991.

Holmes, Su, and Sean Redmond. "A Journal in Celebrity Studies." *Celebrity Studies* 1.1 (2010).

Hughes-Hallett, Lucy. *Cleopatra: Histories, Dreams, and Distortions.* New York: Harper and Row, 1990.

Humbert, Jean-Marcel, Michael Pantazzi, and Christiane Ziegler, eds. *Egyptomania: Egypt in Western Art 1730–1930.* National Gallery of Canada/Réunion de Musées Nationaux, 1994.

Inglis, Fred. *A Short History of Celebrity.* Princeton, NJ: Princeton University Press, 2010.

Jackson, Jeffrey H. *Making Jazz French: Music and Modern Life in Interwar Paris.* Durham, NC: Duke University Press, 2003.

Joannis, Claudette. *Sarah Bernhardt: "Reine de l'attitude et princesse des gestes."* Paris: Éditions Payot & Rivages, 2000.

Jones, Prudence J. *Cleopatra: A Sourcebook.* Oklahoma Series in Classical Culture. Norman: University of Oklahoma Press, 2006.

Jules-Rosette, Bennetta. "Black Paris: Touristic Simulations." *Annals of Tourism Research* 21.4 (1994): 679–700.

Kent, Chris. "Nude Bodies: The Controversial Aesthetics of Exposure." *Victorian Review* 42.1 (Spring 2016): 1–4.

Kerley, Lela F. *Uncovering Paris: Scandals and Nude Spectacles in the Belle Époque.* Baton Rouge: Louisiana State University Press, 2017.

Koda, Harold, and Andrew Bolton. "Paul Poiret (1879–1944)." *Heilbrunn Timeline of Art History.* New York: Metropolitan Museum of Art, 2000–. http://www.metmuseum.org/toah/hd/poir/hd_poir.htm (September 2008)

Kourelou, Olga. "Reclaiming Greece's National Star: Aliki Vougiouklaki, from Sex Kitten to Working Girl." *Journal of Greek Media & Culture* 6.1 (April 1, 2020): 71–90.

Kraut, Aretha. "Between Primitivism and Diaspora: The Dance Performances of Josephine Baker, Zora Neale Hurston, and Katherine Dunham." *Theatre Journal* 55 (2003): 433–50.

Kuhn, Raymond. *The Media in France.* Milton Park, Oxfordshire, UK: Taylor and Francis, 2006.

Larkin, T. Lawrence. *In Search of Marie-Antoinette in the 1930s: Stefan Zweig, Irving Thalber, and Norma Shearer.* London: Palgrave Macmillan, 2019.

Lathers, Marie. "Posing the 'Belle Juive': Jewish Models in 19th-Century Paris." *Woman's Art Journal* 21.1 (Spring–Summer 2000): 27–32.

Lee, Katja. "Reading Celebrity Autobiographies." *Celebrity Studies* 5:1–2 (2014): 87–89.

Lemke, Sieglinde. *Primitivist Modernism: Black Culture and the Origins of Transatlantic Modernism.* New York: Oxford University Press, 1998.

Léon-Martin. *Music-Hall et ses figures.* Paris: Éditions de France, 1928.

Levitov, Karen. "The Divine Sarah and the Infernal Sally: Bernhardt in the Words of Her Contemporaries." *Sarah Bernhardt: The Art of High Drama.* Ed. Carol Ockman and Kenneth E. Silver. New Haven, CT: Yale University Press, 2005.

Lewis, Reina. *Gendering Orientalism: Race, Femininity and Representation.* New York: Routledge, 1996.

Lilti, Antoine. *The Invention of Celebrity, 1750–1850.* Cambridge, UK: Polity, 2017.

Little, Arthur, Jr. *Shakespeare Jungle Fever: National-Imperial Re-Visions of Race, Rape, and Sacrifice.* Stanford, CA: Stanford University Press, 2000.

Lojo Tizón, Mª del Carmen. "Le Mythe de Cléopâtre dans *L'Heure Sexuelle* (1898) de Rachilde." *Jangada* 12 (July–December 2018): 32–51.

Lowe, Lisa. *Critical Terrains: French and British Orientalisms.* Ithaca, NY: Cornell University Press, 2018.

Ludewig, Anna-Dorothea. "Between Orientalization and Self-Orientalization: Remarks on the Image of the 'Beautiful Jewess' in Nineteenth- and Early-Twentieth Century European Literature." *Orientalism, Gender and the Jews: Literary and Artistic Transformations of European National Discourses.* Ed. Ulrike Brunotte, Ludewig, and Axel Stähler. Berlin: De Gruyter OldenBourg, 2015. 221–29.

MacDonald, Joyce Green. "Sex, Race, and Empire in Shakespeare's Antony and Cleopatra." *Literature & History* 5.1 (1996): 60–77.

Mackrell, Judith. *Flappers: Six Women of a Dangerous Generation.* New York: Farrar, Straus and Giroux, 2013.

Maclatchie, Marina. "Foreign Fantasies: Fabricating the Exotic Other in Art Nouveau Jewelry." *Bowdoin Journal of Art* 34.2 (2016).

Maier, Angelica J. 2021. "'Is Cleopatra Black?': Examining Whiteness and the American New Woman." *Humanities* 10.2 (2021): 68. https://doi.org/10.3390/h10020068.

Margadant, Jo Burr. *The New Biography: Performing Femininity in Nineteenth-Century France.* Berkeley: University of California Press, 2000.

Marcus, Sharon. *The Drama of Celebrity.* Princeton, NJ: Princeton University Press, 2019.

———. "Sarah Bernhardt's Exteriority Effects." *Modern Drama* 60.3 (September 2017): 296–321.

Marshall, David P. *Celebrity and Power: Fame in Contemporary Culture.* Minneapolis: University of Minnesota Press, 1997.

Marshall, David, Christopher Moore, and Kim Barbour. "Persona as Method: Exploring Celebrity and the Public Self through Persona Studies." *Celebrity Studies* 6.3 (2015): 288–305.

McBride, Theresa. "Public Authority and Private Lives: Divorce after the French Revolution." *French Historical Studies* 17.3 (Spring 1992): 747–68.

McCombe, John P. "Cleopatra and Her Problems: T. S. Eliot and the Fetishization of Shakespeare's Queen of the Nile." *Journal of Modern Literature* 31.2 (2007): 23–38.

McPherson, Heather. "Sarah Bernhardt: Portrait of the Actress as Spectacle." *Nineteenth Century Contexts* 20.4 (1999): 409–54.

Menon, Elizabeth K. *Evil by Design: The Creation and Marketing of the Femme Fatale.* Urbana: University of Illinois Press, 2006.

Mesch, Rachel. "A Belle Epoque Media Storm: Gender, Celebrity, and the Marcelle Tinayre Affair." *French Historical Studies* 35.1 (Winter 2012): 93–121.

———. *Having it All in the Belle Epoque: How French Women's Magazines Invented the Modern Woman.* Stanford, CA: Stanford University Press, 2013.

Meskell, Lynn. "Consuming Bodies: Cultural Fantasies of Ancient Egypt." *Body and Society* 4.1 (1998): 63–76.

Miles, Margaret M., ed. *Cleopatra: A Sphinx Revisited.* Berkeley: University of California Press, 2011.

———. "Cleopatra in Egypt, Europe, and New York." *Cleopatra: A Sphinx Revisited.* Ed. Miles. Berkeley: University of California Press, 2011.

Mitchell, Robin. "Shaking the Racial and Gender Foundation of France: The Influences of 'Sarah Baartman' in the Production of Frenchness." *Black French Women and the Struggle for Equality, 1848–2016.* Ed. Félix Germain and Silyane Larcher. Lincoln: University of Nebraska Press, 2018. 185–97.

———. *Venus Noire: Black Women and Colonial Fantasies in Nineteenth-Century France.* Athens: University of Georgia Press, 2020.

Morgan, Simon. "Celebrity: Academic 'Pseudo-Event' or a Useful Category for Historians." *Culture and Social History* 8.1 (2011): 95–114.

Needham, Gerald. "Orientalism in France." *Art Journal* 42.4 (Winter 1982): 338–41.

Nochlin, Linda, and Tamar Garb, eds. *The Jew in the Text: Modernity and the Construction of Identity.* London: Thames and Hudson, 1995.

Ockman, Carol. "Was She Magnificent? Sarah Bernhardt's Reach." *Sarah Bernhardt: The Art of High Drama.* Ed. Ockman and Kenneth E. Silver. New Haven, CT: Yale University Press, 2005. 25–37.

———. "When Is a Jewish Star Just a Star? Interpreting Images of Sarah Bernhardt." *The Jew in the Text: Modernity and the Construction of Identity.* Ed. Linda Nochlin and Tamar Garb. London: Thames and Hudson, 1995. 121–39.

Ockman, Carol, and Kenneth E. Silver, eds. *Sarah Bernhardt: The Art of High Drama.* New Haven, CT: Yale University Press, 2005.

Orgeron, Marsha. "Making *It* in Hollywood: Clara Bow, Fandom, and Consumer Culture." *Cinema Journal* 42.4 (2003): 76–97.

Osmond, Suzanne. "'Her Infinite Variety': Representations of Shakespeare's Cleopatra in Fashion, Film and Theater." *Film, Fashion & Consumption* 1.1 (2012): 55–79.

Pellegrini, Ann. "Sarah Bernhardt, Live: A Reply to Allen Allenzweig." *Studies in Gender and Sexuality* 8.1 (2007): 37–44.

Pina Polo, Francisco. "The Great Seducer: Cleopatra, Queen and Sex Symbol." *Seduction and Power: Antiquity in the Visual and Performing Arts.* Ed. Silke Knippschild and Marta Garcia Morcillo. London: Bloomsbury, 2013. 183–96.

Poovey, Mary. *Uneven Developments: The Ideological Work of Gender in Mid-Victorian England.* Chicago: University of Chicago Press, 1988.

Popkin, Jeremy D. *History, Historians, and Autobiography.* Chicago: University of Chicago Press, 2005.

Pucci, Giuseppe. "Every Man's Cleopatra." *Cleopatra: A Sphinx Revisited.* Ed. Margaret M. Miles. Berkeley: University of California Press, 2011. 195–207.

Rearick, Charles. "Song and Society in Turn-of-the-Century France." *Journal of Social History* 22.1 (1988): 45–63.

Redmond, Sean, and Su Holmes, eds. *Stardom and Celebrity: A Reader.* London: Sage, 2007.

Reef, Catherine. *Sarah Bernhardt: The Divine and Dazzling Life of the World's First Superstar.* New York: Clarion, 2020.

Regester, Charlene B. "The Construction of an Image and the Deconstruction of a Star—Josephine Baker Racialized, Sexualized, and Politicized in the African-American Press, the Mainstream Press, and FBI Files." *The Josephine Baker Critical Reader: Selected Writings on the Entertainer and Activist.* Ed. Mae G. Henderson and Regester. Jefferson, NC: McFarland, 2017. 88–126.

Roberts, Mary Louise. "Acting Up: The Feminist Theatrics of Marguerite Durand." *French Historical Studies* 19.4 (1996): 1103–38.

———. *Civilization without Sexes: Reconstructing Gender in Postwar France, 1917–1927.* Chicago: University of Chicago Press, 1994.

———. *Disruptive Acts: The New Woman in Fin-de-Siècle France.* Chicago: University of Chicago Press, 2002.

———. "Out of their Orbit: Celebrity and Eccentricity in Nineteenth Century France." *The Question of Gender: Joan W. Scott's Critical Feminism.* Ed. Judith Butler and Elizabeth Weed. Bloomington: Indiana University Press, 2011. 50–79.

———. "Samson and Delilah Revisited: The Politics of Women's Fashion in 1920s France." *AHR* 98.3 (June 1993): 657–84.

———. "True Womanhood Revisited." *Journal of Women's History* 14.1 (Spring 2002): 150–55.

Rojek, Chris. *Celebrity.* London: Reaktion, 2001.

Roller, Duane W. *Cleopatra: A Biography.* New York: Oxford University Press, 2010.

Rose, Phyllis. *Jazz Cleopatra: Josephine Baker in Her Time.* New York: Doubleday, 1991.

Ross, Andrew Israel. *Public City/Public Sex: Homosexuality, Prostitution, and Urban Culture in Nineteenth-Century Paris.* Philadelphia: Temple University Press, 2019.

Rousseau, François-Olivier. *Missy.* Paris: Pierre-Guillaume de Roux, 2016.

Royster, Francesca. *Becoming Cleopatra: The Shifting Image of an Icon.* New York: Palgrave, 2003.

Ruiz, María Isabel Romero. "Black States of Desire: Josephine Baker, Identity and the Sexual Black Body." *Revista de Estudios Norteamericanos* 16 (2012): 125–39.

Said, Edward. *Orientalism.* New York: Vintage, 1979.

Schiff, Stacy. *Cleopatra: A Life.* New York: Back Bay, 2011.

Schwartz, Vanessa. *Spectacular Realities: Early Mass Culture in Fin-de-Siècle Paris.* Berkeley: University of California Press, 1999.

Scott, Joan Wallach. *The Fantasy of Feminist History.* Durham, NC: Duke University Press, 2011.

———. *Gender and the Politics of History.* New York: Columbia University Press, 1999.

———. *Only Paradoxes to Offer: French Feminists and the Rights of Man.* Cambridge, MA: Harvard University Press, 1997.

Sharpley-Whiting, Tracy Denean. *Black Venus: Sexualized Savages, Primal Fears, and Primitive Narratives in French.* Durham, NC: Duke University Press, 1999.

———. *Bricktop's Paris: African American Women in Paris between the Two World Wars.* Albany: State University of New York Press, 2015.

Smith, Bonnie. *Ladies of the Leisure Class: The Bourgeoises of Northern France in the Nineteenth Century.* Princeton, NJ: Princeton University Press, 1981.

Smith, Margaret Mary DeMaria. "HRH Cleopatra: The Last of the Ptolemies and the Egyptian Paintings of Sir Lawrence Alma-Tadema." *Cleopatra: A Sphinx Revisited.* Ed. Margaret M. Miles. Berkeley: University of California Press, 2011. 150–71.

Smith, Sidonie, and Julia Watson, *Reading Autobiography: A Guide for Interpreting Life Narratives.* Minneapolis: University of Minnesota Press, 2001.

Sohn, Anne-Marie. "Between the Wars in France and England." *Toward a Cultural Identity in the Twentieth Century.* Ed. Françoise Thébaud. Trans. Arthur Goldhammer. Vol. 5 of *A History of Women in the West.* Cambridge, MA: Belknap Press of Harvard University Press, 1994. 114.

Sowinska, Alicja. "Dialectics of the Banana Skirt: The Ambiguities of Josephine Baker's Self-Representation." *University of Michigan Library* 19 (Fall 2005–Spring 2006).

Stovall, Tyler. "Gender, Race, and Miscegenation: African Americans in Jazz Age Paris." *The Modern Women Revisited: Paris between the Wars.* Ed. Whitney Chadwick and Tirza True. New Brunswick, NJ: Rutgers University Press, 2003. 21–34.

———. "The New Woman and the New Empire: Josephine Baker and Changing Views of Femininity in Interwar France." *Scholar and Feminist Online* 6.1–6.2 (Fall 2007/ Spring 2008).

Stovall, Tyler Edward. *Paris Noir: African Americans in the City of Light.* Boston: Houghton Mifflin, 1996.

Sweeney-Risko, Jennifer. "Fashionable Formation: Reclaiming the Sartorial Politics of Josephine Baker." *Australian Feminist Studies* 33.98 (2019): 498–514.

Tarling, Nicholas. *Orientalism and the Operatic World.* London: Rowman and Littlefield, 2015.

Thébaud, Françoise "The Great War and the Triumph of Sexual Division." *Toward a Cultural Identity in the Twentieth Century.* Ed. Françoise Thébaud. Trans. Arthur Goldhammer. Vol. 5 of *A History of Women in the West.* Cambridge, MA: Belknap Press of Harvard University Press, 1994. 21–75.

Thurman, Judith. *Secrets of the Flesh: A Life of Colette.* New York: Ballantine, 1999.

Tilburg, Patricia A. *Colette's Republic: Work, Gender, and Popular Culture in France, 1870–1914.* New York: Berghahn, 2009.

———. "Earning Her Bread: Métier, Order, and Female Honor in Colette's Music Hall, 1906–1913." *French Historical Studies* 28.3 (Summer 2005): 497–530.

Tseëlon, Efrat. *The Masque of Femininity: The Presentation of Woman in Everyday Life.* New York: Sage, 1995.

Turner, Graeme. *Understanding Celebrity.* London: Sage, 2014.

Walker, David. *Outrage and Insight: Modern French Writers and the fait divers.* Oxford: Berg, 1995.

Weber, Brenda. *Women and Literary Celebrity in the Nineteenth Century: The Transatlantic Production of Fame and Gender.* Farnham, UK: Ashgate, 2012.

Wyke, Maria, and Dominic Montserrat, "Glamour Girls: Cleomania in Mass Culture." *Cleopatra: A Sphinx Revisited.* Ed. Margaret M. Miles. Berkeley: University of California Press, 2011. 172–94.

Ziegler, Christiane. "Cleopatra or the Seductions of the East." *Egyptomania: Egypt in Western Art 1730–1930.* Ed. Jean-Marcel Humbert, Michael Pantazzi, and Ziegler. National Gallery of Canada/Réunion de Musées Nationaux, 1994. 554.

Index

Printed in the USA
CPSIA information can be obtained
at www.ICGtesting.com
LVHW092017070224
771238LV00002B/57